History of Christ United Methodist Church

MEMPHIS, TENNESSEE
1955–2002

"Study to shew thyself approved unto God,
a workman that needeth not to be ashamed,
rightly dividing the word of truth."

—II Timothy 2:15 KJV

History of Christ United Methodist Church

MEMPHIS, TENNESSEE
1955–2002

VOLUME I
Dr. Charles William Grant
1955–1969

Harry A. Johnson Jr.

Providence House Publishers
PROVIDENCE PUBLISHING CORPORATION
FRANKLIN, TENNESSEE

Printed in the United States of America

07 06 05 04 03 1 2 3 4 5

Library of Congress Catalog Card Number: 2003103876

ISBN: 1-57736-276-4

Cover design by Lindrel Moates

Cover illustration by R. Brown

Not endorsed by the Executive Committee
of Christ United Methodist Church

PROVIDENCE HOUSE PUBLISHERS
an imprint of
Providence Publishing Corporation
238 Seaboard Lane • Franklin, Tennessee 37067
800-321-5692
www.providencepubcorp.com

DEDICATION

James H. Seabrook Sr.

To the memory of James Hunter Seabrook Sr., who was without a doubt its founding father.

When his father died, Seabrook left the University of Tennessee and returned to Memphis to begin the recovery of the family business, Seabrook Paint Company. He was the oldest of four brothers and the financial survival of the family during the Great Depression rested upon his shoulders. Throughout his struggles to get the business on a firm foundation during the depths of the worst economic period of the century, Jimmy never neglected his commitment to his church. He taught Sunday school and was a leader of Madison Heights Methodist Church, the district and the Memphis Conference. He was mentally and spiritually prepared to become the chair of the Steering Committee that established Christ Methodist Church.

The family business flourished and has become the largest business of its type in the nation. As the business grew, so did Jimmy's generosity of time, energy, and finances to the church throughout the remainder of his life.

The early leadership of the church was outstanding and used its many talents to further the establishment of the church so that its foundation would be that of a solid rock, able to withstand whatever human frailties were presented. James Seabrook was a leader who recognized and appreciated the abilities of others and willingly gave them the projects that best fitted their talents. He was always generous in his praise of others. He laid the foundation for the great missional goals of the church and saw to it that Christ Church supported missions long before the first building was completed. The charter members of this great church who have discussed the subject of leadership foundations of the church have agreed with these recollections and conclusions.

FINANCIAL CONTRIBUTORS TO HISTORY PUBLICATION

Dr. James F. Bigger Jr.
Mr. Earle Billings
Mrs. Dorothy Billings
Ms. Karen Brasfield
Mr. Ben Carpenter
Mrs. Lillie Carpenter
Mrs. Nell Cochran
Mrs. Charlie (Kate) Davenport
Mr. James A. Davenport
Mrs. Mary Davenport
Mrs. Rubye Davie
Mr. Frank Fisher
Mrs. Dorothy Fisher
Judge William H. D. Fones
Mrs. Albert (Alice) Fulmer
Mr. J. Albert Fulmer Jr.
Mr. William L. Hurdle
Mrs. Betty Hurdle
Mr. James C. Ingram Jr.
Mrs. June Ingram
Mr. Harry A. Johnson Jr.
Mrs. Penny Johnson
Mrs. Martha Anne Johnston
Mrs. D. Keith (Mary) Kelley
Mr. David L. Kelley
Mrs. Samuel (Eloise) Mays
Mr. Gordon A. Miles
Mrs. Tennie Miles
Dr. P. D. Miller
Mrs. Greene Miller
Mr. John A. Montgomery
Mr. Raymond E. Moore
Mrs. Virginia Nowlin
Mr. George R. Payne
Mrs. Lou Payne
Mrs. Helen Pipher
Mr. William Poole
Mrs. Elizabeth Poole
Mr. Henry Clay Shelton
Mrs. Harriet Shelton
Mr. Thomas Wade Smith
Mrs. Thomas W. (Nell Carolyn) Smith
Mrs. Alice B. Stolte
Mrs. John (Jane) Stone
Mrs. Jewell Sullivan
Mrs. J. A. (Mary) Summers
Mrs. Jane A. Taylor
Mr. Don Thomas
Mrs. Saralene Thomas
Mr. Jack Wright
Mrs. Martha Wright
Dr. James R. Wyatt
Mrs. Mary Kate Wyatt

CONTENTS

FOREWORD

***Maxie D. Dunnam**, President*
Asbury Theological Seminary

Many of the readers of this book will know the name Brother Lawrence. If you have not read his book, you may have heard a preacher or teacher speak of him. He served in the kitchen of his monastery and said he experienced the presence of God as clearly in washing pots and pans as he did in the blessed sacrament.

For the past twenty-five years, I have kept company with the saints. I mean by that I have lived with the devotional writing of people like William Law, Teresa of Avila, Augustine, Francois Fenelon, Julian of Norwich, and many others. Out of that have come two workbooks: *Keeping Company with the Saints* and *Lessons from the Saints*. One of those saints with whom I have kept company is Brother Lawrence. Many of you know his name.

He is best known for the record of his conversations and writing entitled *The Practice of the Presence of God*. Like many others, Brother Lawrence entered a monastic order believing that he was giving up this world's happiness to become a monk. He discovered a much deeper happiness than he had ever imagined. Reflecting on this turn of events, Brother Lawrence said to God, "You have outwitted me."

Isn't that a delightful phrase? "God, you have outwitted me." What a testimony to the providence of God, the working of God's grace in our lives.

There is a sense in which this history of Christ United Methodist Church is that kind of story. It is certainly that kind of story as it relates to the ministers who have served this church. I count it one of the great joys of my life to have been among those.

Most of us know that we stand on the shoulders of giants. When I came to Christ Church as a third senior minister of that congregation, I knew without question that I was standing on the shoulders of giants. Dr. Charles Grant, the founding pastor, and Dr. Harold Beaty, his successor, were giants—having led the congregation in a remarkable way.

Now, as this history is being published, my successor, Dr. William Bouknight, is continuing in that tradition of leadership.

Here is the story of a remarkable congregation—a congregation that at her best has sought to follow the leading of the Holy Spirit in planning and initiating ministry. The story of the church is not told by its pastors—but by the membership of the church, the laity who are the true ministers. Those of us who are privileged to serve as ordained ministers—representative ministers—know that at our best we are coaches, sometimes cheerleaders, sometimes visionaries—casting a vision which is hopefully inspired by the Holy Spirit—but knowing that no vision comes to fruition apart from the resources of men and women, young people and children, who give themselves passionately to the Lord.

Christ Church is the story of evangelism and church growth. Few churches in our United Methodist denomination have known greater fervor in the evangelistic cause than Christ Church. It is a church that takes mission and outreach seriously. The impact of Christ Church around the world, as the story is told in this volume, is without question.

This is the story of a people of God, called by God, sustained by God, responsive to God, yielded to the Lord's will—being used by the Lord to bring forth a people of God whose ministry continues to be vibrant and alive.

It is wonderful to have been a part of this congregation—having served it for twelve years. The story of my life is not unlike the story of this congregation—seeking to follow the Lord's leading and discovering all along the way that "God outwits us." God's will never takes us where God's grace will not sustain us.

So, I commend this story as one of God's stories with great thanksgiving for having been a small part of it. My wife, Jerry, and our family join me to testify to the grace that abounds within this congregation. We look back upon our life and count it all joy to have spent twelve years as the pastoral leadership team at Christ Church.

Maxie Dunnam

ACKNOWLEDGMENTS

The history books being published in 2003 could not have been completed without the tremendous help provided by the good people pictured on these pages.

Research

Barbara Melton
Worship

Glenn Ragland
Music

D. A. Noel
Land and Buildings

Linda McVean
Day School

Ben Carpenter
Church School

PREPARATION

Beth Sanders

DATA ENTRY

Clara Downen

Rubye Carlile

Ervin H. (Buddy) Wright

Roylyn Parks

INTRODUCTION

Louise Smith was the chairperson of the History and Archives Committee of Christ United Methodist Church for nine years. In 1995 she asked me to write a history of the church. I hesitated, unsure if I was capable of taking on such a project. Louise replied that the committee had appreciated articles I had written for the archives and had full confidence in my ability to do the job. As I had many other responsibilities at that time, I urged her to find someone else to begin the project. She mentioned it once or twice during the next year.

I had not thought about this project in months when Jane Isbell Haynes, past chair of history and archives, called me one night and offered me a key to the archives room so that I could go to work on the history when I was ready. As I was involved in Annual Conference and the refurbishing of the sanctuary and choir areas, I was unable to begin immediately.

Kathy (Mrs. Dwight) Clark has been the chairperson of history and archives since January 1, 2001, and has been most helpful.

The Archival Treasures of Christ Methodist Church

". . . From everyone who has been given, much will be demanded; and from the one who has been entrusted with much, much more will be asked." Luke 12:48b (NIV)

The archives and workroom are on the third floor of the Dunnam Building, directly over the library. I know of no other church with archival facilities that rival those of Christ Church. There are seventy-one bound volumes of meeting minutes, beginning with the Steering Committee and including every year since the church was organized. The original documents represented in the bound volumes are stored in an orderly fashion in locked cabinets.

There are hundreds of photographs, audio and videotapes, as well as original blueprints of the buildings erected on the property. All of this work has been done by volunteers, mostly women of the church, who have invested thousands of hours over the almost half century of the church's existence. Milton Bennett has also contributed many hours to archival work.

Researching and writing this history has taken five years and has been a daunting project. In my opinion, one of the most important life skills we can acquire is the ability to learn from our mistakes and those of others: "Those who cannot remember the past are condemned to repeat it." Just imagine what could

Jane Isbell Haynes

Mrs. Tommy (Louise) Smith

Mrs. Dwight (Kathy) Clark

be done through our ministries to others if we avoid the tremendous amount of physical and mental energy expended when committees try to reinvent the wheel and dream dreams without a practical plan to implement them. Study this history of Christ Church so that God's plan for you on earth will be as fully realized as His gifts to you will allow.

The dictionary defines history as a past that is full of important events. Christ Methodist Church/Christ United Methodist Church in Memphis, Tennessee, has a past of nearly fifty years. That past is chock-full of important events from which a great deal can be learned to benefit the present and enhance the future.

The dictionary states that comprehensive embraces wide and superior content. It includes understanding much, and is broad, extensive, and inclusive. It is my sincere wish and prayer that I have been able to project the meaning of comprehensive history into the four books being published in the year 2003. It is my hope that the content of these books will be attractive and interesting enough to command the attention of the congregation and especially its leaders.

Hopefully it will be read and the actions of those who have gone before will contribute in some measure to the future that I project for this great United Methodist church.

This history will be set up so that it can be added to year after year. It will be divided in such a way as to be readily used by committee chairpersons, members, and anyone else who wants to make the best use of their volunteer or paid staff time for the church.

There will be a section written about major committees, commissions, and work areas. These will contain the facts, the programs, and accomplishments of the work area and be divided into sections relating to the tenure of a particular senior minister. Many pictures will be used so that an accurate view of the project can be fixed in the mind of the reader.

These histories are based on facts contained in documents in the archives. Every effort has been made to ensure that all statements are factual and not based on any individual's memory. Although the greatest care has been exercised, there may still be errors, and I apologize in advance for any mistakes and ask the forgiveness of the reader. Of the nearly fifteen thousand people who have been members of Christ Church over the past forty-seven years, many have performed outstanding ministry to and through the church. Unfortunately, due to space constraints, some accomplishments have had to be omitted. It is my sincere plea that each person not included will know that God and the many people who have known them appreciate and applaud their service to Him and His Church.

History of Christ United Methodist Church

MEMPHIS, TENNESSEE
1955–2002

DR. CHARLES WILLIAM GRANT
1904–1995

First Senior Minister, Christ United Methodist Church, 1955–1969

Charles Grant was born in Mount Vernon Township, Illinois, on March 15, 1904, the second of three sons born to William Nathan Grant and Minnie Hoit Grant. All three sons went into full-time Christian service. Each of them credited his mother's faithful devotion to God and her constant prayers for his life of Christian service.

As this history is being written, there are a dwindling number of people alive who can even imagine the world into which Charles Grant was born and grew up, nearly one hundred years ago. Horses, buggies, wagons, and trains were the predominant modes of transportation. Few people owned automobiles. Roads, even major highways, were gravel. The main streets in cities and towns were mostly gravel; many were dirt (or mud, when it rained). There was no such thing as a television set or radio. There were no high speed or mass methods of communication. The fastest means of communication was hand-sent telegraph. The world was much slower and considerably less complicated.

Grant aspired to be a pharmacist and worked in the Porter and Bond Drug Store in Mount Vernon as a teenager. He started out mopping the floors, clerking, and learning to fill prescriptions at a salary of one dollar per week. Pharmacists were called druggists in those days and almost all learned their trade in what we now call on-the-job training. After six years, having become competent to open and run the store alone, including filling prescriptions, he was making thirty dollars a month. After graduation from high school, as he is pictured, Grant continued to work at the Porter and Bond Drug Store until his brother Edwin graduated two years later. They had no idea about where to go to college until they saw some material on Asbury, at Wilmore, Kentucky, in their Grandfather Hoit's home on a Sunday visit.

Charles and Edwin Grant moved to Wilmore in 1926 to attend Asbury College together. Charles was able to get a job in Sims' Drug Store in Wilmore as a pharmacist. At this writing, Sims' Drug Store in Wilmore still exists and looks and operates much the same as it did in 1926, when he began to work there.

Since all three of her sons were going to school at Asbury and her husband William Nathan was seldom at home, the boys' mother moved to Wilmore and lived just a few blocks from the campus. The family had seen little of William Nathan because of his alcoholism and later the depression, which forced him to seek employment wherever he could find it. He had been a successful merchant in Mount Vernon but lost it all in the 1929 crash. He ended up working in a

paper mill in St. Louis, where he died of apoplexy. Since William Nathan had seldom been present, the raising and nurturing of the three boys was the lot of the mother. They all grew up hating alcohol and its effect on human behavior. She did an outstanding job, as all three served the Lord all of their lives. It was while at Asbury that Charles met his strong, lifelong partner in life and ministry, Mary Anna Edwards. They were married on June 5, 1929, in Nicholasville, Kentucky.

Grant joined the Kentucky Conference in 1930, which was no mean accomplishment during the depths of the depression. His first appointment was to the Methodist church in Whitesburg. This was a very small town amidst the poorest of the poor in the United States. It is in the Appalachian Mountains and in the middle of feuding families that would make today's ghetto look like Sunday school. The air was damp and cold and always full of coal dust. They got paid mostly with chickens and eggs because there wasn't much money in those mountains, even without the depression.

Grant contracted chronic bronchitis or pneumonia, which can put a preacher out of business. For health reasons, they gave him a church a short

Above: *Edwin Hoit Grant, left, went to Asbury College and seminary and was an ordained Methodist minister. John Lawrence Grant, center, went to Asbury College after leaving a career in banking in Mount Vernon, Illinois. He went to China as a Methodist missionary, where he lived, died, and was buried. Charles William Grant, right, went to Asbury College and seminary with his brother Edwin and was also an ordained Methodist minister.* **Opposite Upper Left:** *This picture of Charles sitting on a pony is the only one available of him as a young boy. He was perhaps eight or nine when this picture was made.* **Opposite Upper Right:** *Charles's father, William Nathan Grant.* **Opposite Left:** *Charles Grant in cap and gown at his high school graduation.* **Opposite Right:** *Charles and his mother, Minnie Hoit Grant.* **Opposite Lower Left**: *Mary Anna and Charles Grant when their first child, Martha Ann, was about one year old.* **Opposite Lower Right**: *Mary Anna Edwards in the winter of 1925–1926 when she and Charles Grant met at Asbury.*

GRANT BROS.

Gospel Preaching

UNDER BIG BROWN TENT

6th and Harrison

STARTING TONIGHT

JUNE 15th -- 7:30 P. M.

Grant Brothers were in Mt. Vernon last year. They return this season better equipped for a great meeting. Larger tent, greater seating capacity and the addition of a number of chairs are improvements.
Welcome them tonight.

On April 23, 1927, Charles received his license to preach and he and Edwin started that summer holding tent revivals. They were very successful evangelists, as evidenced by these newspaper articles.

In 1927 and 1928, Edwin and Charles Grant held gospel tent meetings in Mount Vernon, Illinois.

Grant Brothers Open Series of Special Meetings

EDWIN GRANT

CHARLES GRANT

Charles and Edwin Grant, who last summer conducted a successful six weeks' evangelistic meeting in Mt. Vernon, have returned and last night opened a meeting which is expected to last several weeks.

Charles and Edwin compose the Grant brothers evangelistic party. Charles is the elder, being 24 years of age. Edwin is 22 and was recently married.

They are Mt. Vernon men, having been graduated from Mt. Vernon high school, and working here before entering college.

The brothers alternate in preaching and in leading the song services, and their meeting in Mt. Vernon last year was very successful.

The meetings are being held under a large tent which has been pitched on the grounds of the Franklin school at Sixth and Harrison streets.

Both Charles and Edwin are students at Asbury College, Wilmore, Ky. Next year will be their senior year.

distance northeast of Louisville in the town of Eminence, Kentucky. He received his Bachelor of Divinity Degree from Asbury Seminary in Wilmore, Kentucky, in 1935 and served the Methodist churches in Whitesburg, Eminence, Crestwood, and the state capital Methodist church in Frankfort, Kentucky. While serving the church in Fort Thomas, Kentucky, Grant was awarded an honorary doctorate in 1945 from Kentucky Wesleyan College.

It is only a little more than two hundred miles from Whitesburg in the Appalachians to Louisville on the Ohio River, but it probably seemed like another lifetime, in another world when the bishop assigned Grant to the Crescent Hill Church in Louisville. He was the pastor there for six years. During that pastorate, thirteen young people committed themselves to full-time Christian service. Five of them joined the Kentucky Conference in one year. This alone is an enviable accomplishment for any minister and probably helped propel him to his next appointment.

Dr. A. W. Beasley was the pastor of Madison Heights Methodist Church in Memphis, Tennessee, in 1952. He accepted a

GRANT BROTHERS WILL CONDUCT REVIVAL HERE

Mt. Vernon Boys Are Now In Evangelical Work—Meeting in Tent.

The Grant brothers, Charles and Edwin, sons of Mrs. W. N. Grant, will hold a series of open air gospel meetings in Mt. Vernon, starting next Sunday, July 31st.

They are well known in Mt. Vernon. The late W. N. Grant, father of the brothers, was a prominent business man in Mt. Vernon and his widow made her home in this city until a year ago, when she moved to Wilmore, Ky., where Charles and Edwin and another brother, Lawrence, are students.

Charles and Edwin are licensed ministers. This summer they have been working together in holding a number of successful open air meetings. They come to Mt. Vernon from Montier, Mo., where a very successful series was conducted and seventy people professed a desire to be saved.

They will erect a large tent at Sixth and Harrison streets on the grounds of the Franklin school, where the series will be conducted.

Both are graduates of Mt. Vernon Township High school and have many friends here, not only among the younger set but among the older people with whom they were affiliated in their constant church work. Both were employed in business houses in Mt. Vernon and formde many friendships in the contact with the public.

They are still students of Asbury College and will return there this fall to again take up their work. They are studying for the ministry, and although already licensed, will continue their college work.

The meeting scheduled to open next Sunday in Mt. Vernon will last for two weeks. Preaching services and singing will be conducted each evening.

CHARLES GRANT

Charles Grant pictured in newspaper article describing the gospel tent meetings he and his brother Edwin were holding in Mount Vernon, Illinois, in 1927.

position as professor of religion at the Candler School of Theology at Emory University in Atlanta, Georgia. Bishop William T. Watkins was the bishop of the Louisville and Memphis Conferences. Madison Heights was one of the four most prominent churches in Memphis with a membership in excess of three thousand.

James Seabrook, a leader at Madison Heights and in the Memphis Conference, prevailed upon Bishop Watkins to look beyond the confines of the Memphis Conference for a new pastor. Charles Grant was chosen and came to Memphis and to Madison Heights Church in 1952. In 1953 Charles and Mary Anna made an extensive mission trip to Central and South America.

By 1954 Memphis was mushrooming east, and many families were moving from downtown and midtown to the eastern suburbs. Poplar and Highland had been a cotton field just three or four years before this time. First Methodist Church, St. John's, Madison Heights, Union Avenue, and Trinity were still viable and effective churches. They were built and organized when families walked to churches in the neighborhood. With the beginning of the exodus east, the handwriting on the wall was beginning to be very readable.

First Church had made the first move by buying a small wooden house at 4370 Poplar (where the Marsonne Apartments are now) for thirty-two thousand dollars. The intent was to start a small missional church, or outreach ministry of First Church, in east Memphis. James Hunter Seabrook Sr. was the district steward and the Memphis Conference lay leader at this time. Dr. J. E. Underwood was the district superintendent and the presiding bishop was William T. Watkins. These three leaders of the Methodist Church in Memphis saw the compelling need to establish a Methodist church in east Memphis to minister to this fast-growing population.

The decision was made during the summer of 1954, and Bishop Watkins appointed James Seabrook as the chairman of the Steering Committee, which was to be made up of two laymen from each of six Methodist churches, First, Madison Heights, St. John's, Union Avenue, Trinity, and St. Luke's. This was later changed to three from each church. It proved to be a daunting but exhilarating assignment that seemed overwhelming at times. The laypeople on the Steering Committee were outstanding leaders in the local churches, and with the clergy and lay leadership of the district and the conference firmly behind them, they never faltered.

First Methodist Church agreed to give their equity (about seven thousand dollars, leaving a balance of twenty-five thousand dollars) in the house and land, which they owned at 4370 Poplar Avenue. The Conference Committee on Church Extension pledged the unprecedented amount of fifty thousand dollars to the establishment of this new church. This was the largest amount of money that had been pledged, anywhere in Methodism at that time, for the establishment of a new church.

The Steering Committee met at least once each week, usually on Friday at noon, but with additional evening meetings. They began with no money, no place to meet, no pastor, and no congregation. After scouring east Memphis (mostly within a mile or two of Poplar and Highland) for an acceptable temporary home for the church, the Poplar Plaza Theater, at the corner of Poplar and Prescott, was chosen as the only place with the seating capacity and other facilities needed for a church. Augustine Cianciola owned the theater and graciously agreed to move stored equipment to make room for Sunday school classes and have the building clean and ready for services each Sunday morning.

Charles Grant witnessing against gambling in the Louisville, Kentucky, courthouse when he was pastor of Crescent Hill Church and president of the Louisville Ministerial Association.

There was a cry room for babies and their young mothers, a storeroom was fixed up for a nursery, an office available for the Sunday school secretary and treasurer, and plenty of parking space. Mr. Cianciola generously agreed to charge only one hundred dollars per Sunday for the use of the theater. At the invitation of James Seabrook, Clay Shelton and Harry Johnson were in attendance at most of the Steering Committee meetings.

Early on, the Steering Committee began the search for land on which to build the new church and, of course, to come up with a preacher who could inspire the new congregation and set a course that would attract the unsaved and unchurched in east Memphis. These searches were conducted with the help and shared knowledge of the district superintendent and Bishop Watkins. There was a great deal of prayer amidst the growing enthusiasm for this bold step to be taken in east Memphis. There was also a great deal of thought and preparation dealing with what was, at the time, a critical need for a good, solid plan to finance such a project.

Grant Building and Fellowship Hall, the first two buildings. Notice how far it is to the first house north of Fellowship Hall.

Dr. Grant at the pulpit in Fellowship Hall.

In early April 1955, at a meeting of the Steering Committee at the Leader Federal Building on Poplar Avenue near East High School, Harry A. Johnson Jr. was given an almost overwhelming task. He was appointed chairman of the Sunday School Committee and handed the key to the cottage that First Methodist Church had owned. This task included organizing the entire Sunday school to accommodate the five hundred to one thousand people expected the first Sunday. This included recruiting and training 112 teachers, and preparing the cottage and grounds to be used as the church office, Sunday school classes, and all Sunday night and weekly meetings. It also included finding suitable accommodations for the youth and adult classes and purchasing all furniture needed and literature for teachers.

In late April, the final decision was made by the bishop to appoint Charles W. Grant as the first senior minister. This was as near perfect a choice as a human could possibly make. It took a whale of a lot of courage for him to accept this appointment because he had spent thirty years of work and preparations to be the pastor of one of the better appointments in Methodism, at Madison Heights. The possibility of a mediocre or failed beginning of this new venture could have effectively ended his career.

The first parsonage was a rented apartment at Poplar and Highland, then a house in Belle Meade that served the Grant family and later the Beaty family. Charles and Mary Anna took daily walks down Poplar Avenue. They walked several miles each day.

On Sunday, June 19, 1955, everything was as ready as it could possibly be. Between nine hundred and eleven hundred people showed up for the first church service and almost 100 percent of them came early for Sunday school. There was a rented organ, a choir, greeters, and ushers as well as the 112 trained Sunday school teachers. Jesse Anderson, a lay volunteer, was the first choir director.

Grant preached his first sermon to this new congregation. There were many who came thinking that the Plaza Theater showing *To Hell and Back* on its screen could not possibly be a good place for a worship service. What a surprise! Grant's sermon "The Birth of a Church" inspired a very receptive and enthusiastic congregation; and the atmosphere could not have been more worshipful. Every attending soul was uplifted by the experience. There were two hundred folding chairs set up on the lawn at the little cottage for Sunday night services and there was standing room only. Grant preached from a lectern on the front porch.

Upper Left: *Mary Anna and Charles, Joy and Keith Weisinger. Joy was chair of the going-away reception for Charles after fourteen years.* **Upper Right:** *Mary Anna and Charles at reception after fourteen years as senior minister at Christ United Methodist Church.* **Above:** *Dorothy Billings, secretary to Dr. Grant from 1955 to 1967. Mrs. W. J. Templeton, Charles, and Mary Anna at reception.*

Dr. Grant's and Dorothy Billings's (secretary) offices were in the southeast corner breakfast room of the cottage. All meetings, including the Board of Stewards, all commissions, the Men's Club, Woman's Society of Christian Service, met in the living room and dining room of this little house.

After seeing the initial response, the necessity for a better place for all of these meetings was evident to all concerned. A wooden building was built to be ready before the fall rains began and was erected next to the house. It had a toilet on each side of the entrance and one large room. The room could hold about 250 people seated but was used for parties as well as worship services and meetings. Grant would not allow card tables in the church; therefore, utility folding tables (these were card tables with another name) had to be used. There could not be dances of any kind on the premises either, but folk games were allowed, which strangely resembled square dances.

Volunteers performed every chore because the only paid staff member was Dorothy Billings. Evangelistic visitation teams went out every Monday night, with hundreds participating in pairs. Six hundred people became charter members, and with the enthusiasm of these people, and the leadership of Dr. Grant, the church began a steady growth. During his fourteen-year tenure as the first senior minister, 4,332 members were received in the church.

Both Dr. Grant and Jimmy Seabrook were very committed to missions; therefore, the church began to support two missionaries—a hospital in Borneo and a church in Frayser—before the first building was built. In 1961 Christ Church sent Dr. Grant and his wife to Korea, Singapore, Borneo, and other Southeast Asian countries. This included a visit with the missionaries at the hospital in Sarawak.

In 1966 Charles and Mary Anna were delegates to the World Methodist Conference in London.

In 1969, Dr. Grant decided it was time to make a move and accepted the pastorate of Grace United Methodist Church in Whitehaven. The demands on him were lessened and helped him to ease into retirement, which he almost did after five years when he became an associate minister at St. Luke's Methodist Church in 1974.

After a prolonged illness, Mary Anna Grant died on November 28, 1983. Grant lived alone until 1990 when he went to live with David and Sallie Grant and their family, where he died on January 12, 1995, leaving two children, six grandchildren, and three great-grandchildren. He had spent nearly forty-four years of his life as an active minister of the Methodist Church.

When he came back to Christ Church as its pastor emeritus, Dwight Koenig would pick him up every Wednesday night and bring him to the Wednesday night suppers. They invariably sat next to Harry Johnson, and they had a great old time remembering the many nights when they worked until midnight, or after, trying to solve the church's problems. They didn't always agree, but they always supported each other after they arrived at a decision. Harry always wrapped up a piece of pie for Dr. Grant to take home for a late night snack. When he was going out of town he would always say, "Harry, cast my vote for everything that is right and against everything that is wrong."

Harry went to see him with a half-gallon of ice cream, after he had been homebound for some time. The first thing he told him was exactly how many weeks it had been since he had seen him. Although he was ninety years old and in poor health, Dr. Grant still expressed himself with a smile and a quick comeback to whatever Harry said. He was still remembering the happy times, although sometimes exhausting, during the first years of the church.

COMMENTS BY DAVID LAWRENCE GRANT

January 3, 1997

Personal memories of my father are by nature connected to him in the pulpit at the church. It is impossible for me to separate home and church because in my mind they were one and the same. In a very real sense the church was a part of my home.

In early days, the parsonage, or home, was adjacent to the church building. A pastor, like my dad, was literally on call or on duty twenty-four hours a day, seven days a week with weekends being the heaviest days of duty. There is always something going on at a big and growing church, and a pastor is at the beck and call of every single member of the church and also many nonmembers who quite frequently need spiritual, emotional, and financial help. I remember my dad wearing many hats or being responsible for many duties. In addition to preaching and teaching, which is quite a task in itself, he was also responsible for church and home building, scheduling, counseling, funerals, weddings, special ceremonies, radio broadcasts, and many civic and community responsibilities as well.

Many things we did as a family were centered around the church. I remember one very special surprise party they had on my eighth or ninth birthday. Every child at Crescent Hill Methodist in Louisville, Kentucky, was invited, plus some friends who were not members. I remember my dad blowing up balloons the old-fashioned way for every single child there. This, of course, was held in the church fellowship hall, complete with Woody Woodpecker cartoons, cake, ice cream, and games for all. It was a wonderful birthday party that he had planned and executed with the help of my wonderful mother. They always did things together and were a great help to one another.

On another occasion, my dad had meticulously put together a Lionel train set on a plywood board in the church basement. The tracks were nailed or screwed down in perfect order and it was a complete surprise for me on Christmas at age six or seven. That, to me, was one of the greatest Christmases I could remember.

Words really are inadequate to express a lifetime of memories of two people like my mother and dad. They were behind the scenes as they appeared in public, dedicated to what was right, even in the face of opposition, simply purposed in fulfilling the Lord's will for their lives; tireless workers constantly focused on their task at hand and loving every minute of it.

My dad once remarked that he could not believe that someone would pay him to do a job that he enjoyed as much as the one he had—he would have been happy to have done it for nothing. With my mother, you really did get two for the price of one because she tirelessly helped him with all his projects, which were many.

Comments by Sallie Grant

January 3, 1997

The life of my father-in-law was characterized by his seeing everything as a gift from a loving heavenly Father and himself therefore as a steward. First, he was careful to use wisely, and care for, meticulously everything in his life. He was a steward of his body; so, as much as possible, he exercised daily by walking up to five miles a day and by eating a balanced diet so he could serve God with all his strength. He was also a steward of the financial resources that God had entrusted to him; so he gave generously, invested prudently, and spent judiciously. In so doing, he served God with his tithes and offerings.

He viewed his relationships with people as a gift given by God, so he never allowed any act or unkind word to remain unforgiven. He was always quick to forgive and he refused to hold a grudge against anyone. He truly prayed for, forgave, and treated even his opponents with respect and grace. He served God with his heart and mind. He always maintained his keen sense of humor. Even when he was incapacitated he still could see the humor in life and always enjoyed a good laugh.

He also loved music. He enjoyed listening to classical and sacred music, especially the old standards of the faith. When his younger brother Edwin (who has since also passed away) would come for a visit to our home, they would sing as they had sung sixty years earlier when they began their ministries as itinerant tent preachers in the 1920s. Edwin would sing the lead and Charles would sing the harmony.

A few weeks before he died, he asked me to get the tape recorder; he wanted to sing. He had never requested a taped solo before so I was a little surprised, but delighted. I found a cassette recorder and he began to sing in a weak, but heartfelt voice:

> There is a fountain filled with blood, drawn from Emmanuel's veins;
> And sinners plunged beneath that flood lose all their guilty stains.

That was his conviction. That was his life; he died as he had lived.

Comments by Grandson Charles Kevin Grant

December 1996

My grandfather was the first public figure I ever wanted to emulate. When my family would go on Sunday nights to hear my grandfather preach at St. Luke's Church on Highland, I would watch him stand behind the pulpit and I would listen as a silence fell over the congregation. I noticed that people were very interested in what he had to say. They were taking notes and underlining words in their Bibles as he spoke.

When I listened, I always wondered if he would mention my name or use me as an example in one of his illustrations. Sometimes he did and sometimes he didn't. Even if he didn't, I never for a minute doubted that he was aware of my presence in the congregation. When the sermon was over, he would then invite people to come forward and pray if they wanted to. As soon as he did that, I would slip out of the pew and make a beeline to the altar rail, usually on the left-hand side of the chancel where I would kneel down like I was praying. But I wasn't praying, I was waiting—waiting for my grandfather to make his way over to where I was kneeling.

In just a moment, I would feel the presence of a big, black robe in front of me followed by a soft hand touching mine. I would look up to see his smiling face as he said, "Hey pal." I'll never forget how good it made me feel to be acknowledged by my grandfather on Sunday evenings at church. It made me feel like a million dollars! In my mind, he will always be the great minister whose priorities still had room for a curious little boy at the prayer rail on Sunday nights.

Not too long ago, my Sunday school class was talking about values and virtues. Each member of the class was asked to relate an experience from their own family that illustrated a particular value or virtue. When it came around to me, my mind was spinning with at least a hundred different memories that mean so much to me. Then I began to describe a time when I spent the night with my grandparents (we called them Nannie and Bigdaddy). Try to imagine the feeling of total serenity, security, and acceptance. That's how I felt when I stayed with them. After they had put me to bed, sang songs to me, and said prayers over me, I can remember seeing across the hallway my grandfather and grandmother kneeling at their own bedside to thank God for his blessings and to intercede for others. What an impression that made on me.

When morning came, they got up early. Rather than changing their routine, they invited me right into their daily rituals and I loved every minute of it. We ate breakfast in a small area beside the kitchen that overlooked the giant pine trees in the backyard. The early morning sunshine made everything look so fresh, so full of life. We ate a simple breakfast of fruit juice, toasted muffins, and different kinds of jellies. One thing that stands out in my memory is the peacefulness of those morning hours at their house. They didn't turn on television sets or radios to fill the house with sound. Just the soft-spoken greeting to each other and to me as their guest.

When breakfast was over they would clear off the table and take out their Bibles and devotional books. Since I was there, my grandparents took it as an opportunity to teach me something. They let me read the Scripture passages and helped me to understand them. I always had questions that came to mind and I loved to hear my grandfather explain them to me. When I would ask, for example, "What does repentance mean?" he would instruct me to read the text again. Then he would explain to me in straightforward terms what the concept was all about.

They typically spent some thirty to forty-five minutes every morning reading the Bible and praying for people they knew. Then they took their walks. For miles they would walk, one block after another, incline after incline, and I would be worn out after just a short time, but they had the stamina of athletes less than half their age! What a rich blessing these and many other memories are to me.

When I told some of these things to my Sunday school class, the value or virtue I was trying to illustrate was, in a word, authenticity. The man who stood in the pulpit on Sunday was the same man who knelt at his bedside every night. The man who consistently opened the door for his wife in public was the same man who opened and held the door for her in private. I can honestly say after looking back over so many years of memories that the greatest sermon I ever saw was the one my grandfather lived every day of this life. He was not a perfect man and he would be the first to freely admit it, but he said what he meant, he walked what he talked to the best of his ability, and by God's grace he finished the course with faithfulness.

✣ ✣ ✣

Dear Dr. Grant:

What a joy it was to share with you on Sunday. It was a high-water mark in the life of this church affirming your leadership as the crucial founding leadership of this great congregation.

I thought you might be interested in what I had to say in light of the comments of so many people. This is partly constructed from my notes and my memory.

> There is a sense of which institutions are the extended shadows of great men. Democracy is a governmental ideal in the United States, is the extended shadow of our founding fathers, especially Thomas Jefferson. Modern communism is the extension of the shadow of Karl Marx.
>
> This church is the extension of the shadow of many dedicated persons—but especially Charles W. Grant. As the founding Pastor of this church, Dr. Grant shaped the mission and ministry—the very personality of this great congregation. He and his wife Mary Anna poured their total life and energy into this body. They breathed into this body the breath of life.
>
> In an effort to express our gratitude and honor to this great man, our Administrative Board has named him Minister Emeritus. When I shared this word with Dr. Grant, he was overwhelmed with emotion, and said to me that this was the most signal honor of his life.
>
> That word alone reflects his deep commitment and the place in his heart that he holds this congregation.

Dr. Grant, while we seek to honor you in the bestowal of this title, I want you to know that you have honored us far more than we could ever honor you. You've honored us by giving us this church, the fruits of your labor. You've honored us by giving us a living witness of Christian discipleship. Most of all, you've honored us in showing what it means to be a faithful minister of the gospel of Jesus Christ. Reverend, Sir, we salute you!

It's good to have you as a part of this body in this fashion, and I'm grateful for the legacy you have bestowed upon me.

Grace and peace,
Maxie [Dunnam, the third senior minister of Christ United Methodist Church]

THE BOOK OF DISCIPLINE

It is doubtful that more than a small percentage of Methodist Church members have ever seen, much less read, a copy of the *Book of Discipline.* A new Discipline is published every four years after the General Conference has met.

In order to better understand Christ Methodist Church and its history, a history of the Memphis Conference and the historical statement from the 1960 *Discipline*, The Episcopal Greetings, and The Declaration of Union are included in this volume.

The Declaration of Union printed in this volume describes the union of the Methodist Episcopal Church, the Methodist Episcopal Church, South, and the Methodist Protestant Church as they joined and adopted The Methodist Church as their name.

The Declaration of Union printed in this volume is not the beginning of the United Methodist Church as we know it but the first major step in that direction. The United Methodist Church did not come into existence as such until 1968 when the Methodist Church and the Evangelical United Brethren Church came together to form the church of which we are now a part. The 1968 Historical Statement from the *Discipline* will be included in Volume II of this history.

Historical Statement

The Book of Discipline, 1960

The Methodist Church is a church of Christ in which "the pure Word of God is preached, and the Sacraments duly administered." This church is a great Protestant body, though it did not come directly out of the Reformation but had its origin within the Church of England. Its founder was John Wesley, a clergyman of that church, as was his father before him. His mother, Susanna Wesley, was a woman of zeal, devotion, and strength of character who was perhaps the greatest single human influence in Wesley's life.

Nurtured in this devout home, educated at Oxford University, the young John Wesley, like a second Paul, sought in vain for religious satisfaction by the strict observance of the rules of religion and the ordinances of the church. The turning point in his life came when, at a prayer meeting in Aldersgate Street, London, on May 24, 1738, he learned what Paul had discovered, that it is not by rules and laws, nor by our own efforts at self-perfection, but by faith in God's mercy as it comes to us in Christ, that man may enter upon life and peace.

The gospel which Wesley thus found for himself he began to proclaim to others, first to companions who sought his counsel, including his brother Charles, then in widening circles that took him throughout the British Isles. His message had a double emphasis, which has remained with Methodism to this day. First was the gospel of God's grace, offered to all men and equal to every human need. Second was the moral ideal which this gospel presents to men. The Bible, he declared, knows no salvation which is not salvation from sin. He called men to holiness of life, and this holiness, he insisted, is "social holiness," the love and service of their fellow men. Methodism meant Christianity in earnest. The General Rules which are still found in our *Discipline* are the directions which Wesley gave to his followers to enable them to test the sincerity of their purpose and to guide them in this life. Wesley did not plan to found a new church. In his work he simply followed, like Paul, the clear call of God, first to preach the gospel to the needy who were not being reached by the Established Church and its clergy, second to take care of those who were won to the Christian life. Step by step he was led on until Methodism became a great and transforming movement in the life of England. He gathered his people in groups, in classes, and societies. He appointed leaders. He found men who were ready to carry the gospel to the masses, speaking on the streets, in the open fields, and in private homes. These men were not ordained ministers but lay preachers or "local preachers" as they were called. He appointed these men, assigned them to various fields of labor, and supervised their work. Once a year he called them together for a conference just as Methodist preachers meet in their Annual Conference sessions today.

Wesley thus united in extraordinary fashion three notable activities in all of which he excelled. One was evangelism. "The world is my parish," he declared. His preachers went to the people; they did not wait for people to come to them and he himself knew the highways and byways of England as did no other man of his day. The second was organization and administration, by which he conserved the fruits of this preaching and extended its influence. The third was his appreciation of education and his use of the printed page. He made the press a servant of the Church and was the father of the mass circulation of inexpensive books, pamphlets, and periodicals.

From England, Methodism spread to Ireland and then to America. In 1766 Philip Embury, a lay preacher from Ireland, began to preach in the city of New York. At about the same time Robert Strawbridge, another lay preacher from Ireland, settled in Frederick County, Maryland, and began the work there. In 1769 Wesley sent Richard Boardman and Joseph Pilmore to America, and two years later Francis Asbury, who became the great leader of American Methodism.

Methodism was especially adapted to American life. These itinerant preachers served the people under conditions where a settled ministry was not feasible. They sought out the scattered homes, followed the tide of migration as it moved west, preached the gospel, organized societies, established "preaching places," and formed these into "circuits." Thus by the close of the American

Revolution the Methodists numbered some 15,000 members and 80 preachers.

In the beginning, Wesley had thought of his fellows not as constituting a church but simply as forming so many societies. The preachers were not ordained, and the members were supposed to receive the Sacraments in the Anglican Church. But the Anglican clergy in America were few and far between. The Revolution had severed America from England, and Methodism to all intents and purposes had become an independent church. Wesley responded to appeals for help from America by asking the Bishop of London to ordain some of his preachers. Failing in this, he himself ordained two men and set aside Dr. Thomas Coke, who was a presbyter of the Church of England, to be a superintendent, "to preside over the flock of Christ" in America. Coke was directed to ordain Francis Asbury as a second superintendent.

At the Christmas Conference, which met in Baltimore December 24, 1784, some 60 preachers, with Dr. Coke and his companions, organized the Methodist Episcopal Church in America. Wesley had sent over *The Sunday Service*, a simplified form of the English *Book of Common Prayer*, with the Articles of Religion reduced in number. This book they adopted, adding to the articles one which recognized the independence of the new nation.

Our present Articles of Religion come from this book and unite us with the historic faith of Christendom. Our Ritual, too, though it has been modified, has this as its source. However, the forms for public worship taken from the *Book of Common Prayer* were not adapted to the freer religious life of American Methodism and never entered into common use. Instead, Methodism created a book of its own, its *Discipline*. This contains today the Articles of Religion, Wesley's General Rules, the Ritual and other forms of worship, and a large section which deals with the ministry, the various church organizations, and the rules governing the life and work of the church.

In the history of Methodism two notable divisions occurred. In 1828 a group of earnest and godly persons, largely moved by an insistence on lay representation, separated and became the Methodist Protestant Church. In 1844 there was another division, the cause being construed by some as the question of slavery, by others as a constitutional issue over the powers of the General Conference versus the episcopacy. After years of negotiation a Plan of Union was agreed upon; and on May 10, 1939, the Methodist Episcopal Church, the Methodist Episcopal Church, South, and the Methodist Protestant Church united to form the Methodist Church.

The Methodist Church believes today, as Methodism has from the first, that the only infallible proof of a true church of Christ is its ability to seek and to save the lost, to disseminate the Pentecostal spirit and life, to spread scriptural holiness, and to transform all peoples and nations through the gospel of Christ. The sole object of the rules, regulations, and usages of The Methodist Church is to aid the church in fulfilling its divine commission. United Methodism thanks God for the new life, and strength which have come with reunion, while realizing the new obligations which this brings. At the same time it rejoices in the fact that it is a part of the one Church of our Lord and shares in a common task. Its spirit is still expressed in Wesley's words: "I desire to have a league, offensive and defensive, with every soldier of Christ. We have not only one faith, one hope, one Lord, but are directly engaged in one warfare."

THE DECLARATION OF UNION

The Book of Discipline, 1960

WHEREAS, The Methodist Episcopal Church, The Methodist Episcopal Church, South, and The Methodist Protestant Church did through their respective General Conferences appoint Commissions on Interdenominational Relations and Church Union; and

WHEREAS, These Commissions acting jointly did produce, propose, and present to the three Churches a Plan of Union; and

WHEREAS, These three Churches, each acting separately for and in its own behalf, did by more than the constitutional majorities endorse and adopt this Plan of Union, in accord with their respective constitutions and disciplines, and did effect the full consummation of union in accordance with the Plan of Union; and

WHEREAS, These three Churches in adopting this Plan of Union did authorize and provide for a Uniting Conference with certain powers and duties as therein set forth; and

WHEREAS, The Uniting Conference duly authorized and legally chosen in accordance with the Plan of Union is now in session in the city of Kansas City, Missouri:

Now, THEREFORE, We, the members of the Uniting Conference, the legal and authorized representatives of The Methodist Episcopal Church, The Methodist Episcopal Church, South, and The Methodist Protestant Church, in session here assembled on this the 10th day of May, 1939, do solemnly in the presence of God and before all the world make and publish the following Declarations of fact and principle:

I. The Methodist Episcopal Church, The Methodist Episcopal Church, South, and The Methodist Protestant Church are and shall be one United Church.

II. The Plan of Union as adopted is and shall be the constitution of this United Church, and of its three constitutent bodies.

III. The Methodist Episcopal Church, The Methodist Episcopal Church, South and the Methodist Protestant Church had their common origin in the organisation of the Methodist Episcopal Church in America in 1784, A.D. and have ever held, adhered to and preseved a common belief, spirit and purpose, as expressed in their common Articles of Religion.

IV. The Methodist Episcopal Church, The Methodist Episcopal Church, South and the Methodist Protestant Church, in adopting the name "The Methodist Church" for the United Church, do not and will not surrender any right, interest or title in and to these respective names, which, by long and honored use and association have become dear to the ministry and membership of the three uniting Churches and have become enshrined in their history and records.

V. The Methodist Church is the ecclesiastical and lawful successor of the three united Churches, in and through which the three Churches as one United Church shall continue to live and have their existence, continue their Institutions and hold and enjoy their property, exercise and perform their several trusts under and in accord with the Plan of Union and Discipline of the United Church; and such trusts or corporate bodies as exist in the constituent Churches shall be continued as long as legally necessary.

VI. To the Methodist Church thus established we do now solemnly declare our allegiance, and upon all its life and service we do reverently invoke the blessing of Almighty God. Amen.

(Unaminously adopted by the Uniting Conference, Kansas City, Missouri, May 10, 1939.)

THE MEMPHIS CONFERENCE

by Paul F. Blankenship

The present geographical area occupied by the Memphis Conference was originally used as hunting grounds by the Chickasaw people until it was purchased by the government of the United States on October 18, 1818. Since this agreement was negotiated by General Andrew Jackson (along with Isaac Shelby, former governor of Kentucky), the new territory was referred to as the Jackson Purchase and the portion of this land in extreme western Kentucky is still called the Purchase. The boundaries of this new area and the present Memphis Conference are the Mississippi River on the west, the Tennessee River on the east, the Ohio River on the north, and the Mississippi state line on the south, including the Purchase area of Kentucky and West Tennessee, one of the three grand divisions of the state.

This area probably had a European American and African-American population of something over twenty-five hundred by 1820 when the first Methodist circuit riders were appointed to witness to these new settlers. When the Tennessee Conference met at Hopkinsville, Kentucky, in 1820, Hezekiah Holland and Lewis Garrett were appointed to the mission in Jackson's Purchase. Benjamin Peeples replaced Holland before the work began, and he and Garrett divided their work along the south fork of the Obion River.

A Quarterly Conference was held in the mission in Jackson's Purchase as early as June 9–10, 1821, from a stage in the woods by the Forked Deer River, led by presiding elder Thomas L. Douglass with around six hundred people in attendance. By 1823, this new mission area was named the Forked Deer District with circuits named primarily for rivers: Wolf, Hatchie, Forked Deer, Gibson, Sandy, Clark's River, Beech, and Henderson. Camp meetings and other outdoor preaching services as well as worship, preaching, and society meetings in homes characterized this early stage of the mission. Two present-day camp meetings, Tabernacle, near Brownsville, Tennessee, and Joyner's Campground in Fayette County, Tennessee, echo these early camp meetings. Both Manley's Chapel (1821) in Henry County, Tennessee, and Cowell's Chapel, near Camden, Tennessee (1824), were organized and built church buildings during this period. Both trace their history back to the efforts of Benjamin Peeples. Several other congregations, including First Church Brownsville (1824) and First Church Memphis (1826), had their beginnings in the 1820s.

Because of the rapid growth of Methodism in the new mission area during the 1820s and 1830s, the General Conference of 1840 formed the Memphis Annual

Conference, consisting of the original Jackson Purchase and a substantial northern portion of the State of Mississippi north of a line from the southwest corner of Tallahatchie County, thence due east to the southeastern corner of Oktibbeha County, thence due east to the Tombigbee River. Memphis had a population of only 1,799 in 1840 when the new conference was given its name. The first meeting of the Memphis Conference convened in Jackson, Tennessee, on November 4, 1840, under the leadership of Bishop James O. Andrew and reported 12,497 white and 1,995 black members, served by 183 local and 68 traveling preachers.

When the Methodists of the south separated from the Methodist Episcopal Church in 1844—reacting to that General Conference's chastisement of Bishop Andrew for being a slave owner—and formed the Methodist Episcopal Church, South, in 1845, the delegates from the Memphis Conference voted with the southern delegates on every issue. One of the Memphis Conference delegates to the 1844 General Conference was George W. D. Harris, who was admitted on trial in 1824 and retired in 1870, two years before his death. Because he served as a presiding elder continuously for twenty-nine years, he was considered by many to be the unofficial bishop of Memphis Conference Methodism and actually presided over the 1863 and 1864 advisory sessions of the conference in West Tennessee behind federal lines while the regular sessions were being held in Mississippi.

The records of the Memphis Conference do not reflect opposition to African slavery or to the forced removal of Native Americans west of the Mississippi River. Instead, the conference's attention was focused on proclaiming the gospel to the slaves and urging their owners to treat them fairly. By 1860, there were 7,002 colored and 28,838 white members of Memphis Conference congregations. Approximately half of these African-American Methodists were members of at least eight colored missions that were in place by 1862, including the present Collins Chapel and Greenwood C.M.E. churches in Memphis. The other half were members of white congregations and usually sat in slave balconies or in other designated areas of the church sanctuaries.

When the Civil War broke out in 1860, the Memphis Conference gave solid support to the Confederacy. Over a dozen Memphis Conference clergy served as chaplains to various regiments of the Confederate Army and several joined the fighting ranks of the army. One of these, Amos B. Jones, served as a captain in the Sixth Tennessee and later became president of the Memphis Conference Female Institute (M.C.F.I.), the position that his father had held earlier.

The African-American membership of the Memphis Conference congregations declined rapidly after the war ended and slavery was abolished: 4,025 in 1865; 2,213 in 1867. Many of those who left the Methodist Episcopal (M.E.) Church, South, became members of the Methodist Episcopal Church, the African Methodist Episcopal Church, or the African Methodist Episcopal Church, Zion, who were actively recruiting members in the Memphis Conference area during and following the war. Alexander Chapel, in the present

Brownsville District, is the oldest black congregation in the present Memphis Conference. It was organized in 1858, probably as a colored mission of the M.E. Church, South, and became a part of the M.E. Church during or following the Civil War. Centenary Church in Memphis was organized in 1865 as a congregation of the M.E. Church.

Finally, those African-Americans remaining in the M.E. Church, South, were included in the Colored (later Christian) Methodist Episcopal (C.M.E.) Church which was organized in Jackson, Tennessee, in 1870 with the encouragement and support of the M.E. Church, South. In anticipation of this development which was authorized by the history-making 1866 M.E. Church, South, General Conference, three African-American preachers (Silas Phillips, Stepney Graves, and Isaac Lane) were ordained deacons by Bishop Robert Paine "at the Colored Methodist Church" during the 1866 session of the Memphis Conference. Lane soon became an outstanding leader and bishop of the C.M.E. Church as well as founder of Lane College in Jackson, Tennessee.

The 1866 General Conference also began the process that provided for the election of lay delegates to Annual and General Conference, leading the North Mississippi District of the Methodist Protestant Church to unite with the Memphis Conference in 1869. The first lay delegates (all men) to the Memphis Annual Conference had been seated in Paducah, Kentucky, in 1867. In 1870 the Mississippi portion of the Memphis Conference was set apart to become the North Mississippi Conference. Since 1870 the geographical boundaries of the Memphis Conference have remained unchanged.

The last thirty years of the nineteenth century and the first sixty years of the twentieth century were years of strong emphasis on evangelism, missions, and education. Revivals were a typical means of evangelistic outreach through the 1950s and membership growth continued at a rapid pace, from 57,980 in 1900, to 97,007 in 1939, to a high of 123,076 in 1965. Overseas missions received special emphasis during this period, especially after the organization of the Woman's Missionary Society in 1878. Miss Lochie Rankin of Milan, Tennessee, responded to the call to the mission field in October 1878 and became the first woman missionary to represent the M.E. Church, South, in a foreign land, giving forty-two years of service in China.

The conference supported a number of local high schools and colleges in the late nineteenth and early twentieth centuries before public schools were organized. The conference gave strong support for public schools and as public elementary and high schools became available, the church-sponsored schools either became public schools or were closed. Support for colleges was eventually focused on the Memphis Conference Female Institute (M.C.F.I.) which became Lambuth College (now Lambuth University) in 1924, a coeducational institution named for missionary Bishop Walter Russell Lambuth who died in 1921. The college's first president, Dr. Richard E. Womack, led Lambuth from its beginning until his retirement in 1953. Much later, in 1973, the conference's concern for education of clergy led to its establishing a Chair of Methodist Studies at Memphis Theological Seminary of the Cumberland Presbyterian Church which it continues to support today.

During this same period local churches became more organized for education and youth ministries. The Sunday school movement was warmly endorsed by the conference and flourished under the leadership (beginning in late 1880s) of I. R. Pepper, a layperson in Memphis First Church. Epworth Leagues were first organized in 1890 and became a vital arm of the church's outreach to youth, with its name changing to Methodist Youth Fellowship in 1939 and United Methodist Youth Fellowship in 1968, reflecting the denominational unions of those years. The first conference-owned summer youth camp, Lakeshore Camp, opened in 1948 on Kentucky Lake near Camden, Tennessee, and has grown to become year-round Lakeshore Assembly.

The conference's social concern has been expressed especially through institutions, primarily settlement houses and hospitals. Wesley House (later Wesley Institute) was organized in Memphis in 1906 to minister among the poor, and Goodwill Industries was added to this ministry in 1923. Bethlehem Center emerged in Memphis in the 1930s for work among the poor of the African-American community. Today these ministries (except Goodwill Industries) are included in United Methodist Neighborhood Centers which ministers effectively in various poverty-stricken areas of Memphis. Reelfoot Rural Ministries was organized in the early 1960s to carry out a similar ministry in the Reelfoot Lake area of northwest Tennessee and continues its effective work today.

Methodist Hospital opened in Memphis in 1924 after years of planning and fund-raising by the Memphis, North Mississippi, and the North Arkansas Conferences. This ministry, owned by these three Conferences, has grown into a chain of hospitals and other medical facilities now known as Methodist Le Bonheur Healthcare and may be the largest private nonprofit health care system in the United States.

Ministry with older adults received special emphasis in 1972 when the Wesley Housing Corporation (now Wesley Senior Ministries) was formed to provide housing for low-income senior citizens, making use of government grants. Wesley Senior Ministries now has facilities in each of the seven districts of the Memphis Conference and is the largest provider of housing and health care for the elderly in the midsouth.

There have been a variety of conference newspapers during the history of the Memphis Conference. The *Western Methodist*, *Memphis Christian Advocate*, and *Epworth Messenger* appeared in the late 1800s. A *Memphis Conference Daily* was printed for the 1881 conference session. The *Midland Methodist* and the *Methodist* appeared during the first quarter of the twentieth century. After a long time without a conference newspaper, the conference approved the idea of a monthly news organ or newspaper in 1969. This action was not carried out, however, until the weekly *United Methodist Reporter* of the Memphis

Conference was established in 1980 in conjunction with the *United Methodist Reporter* of Dallas, Texas. The *Reporter* continues to serve a vital communications role in the conference.

The Methodist reunion of 1939 meant that a small number of members and preachers from the Methodist Episcopal Church and an even smaller number of members and preachers from the Methodist Protestant Church were included in the new Memphis Conference with appropriate organizational name changes. The Methodist union with the Evangelical United Brethren (E.U.B.) Church in 1968 did not bring E.U.B.s into the Memphis Conference (since no E.U.B. Churches were located in this area), but it did bring into focus the African-American Methodists who were included in the new Memphis Conference as a part of the Plan of Union with the abolition of the Central Jurisdiction. Since 1968 they have made a significant contribution in the life and ministry of their conference. Two African-American men have served as district superintendents and we were led by Bishop Ernest Newman, an African-American, from 1984 to 1992; but cross-racial pastoral appointments have been few, and we know we have a long way to go in dealing successfully with racism.

Routine issues such as how to figure conference apportionments, conference structure, declining membership (92,544 in 1998), whether to unite with the Tennessee Conference (both conferences have said no three times during the past thirty years), and ministers' pensions continue to be discussed. However, inclusiveness is probably our most obvious present challenge: how to employ most effectively our increasing number of women clergy (two have served as district superintendents as of 1999); how to be racially inclusive in a still-segregated society; how to share the gospel with people of all classes, races, nationalities, and conditions and welcome them in our congregations. Bishop Kenneth Carder is effectively leading us to face up to these challenges.

Note: Most of the information in this historical sketch is from *Methodism in the Memphis Conference: 1840–1990*, edited by Kenneth Wilkerson and published by the Memphis Conference Commission on Archives and History in 1990 for the sesquicentennial of the Memphis Conference.

✣ ✣ ✣

1. Memphis' First United Methodist Church is the oldest house of worship in the city. Organized in 1826, the present building was built in 1892. It has closed only once, during the yellow fever epidemic. During federal occupation during the Civil War, a minister detailed by the Union commander occupied the pulpit.

2. St. John's United Methodist Church was established in 1889 as Central Church Mission on Union Avenue. It was built on its present site in 1907 and renamed St. John's. The first church health center in the Memphis Conference is located here.

3. United Methodist Neighborhood Centers started in 1907; Neighborhood Centers today has four day care centers and three social service centers. Its main offices are located at 175 N. Tillman in Memphis. The social service centers help pay utilities, provide food and clothing, and offer GED classes and tutoring. The day care centers have paying customers and children whose care is sponsored by the Department of Human Services.

4. Methodist Hospitals, which first opened in 1921, are jointly owned by the Memphis, North Mississippi, and North Arkansas Conferences. They were hailed as the result of a triumphant laymen's movement. The present site of the main hospital on Union Avenue was occupied in 1923.

5. Randolph United Methodist Church is in the town of Randolph, Tennessee, that was settled in the early 1800s and became a large river port. Rev. Samuel Davidson was appointed as the first pastor by the Tennessee Conference in 1834. During the Civil War, the town was burned for firing on the Union troops from the bluff. The second church was built on the bluffs in 1883. Bishop William C. Martin, president of the Council of Bishops, grew up in this church.

6. The Reverend James McFerrin's gravesite in the cemetery of the Charleston United Methodist Church is the resting place of this 1812 soldier and farmer who was converted at a camp meeting and was a Methodist preacher for twenty years. He came to Charleston in 1834 and died in the year the Memphis Conference was formed. His sons, John Berry, A. P., and William McFerrin became prominent Methodist ministers in Tennessee. Other family members carried Methodism to Arkansas and Texas. Bishop McFerrin Stowe is a descendant.

7. The home of Alex Haley, author of *Roots*, in Henning, Tennessee, has been developed into a museum and is open to the public. Haley attended Lane College, which has close ties to the Memphis Conference.

8. Dancyville United Methodist Church was deeded its site in 1835. In 1837, a log church was built and in 1850 the present building was completed. It is constructed of hand-sawed timbers cut on the grounds. It survives as the oldest United Methodist church building in West Tennessee in continuous use for worship. The cemetery dates back to 1830. The Brownsville District High School was located here from 1882 to 1890.

9. Wesley was a town once located on U.S. Highway 70, approximately one mile southeast of Stanton, Tennessee. Named for John Wesley, the town was laid off northwest of its Methodist church in 1829. The old Wesley Circuit, which covered most of southwest Tennessee, took its name from this church and town. The town was removed and named for Joseph B. Stanton with the coming of the railroad.

10. Joyner's Campground is two miles off Highway 76 between Dancyville and Somerville. The campground has been in service for over a century. The annual camp meetings held in late July used to attract thousands and are still very popular in the area. The open-air pavilion has log seats and a dirt floor, and families who come for the week stay in small cabins on the grounds.

11. LaGrange, Tennessee, was settled in the early 1820s by very prominent folk from the Carolinas and Virginia. Elegant homes abound in this small area. The town once rivaled Memphis but died out when the railroad failed to connect them to a main line. The United Methodist church is still active and the Episcopal church is used only occasionally for special events.

12. Brownsville's First United Methodist Church was the first church built in the town in 1832. The church moved to the present site in 1898. Eight sessions of the Annual Conference have met at this church, including the 1937 conference when unification was voted and passed 179 to 92. The first Woman's Missionary Society in the Memphis Conference was formed here. The stained-glass windows are of special interest.

13. Tabernacle United Methodist Church and Kinfolks Campground were organized by Edmund Taylor and his four brothers in 1826. This church, named for their church in Virginia, has been in continuous service since that day. It is famous for the Kinfolks Campmeeting, the annual Taylor Family reunion which now draws about five hundred people. The campsite is on the grounds of the original home place of the Taylors and is still in use by Edmund Taylor, great-great grandson of the original.

14. Reelfoot Rural Ministries serves the three northwest counties of Tennessee: Dyer, Lake, and Obion. There are twenty-one different programs which include two day cares, two thrift stores, two senior meal programs, four clinical programs, arts and crafts, a Christmas toy store, and summer work camps. More than 1,020 people were served per month in 1989. It has been in operation since 1963. It is located on Minnick Road between Obion and Ridgely, Tennessee.

15. Lambuth College (now Lambuth University) on Lambuth Boulevard in Jackson, Tennessee, was chartered in 1843 as the Memphis Conference Female Institute. The school became coeducational and moved to its present site in 1923. It was named for Bishop Walter Russell Lambuth, the great missionary who often visited this conference. It opened in 1924 with Richard E. Womack as its president. The original building has been named Jones Hall for the long-time president of M.C.F.I., Amos W. Jones. Behind the main building is the Womack garden and statue; under the flagpole is a cornerstone from

Memphis Conference
Map of Methodist History

Legend

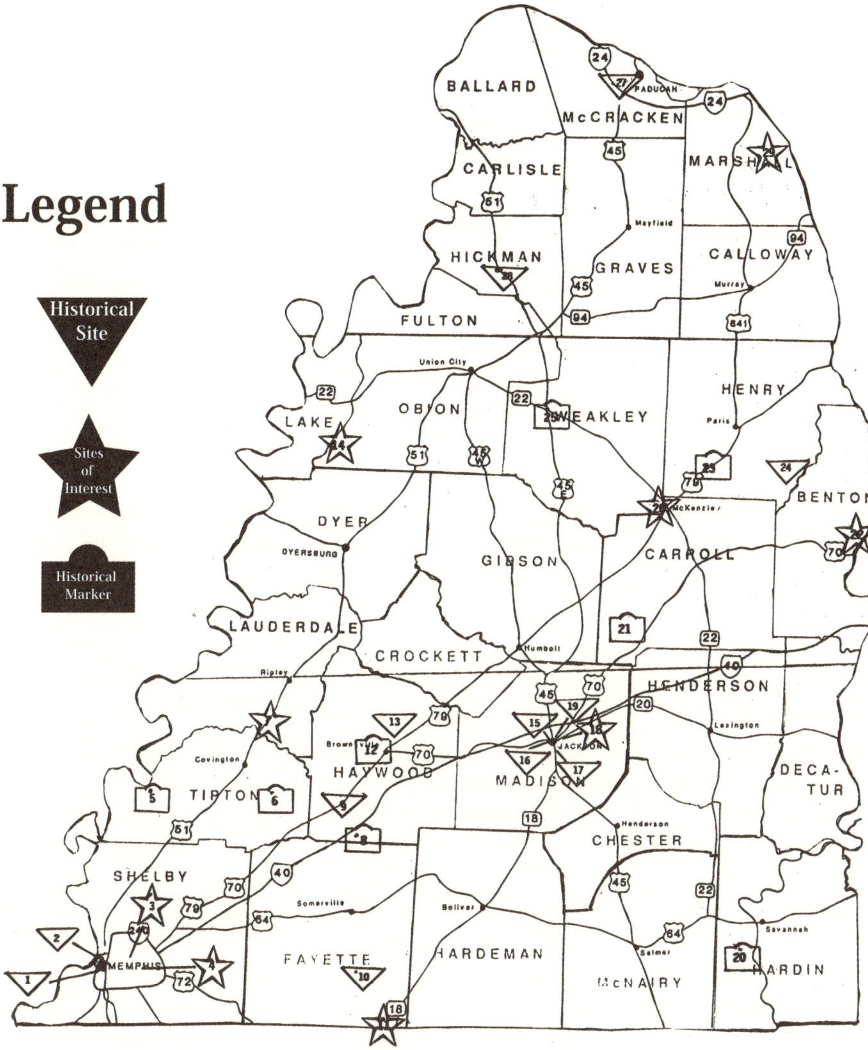

M.C.F. I.; in the chapel is a Womack display; and in the library, the Treasure Room, and archives there are a number of historic displays.

16. The Memphis Conference Female Institute site has a marker near the fire station on the Jackson Civic Center parking lot showing the original location. It was built in 1843 on land formerly used as a racetrack and donated by William O. Butler. It flourished for eighty years as an eminent school for young ladies mostly under the leadership of Amos W. and Amos B. Jones. During the Civil War, Union forces took it over for a hospital, and it was closed for two sessions. Some students met in the president's home during this time. It closed after graduation in 1919 to become a coeducational college.

17. Mother Liberty Christian Methodist Episcopal Church was the first official church of the new denomination. The General Conference of the Methodist Episcopal Church, South, met in Memphis in 1870 and authorized the formation of a separate denomination for its Negro members. The organizational meeting was held in the basement of Jackson's First Methodist Church.

18. Jackson's First United Methodist Church was organized with eight members by Rev. Thomas Neely in 1826. The first building was across the street from the present structure, which was built in 1914. Members from this church helped establish missions in east Jackson which became East Trinity United Methodist Church. The C.M.E. Church was organized here in 1870. Bishop Isaac Lane often worshiped here and prayed from the balcony. Many preachers came from this congregation, including the late Bishop Walter Lee Underwood whose father was once pastor.

19. Lane College at 545 Lane Avenue in Jackson was founded in 1882 by the Colored Methodist Episcopal Church as a high school under the direction of Bishop Isaac Lane. It became Lane Institute in 1883. In 1886 the trustees asked the Memphis Conference to send them a teacher of theology. Dr. Thomas F. Saunders, a Memphis Conference preacher, answered the call. He served from 1887 to 1903 and then Lane became a college in 1895. He was the first president.

20. Shiloh United Methodist Church and the Shiloh National Battlefield are near Savannah, Tennessee, three miles south of Highway 64. In 1851, John Ellis donated four acres to build a church. The original structure was of rough-hewn logs. Shiloh, from which the Civil War battle takes its name, means house of peace. In 1862, on April 6–7, the church was the scene of heavy fighting between Union and Confederate forces. The church was destroyed after the battle. The present church is located on the original site inside the National Military Park, which bears its name.

21. McLemoresville United Methodist Church, McLemoresville Collegiate Institute, and the site of the Public Land Office can be found on Highway 70. In 1820, missionaries Benjamin Peeples and Lewis Garrett met at the Public Land Office in McLemoresville to divide their territory. Garrett took the southernmost area and did much work around Jackson. Peeples remained in the northern area. The church was organized by the northern Methodist Episcopal Church. When they founded the McLemoresville Collegiate Institute in 1886, a part of the school building was dedicated to worship and used by the church until the present building was erected in 1926. Before joining the Memphis Conference at Unification in 1936, this church was a vital force in the Central Tennessee Conference of the Methodist Episcopal Church.

22. Lakeshore Assembly and Nathan Bedford Forrest State Park are near Eva, Tennessee. The camp was begun in 1948 and has been in continuous use since then. Most of the buildings were constructed in the early 1970s. There are presently fifteen cabins, a conference center, a swimming pool, a waterfront, and a tent and trailer site. The camp is used year-round for local church and conference retreats as well as summer camps for children and youth. More than forty-five hundred people used the facilities in 1989.

23. The Benjamin Peeples gravesite at Henry United Methodist Church is located near Highway 79 on his farm, three miles on the Henry-Mansfield Road. Peeples was one of two missionaries sent to the Jackson Purchase area in 1820. He organized churches and formed the Sandy River Circuit. To support his family, he located in Henry County, studied medicine, and practiced for thirty years. He was also a judge. Ten ministers were reared in his home: five sons, three brothers-in-law, and two orphans. In 1869, he rejoined the Memphis Conference and served until his death.

24. Manley's Chapel, which is near Highway 641, was organized before 1820 by the Reverend John Manley who had been a circuit rider in the old Western Conference since 1810. He was probably ordained by Bishop Francis Asbury during his early ministry. He located in 1814 in the newly formed Tennessee Conference. When the Jackson Purchase was opened to settlers in 1818, he moved his family across the river and took up land. When Benjamin Peeples arrived in 1820, he found Manley preaching to settlers. They organized a church with this group and Manley continued as a local preacher.

25. McFerrin College site at the University of Tennessee at Martin is on Highway 45. This Methodist liberal arts college and preparatory school was financed and built by the Methodists of Martin and deeded to the Methodist Episcopal Church, South. It was named for John B. McFerrin, prominent preacher, editor, and administrator. It was opened in 1890 with J. T. Williams as

its first president. It closed in 1924 when Lambuth College was opened. Its building was used by Martin High School, Weakley County Hospital, and now by the Martin Primary School.

26. McTylere College is in McKenzie, Tennessee, on Highway 79. Begun as Caledonia College in 1858 under the presidency of E. H. Randall, the original school was burned during the Civil War. McKenzie College was chartered in 1871 and run by H. C. Irby. When Irby retired in 1874, the school was bought by Professor Randall. It was renamed McTylere Institute in 1882 and the Methodist Church gave its support. In 1899, James S. Robins took over the school and remained its president until its closing in 1931.

27. Broadway United Methodist Church is the oldest institution in Paducah, Kentucky. The original church was founded in 1832, and a building was erected on northwest Broadway at Fourth Street in 1842. The church relocated in 1879 to a site on the southeast corner of Broadway and Seventh Street, then moved to its present location on the north corner of Broadway and Seventh Street in 1896. The building was destroyed by fire in 1929 and rebuilt in 1930. William Sutton Bishop, the "Old Judge Priest" of Irvin Cobb stories, was a member here, along with Alben W. Barkley, vice-president of the United States.

28. Marvin College in Clinton, Kentucky, on Highway 51 was a Methodist school built in 1894. It operated until 1922 when it was closed because of the advance of public education. Alben W. Barkley, congressman, senator, and U.S. vice president, graduated here in 1897. He worked his way through school by doing janitorial work, giving rise to the phrase, "Barkley swept here."

29. Lakeland Wesley Village and the Land Between the Lakes is just off Highway 68. The village is a retirement facility at Jonathan Creek that is run by the Paducah District of the Memphis Conference. The Land Between the Lakes is a vacation spot featuring fishing, boating, and lovely scenery. There is a summer program of church-related activities offered to the vacationers and a constant variety of activities for the retirees.

THE BIRTH OF CHRIST METHODIST CHURCH

One of the Greatest Churches in United Methodism

After a great deal of thought, prayer, talk, and research by Bishop William T. Watkins, J. E. Underwood, the district superintendent, and James H. Seabrook, the district steward, a Steering Committee was formed to organize a new Methodist congregation in east Memphis. This committee met for the first time on December 10, 1954, in the office of the district superintendent, which was in the Falls Building, situated on the corner of Front Street and "Whiskey Chute." "Whiskey Chute" was an alley, a passage between Main Street and Front Street a half-block north of Madison Avenue.

✣ ✣ ✣

The original committee was as follows:

Howard L. Davenport (First Methodist Church)
Everett C. Handorf, Secretary (First Methodist Church)
L. G. Bone (Union Avenue Methodist Church)
John A. Parsons, Treasurer (St. John's Methodist Church)
E. H. Tenent (St. Luke's Methodist Church)
Gerald T. Owens (Madison Heights Methodist Church)
L. Palmer Brown III* (St. John's Methodist Church)
Lee B. McCormick, Vice Chairman (St. Luke's Methodist Church)
James H. Seabrook, Chairman (Madison Heights Methodist Church)
Conrad R. McDaniel (Madison Heights Methodist Church)

These were added at later dates:

William E. Drenner (First Methodist Church)
Albert C. Jones* (Union Avenue Methodist Church)
C. B. Johnston* (Trinity Methodist Church)
Samuel Mays (St. John's Methodist Church), April 1, 1955
Fred Ridolphi (Trinity Methodist Church), April 29, 1955
W. J. Templeton (St. Luke's Methodist Church), May 6, 1955
Clifford D. Pierce* (Union Avenue Methodist Church)
H. W. Durham* (Trinity Methodist Church)

*These five members of the Steering Committee opted to remain at their home churches and not to join Christ Church.

✣ ✣ ✣

In January 1955, Harry A. Johnson Jr. was asked to be the chairman of the Church School and Youth Committees, to organize all departments of the Sunday school and Methodist Youth Fellowship, to find places for them to meet, to clean up and ready the cottage at 4370 Poplar Avenue, to find and train the teachers for all areas, and buy appropriate furniture for the church school, services at the cottage, and the pastor's offices. In February and March, Mrs. Charles M. Henderson was given the task of organizing the Woman's Society of Christian Service and the Wesleyan Service Guild. Jesse Anderson was to chair the music and choir organizational meetings and C. R. McDaniel was to take care of finding a parsonage for the new pastor.

First Methodist Church gave the new church their equity in a tract of land and a cottage at 4370 Poplar Avenue (where the Marsonne Apartments are now). The new church assumed the mortgage for $25,000. Everett Handorf tendered this property to the Steering Committee on December 17, 1954.

At the same meeting the committee was informed that the Wallace property (where the playing fields are now) was available for $114,000 cash. This amount of cash was not available. This proved to be a long-range benefit for the new church. Emmett Joyner and L. Hall Jones owned 6.4 acres of land at the corner of Poplar and the proposed new street, Grove Park Road. The parcel was offered to the church for $125,000 and that amount and the terms of payment were negotiable. A buffer was needed between the proposed Laurelwood Shopping Center and the surrounding homes, and this new church would give them the buffer.

After much negotiation the church was given an easement for parking (nights and Sundays) on the shopping center property. This was the first time the city had allowed such an arrangement. The parking agreement with the city was the skillful work of Jesse Vineyard, the volunteer church attorney. The property was finally purchased for $95,000. The Steering Committee appointed three temporary trustees to handle the property legalities. They were Howard Davenport, Edgar Tenent, and C. R. McDaniel. This was done at the January 28, 1955, meeting. There were more than thirty parcels of land considered before the final decision to buy the 6.4 acres at Poplar and Grove Park. The parking arrangement was a lifesaver for the church.

On March 28, 1955, the Memphis District Committee on Church and Society offered $50,000 for the new church project. This meeting of the Steering Committee had a profound effect on the future of the church. The $50,000 was a tremendous financial boost, but the most far-reaching action taken was the naming of the new church, "Christ Methodist Church."

The meeting place for the church was finally settled on April 22, 1955. Mr. Augustine Cianciola, who owned the Plaza Theater, offered it for $100 per Sunday. The rent included air-conditioning, heat, cleanup before and after services, stage and office space for Sunday school, and storage for chairs, piano, and organ.

It was learned in late April who the pastor for the new church would be—Charles W. Grant, pastor at Madison Heights Methodist Church.

At the May 6 Steering Committee meeting the pastor's salary was set at $9,000 and authority to rent an apartment in Camellia Gardens, 174 Windover, Apt. 2, as the temporary parsonage. The rent for the apartment was $135 per month. A car allowance for the pastor was set at $600 per year.

✣ ✣ ✣

Following are the reports on the organization of the essential committees made on May 23, 1955, and June 10, 1955:

Church School and Youth Committee
Harry Johnson, Chairman (Madison Heights)
Mrs. Charles McVean (St. John's)
Mrs. Richard Kite (St. John's)
Clarence Colby (First Methodist)
J. B. Emerson (First Methodist)
Mrs. A. A. Sippel (Trinity)
Leland W. Helms (Trinity)
Mrs. Leland W. Helms (Trinity)

Woman's Society of Christian Service
Mrs. C. M. Henderson, Chairman (Madison Heights)
Mrs. Hugh Carey (Madison Heights)
Mrs. Percy Whitenton (First Methodist)
Mrs. J. C. Ingram (First Methodist)
Mrs. Thomas West (St. John's)
Mrs. Richard Taylor (St. John's)
Mrs. Oscar Crofford (Trinity)
Mrs. F. M. Ridolphi (Trinity)
Mrs. J. V. Thomas (St. Luke's)
Mrs. H. C. Shelton (St. Luke's)

Music and Choir
Jesse Anderson, Chairman (First Methodist)
Mrs. John Parsons (St. John's)
Mrs. W. J. Templeton (St. Luke's)
Mrs. Herbert Dunkman (Madison Heights)
Jack B. Caskey (Trinity)
Les Bone (Union)

These three movies were shown at the Plaza Theater in Christ Church's first few months of existence. They created many conversations about the new church.

Parsonage
C. R. McDaniel (Madison Heights)

The following is the proposed organization and physical arrangement of the church school and was unanimously approved by the Church School Committee of Christ Methodist Church, May 23, 1955:

Children's Division
Mrs. Leland Helms, Superintendent (Trinity)

Department, Superintendent (Church)
Nursery, Mrs. Charles McVean (St. John's)
Kindergarten, Mrs. A. A. Sippel (Trinity)
Primary, Mrs. V. Hugo Akin (Madison Heights)
Junior, Mrs. E. L. Carpenter (Madison Heights)

Youth Division
Sam Mays, Superintendent (St. John's)

Department, Superintendent (Church)
Intermediate, Mrs. Richard Kite (St. John's)
Senior, Sam Reid (First Methodist)
Older Youth, Mr. & Mrs. Percy Whitenton (First Methodist)

Adult Division
J. B. Emerson, Superintendent (First Methodist)

Department, Superintendent (Church)
Young Adult, Clarence Colby (First Methodist)
Young Adult, Mrs. C. M. Henderson (Madison Heights)
Adult, John Parsons (St. John's)

Church School Secretary, Clay Shelton (St. Luke's)
Church School Treasurer, Leland Helms (Trinity)

✣ ✣ ✣

We propose that the Kindergarten, Primary, and Junior Departments meet at 4370 Poplar for church school and for expanded sessions during church. This will eliminate the necessity of parents making the five-mile trip between church school and church to pick up their children.

The Nursery will use the Cry and Party rooms at the Plaza Theater during both church school and church.

The Intermediate, Senior, Older Youth, and all Adult classes will meet in the theater for an assembly program.

These classes will then split up with the Intermediate Department meeting in the west lobby, the Senior and Older Youth Departments will meet together in one corner of the theater proper, the two Young Adult and the Adult Class will meet in the other three corners of the theater.

A Methodist Youth Fellowship (M.Y.F.) for Intermediates, Seniors and Older Youth will meet at 4370 Poplar on Sunday evenings.

We further propose that a Boy Scout Troop be organized as soon as possible.

Harry A. Johnson Jr.
Chairman

STEERING COMMITTEE
Twenty-First Meeting, June 10, 1955
The meeting was opened and closed by Chairman James Seabrook

Sunday School Committee. Harry Johnson reported on plans for Sunday school beginning on June 19. Attached is a copy of his report. In addition, he received permission from the Steering Committee to order 125 folding chairs and the necessary oak chairs that will be needed on June 19, also to rent a piano for the Sunday school, to have a sign put in front of the building at 4370 Poplar that would read "Temporary Office Christ Methodist Church" and furniture for the preacher's study.

We have had donated to us two large window fans, a desk and chair for the secretary, a mimeograph machine and a typewriter. Mr. Johnson pointed out some repairs that would need attention and the need for keeping the yard cut.

Choir. Jesse Anderson reported that we have a Hammond organ installed for our use for the next four Sundays starting June 19 and at no charge to us. He introduced Mrs. Dunkman, who has agreed to play the organ temporarily. It was decided the choir would not have a trained leader. Jesse Anderson is to lead the congregation in singing. The Choir Committee plus any additional people interested in the choir would sit together to assist. Mr. Anderson reported that he would have 300 Cokesbury Song Books and a rostrum and light for the preacher. He also said that he would contact Dr. Grant about special music for the service.

Publicity. It was moved by Lee McCormick, seconded by Mr. Davenport and passed that Bill Grumbles run advertisements in both newspapers for the next four weekends announcing the services of Christ Church and inviting people to attend. Mr. McCormick pointed out that we should also capitalize on all news stories for additional publicity.

Charter Members. It was moved by Jesse Anderson, seconded by Clay Shelton and passed that charter memberships remain open for the first four Sundays, closing July 10, 1955.

WSCS Mrs. Henderson reported that her committee members have been contacted and a meeting was planned for June 14 at 4370 Poplar.

New Committees. Ushers Committee: Dr. W. J. Templeton, Chairman (St. Luke's), Sam Reed, James M. Doyle (First), Earl Billings, Jac Gates, Ernest Hall (Madison Heights), Ralph McCool, Charles McVean, Haskell Gass (St. John's)

Greeting Committee: C. R. McDaniel, Chairman (Madison Heights), R. H. Norris (St. Luke's), J. W. Pattinson, C. P. Harris (St. John's), Percy Whitenton, Ray Drenner (First), Harry Johnson (Madison Heights), Les Bone (Union Avenue), Jack Caskey, Fred Ridolphi (Trinity)

Nominating Committee: (For Official Board and the Four Commissions) Dr. Charles Grant, Chairman, Mr. H. L. Davenport, Lay Chairman (First), James Seabrook (Madison Heights), Lee McCormick (St. Luke's), John Parsons (St. John's), Fred Ridolphi (Trinity), Les Bone (Union Avenue)

Building Fund. Campaign Planning Committee: John A. Parsons, Chairman (St. John's), H. L. Davenport (First), C. R. McDaniel (Madison Heights), E. H. Tenent (St. Luke's), H. W. Durham (Trinity), A. C. Jones (Union Avenue)

Architect Committee: In addition to Lee McCormick and E. C. Handorf, Harry A. Johnson Jr. was approved for the committee; two other members to be recommended by those three. This committee is to get to the point where all of the information can be presented to the Official Board with a recommendation.

Church Office. Mrs. Billings, who has been Dr. Grant's secretary at Madison Heights on a part-time basis, was approved on a temporary basis. Mrs. Billings is not interested in a permanent job but will work until a permanent secretary is hired. The office is to be opened at 4370 Poplar on Monday or Tuesday.

Membership and Records. Mrs. P. B. Whitenton is to receive all membership cards from each of the churches. She will compile this to be used for letters that will be gotten out instructing the membership about plans for our first meeting on June 19.

Samuel H. Mays
Acting Secretary

Steering Committee

Twenty-Second Meeting, June 17, 1955

The meeting was called to order by Chairman James Seabrook and opened with a prayer by Dr. Grant.

Mr. Seabrook said the purpose of the meeting was to have reports from the committees to see if we were prepared for services on our first Sunday, June 19, 1955.

Choir. Jesse Anderson reported that the songbooks had not arrived, but if they were not here in time for the services, arrangements would be made to borrow the necessary number from First Methodist. The chairs for the choir are already in the theater and the Hammond organ has been installed.

Sunday School. Harry Johnson reported that everything was ready for the Sunday school. He requested that the Hospitality Committee be on hand at 9:30 A.M. to greet the people coming to Sunday school and also that the Ushers Committee take the offering for Sunday school as well as the church service.

Jesse Anderson moved, C. B. Johnston seconded it, and it was unanimously passed that the Memphis House Cleaning Company clean up the cottage at 4370 Poplar at four dollars per day and that Harry Johnson have the lawn mowed as needed.

It was reported that the sign had been put up in front of the cottage, that collection plates and envelopes had been secured, and that arrangements had been made to handle the traffic problem at 4370 Poplar.

Ushers. Dr. Templeton reported that the ushers had been contacted and would be on hand at 9:00 A.M.

Hospitality Committee. Mr. McDaniel said that he had contacted all of his committee except one person, and that they would also be on hand at 9:00 A.M.

WSCS Mrs. Henderson said that there would be another meeting on Tuesday to plan for the organizational meeting of the WSCS, which would be held on June 28 at 10:10 A.M. at the cottage. She asked that anyone wanting to place flowers on the altar as memorials contact her so that this could be arranged for the church services.

Dr. Grant. Dr. Grant said that he knew we had planned M.Y.F. for 6:30 P.M. but wondered if maybe there should be a Sunday evening service of some type. With all the enthusiasm that we have, every avenue possible should be explored. He said he would like to throw things into high gear as soon as possible.

Building Fund Campaign Planning Committee. John Parsons is to have a meeting as soon as possible to organize a plan for raising the funds, and be prepared to present it to the Official Board.

Publicity. At Ed Tenent's suggestion, Bill Grumbles is to be contacted about pictures of the congregation in front of the Plaza Theater both for television and newspaper publicity. The Chairman asked about a sign near the street that would point toward the theater advertising our church services. Mr. Helms is to be contacted on this.

The meeting was closed with a prayer by John A. Parsons.

Samuel H. Mays
Acting Secretary

✣ ✣ ✣

PROPOSED BUDGET FOR CHRIST METHODIST CHURCH
1955–1956

Methodist Conference Work

World Service & Conference Benevolences	1,000.00
General Administration Fund	5.00

Jurisdictional Conference Fund 5.00
District Work Fund 5.00
City Missions Fund 75.00
District Church Extension Fund 100.00
District Superintendent's Salary 50.00
Ten-in-One Offering 312.00
Wesley Foundation & Student Work 5.00
Minimum Salary Fund 112.50
Conference Claimants 1,350.00
Bishop's Fund 180.00
Lambuth College Sustaining Fund 300.00
Total $3,499.50

Salaries
Pastor's Salary 9,000.00
Pastor's Automobile Exp. Allowance 600.00
Secretaries (estimated) 3,600.00
Janitor Service (estimated) 1,500.00
Total $14,700.00

Rents and Utilities
Rent—Plaza Theater 5,200.00
Rent—Parsonage 1,620.00
Utilities—Parsonage 480.00
Utilities—Little Cottage 400.00
Total $7,700.00

Office Supplies & Postage
Estimated Total $5,000.00

Publicity
Newspaper Advertising 4,500.00
Christ Methodist Courier 2,000.00
Total $6,500.00

Music
Organ (Theater, later Edu. Building) 5,000.00
Minister of Music (Approx. 6 mos.) 2,500.00
Organist (Approx. 6 mos.) 1,000.00
Sheet Music for Choir 500.00
Hymnals for Sanctuary 1,000.00
Total $10,000.00

Youth Work and Nursery
Youth Center and Activities 1,000.00
Nursery 500.00
Total $11,500.00

Maintenance, Repairs, Interest, Etc.
Interest on Indebtedness 4,765.00
Insurance on Property 100.00
Maintenance & Repairs (Est.) 3,000.00
Total $7,865.00

Kitchen Supplies – Dishes, etc. $1,000.00

Contingent Fund – Miscellaneous Items $7,235.50

Sinking Fund
To provide for purchase of furniture
and equipment for church when built $25,000.00

Grand Total of All Items $90,000.00

✣ ✣ ✣

The following is the first presentation made to the congregation of Christ Church. It was made at the Plaza Theater at 9:45 A.M. to the assembly for the first session in the Sunday school, June 19, 1955:

> On behalf of the temporary Sunday school Committee, I am pleased to welcome you to the first session of the Sunday school of Christ Methodist Church. We'd like for you to meet our Pastor, Dr. Charles W. Grant, who has a few words to say to us, after which he will offer our first prayer.
>
> The temporary Sunday school Committee, which I represent, has made every effort to organize the Sunday school in such a way that it will serve you best and be as efficient as possible. We think that the arrangement we have is the best, considering the physical facilities available. We know it isn't perfect and that there will be inconveniences, but with your patience and help we are sure our purposes can be accomplished.
>
> It has been a great pleasure for me to work with this committee and the teachers who are on the job this morning. Everyone has been so cooperative and enthusiastic about all the work that has been done, and is yet to be done. Without exception everyone we have called on has enthusiastically accepted whatever job needed to be done and only asked when it should be finished.
>
> We have already some of the finest teachers in Memphis to care for your children. As you know, the Kindergarten, Primary and Junior Departments are meeting at 4370 Poplar

for Sunday school and extended sessions during church. We ask you to cooperate with these teachers by leaving your children there through the church hour. If for any reason you need to pick them up after Sunday school, please notify the teacher before Sunday school. They will have your child ready and it won't disrupt their program when you come for them.

Nursery teachers will care for the babies from the cradle through three years here at the theater, also through the church hour. Their teachers have even made arrangements to give them juice and cookies to tide them over until lunch. Church will be over at 11:45 A.M. so you can pick your children up at 4370 Poplar without making it too late to get home for lunch. With such an extensive children's program as this, we need more leaders, teachers and workers for every department, so whether you feel qualified or not, please give us your name and the area in which you'd like to work. We need you now and hope that the need will grow each week.

[Scripture and Offering]

There will be Methodist Youth Fellowship meetings for the Intermediates, Seniors and Older Youth at 4370 Poplar every Sunday evening at 6:30 P.M. Mr. Sam Mays has arranged our initial youth program for us. Immediately after this assembly each Sunday, the Intermediates will go to the lobby and have their lesson period under the direction of Mrs. Richard Kite, the Seniors and Older Youth will assemble in the southeast corner of this theater with Mr. Sam Reid.

There will be three adult classes initially with Mr. J. B. Emerson taking responsibility of organizing the adult division. We hope there will be a need for many more. The first is a class for young adults in the general age group of 24–35 with Mr. Clarence Colby as teacher. They will meet in the southwest corner of the theater. The second is, for lack of a better name, the middle adults, in the general age group of 30–45. They will meet with Mrs. Charles Henderson in the northeast corner of the theater. The third class, which will have no age limitation at all, anyone from 24 and up will meet with Mr. John Parsons in the northwest corner.

The Committee wants you to help us with your constructive criticism of the entire Sunday school program and changes will be made to meet your needs when possible. If you are undecided as to which group you should belong, try each of them and then settle in the one which fills your need best.

May God bless and nourish this, His Church and Church School and may all things we do be in the name of Jesus Christ and to His Glory.

Harry A. Johnson Jr.

Dr. Grant's sermon was "The Birth of a Church." There was a solo sung by Miss Zetta Walker and the choir was directed by Mr. Jesse Anderson. Mrs. Herbert Dunkman played the organ. Dr. Grant announced the theme for the new church would be *Tell Ten, Bring Two.*

OFFICIAL FAMILY

Steering Committee, 1954–1955

Les G. Bone	Union Avenue Methodist Church
L. Palmer Brown III*	St. John's Methodist Church
Howard L. Davenport	First Methodist Church
William E. Drenner	First Methodist Church
H. W. Durham*	Trinity Methodist Church
E. C. Handorf	First Methodist Church
C. B. Johnston*	Trinity Methodist Church
A. C. Jones*	Union Avenue Methodist Church
Samuel H. Mays	St. John's Methodist Church
Lee B. McCormick	St. Luke's Methodist Church
C. R. McDaniel	Madison Heights Methodist Church
Gerald T. Owens	Madison Heights Methodist Church
John A. Parsons	St. John's Methodist Church
Clifford D. Pierce*	Union Avenue Methodist Church
Fred M. Ridolphi	Trinity Methodist Church
James H. Seabrook Sr.	Madison Heights Methodist Church
Dr. W. J. Templeton	St. Luke's Methodist Church
Ed H. Tenent	St. Luke's Methodist Church

*served on the steering committe but did not come to Christ Methodist Church

It was decided at the June 10, 1955, meeting of the Steering Committee to hold the charter membership open until July 10, 1955.

James H. Seabrook Sr.
Chairman, Madison Heights Methodist Church

Lee B. McCormick
Vice Chairman, St. Luke's Methodist Church

E. C. Handorf
Secretary
First Methodist Church

STEERING COMMITTEE, 1954–1955

**Les G. Bone, Union Methodist Church, Photo Unavailable*

Ed H. Tenent
St. Luke's Methodist Church

Howard L. Davenport
First Methodist Church

William E. Drenner
First Methodist Church

Samuel M. Mays
St. John's Methodist Church

C. R. McDaniel
Madison Heights Methodist Church

Gerald T. Owens
Madison Heights Methodist Church

John A. Parsons
St. John's Methodist Church

Fred M. Ridolphi
Trinity Methodist Church

Dr. W. J. Templeton
St. Luke's Methodist Church

Membership of the First Official Board 1955–1956

James H. Seabrook Sr.
Chairman

Howard L. Davenport
Church Lay Leader

Lee B. McCormick, First Vice Chairman
Fred M. Ridolphi, Second Vice Chairman
Charles Tate, Secretary

Jesse Anderson
Charles Baker
Roy Barron
Earle Billings
Dr. Howard Boone
Jack Byrne
Tom Campbell
James Canfield
Hugh Carey
Jack Caskey
James Clay Jr.
Clarence Colby
L. A. Conolly
Charles Cunningham
Harry DeZonia
James Doyle
Ray Drenner
William Drenner
Horton DuBard
Herbert Dunkman
Dennis Earles
J. B. Emerson
Ned French
Haskell Gass
Fred Graham
William Grumbles
E. C. Handorf
B. F. Hardin
C. P. Harris
Henry Harry
Horace Harwell
Leland Helms
John Huckabee
J. C. Ingram Jr.
Harry Johnson Jr.
Jesse Joyner
Keith Kelley
Frank Liddell
W. K. Martak
Sam Mays
Porter McClean
Ralph McCool
Lee McCormick
C. R. McDaniel
J. M. Meadows
Early Mitchell
Y. O. Mitchell
Earl Montgomery
D. A. Noel
R. H. Norris
Gerald Owens
Frank Prichard
Sam Reid
E. R. Richmond
Fred Ridolphi
Lloyd Sarber
Clay Shelton Jr.
Carey Stanley Sr.
H. C. Stroupe
Charles Tate
Dr. W. J. Templeton
Edgar Tenent
Jesse Vineyard
Russell Weaver
Percy Whitenton
Mrs. Percy Whitenton
W. A. Wren
Paul Yarbrough

Christ Methodist Church

Organized
June 26, 1955

Charles W. Grant, D.D., Pastor

J.E. Underwood, District Superintendent
W.T. Watkins, Bishop

This Membership Book Presented
by
Dr. & Mrs. Grant and David Lawrence Grant

In Memory of
Mrs. William Nathan Grant
Mother of our First Pastor
Who Gave Three Sons to the Christian Ministry

CHARTER MEMBER SIGNATURES

No.	Name	Date	Manner	No.	Name	Date	Manner
1	James H Seabrook	6/26/55	C.	36	Carey P Stanley, Sr.	6/26/55	C.
2	Lee D. McCormick	"	C.	37	Mrs Carey P Stanley	"	C.
3	Samuel H. Mays	"	C.	38	Mrs R. G. Stanley	"	C.
4	J.O. Parsons	"	C.	39	Mrs. B. N. Fain	"	V.
5	Everett E Handel(?)	"	C.	40	B N Fain	"	B.
6	Fred M Ridolphi	"	C.	41	Sam B. Reid	"	C.
7	W.J. Templeton DDS.	"	C.	42	Mrs. Sam B Reid	"	C.
8	Conrad R. McDaniel	"	C.	43	S. A. Noel	"	C.
9	Edgar H Tenent Sr	"	C.	44	Mrs S A Noel	"	C.
10	Howard L Davenport	"	C.	45	Carrie Anne Noel	"	C.
11	Mrs. Howard L. Davenport	"	C.	46	Mrs. Oscar B. Crofford Sr.		C.
12	William E. Drenner	"	C.	47	Dr. Oscar B Crofford	"	C.
13	Mrs William E Drenner		C.	48	Mrs F. J. Cassels(?)	"	C.
14	Mrs. Chas. Henderson	"	C.	49	F. J. Cassels(?)	"	C.
15	Mrs F. R. Thomas	"	C.	50	William Barry DeZonia	"	C.
16	D. K. Kerr(?)	"	C.	51	Mrs. William Barry DeZonia	"	C.
17	Mrs. L. N. Talley	"	C.	52	Robert Harris DeZonia	"	C.
18	Letta Walker	"	C.	53	Mrs Harry F. DeZonia		C.
19	Mrs. H. F. Pickering	"	C.	54	Harry F DeZonia	"	C.
20	Harold F. Pickering(?)	"	C.	55	William McKnight	7/10/55(?)	C.
21	Earle N. Billings	"	C.	56	Mrs William McKnight	"	C.
22	Mrs. Earle N. Billings	"	C.	57	Mrs. Herbert H. Dunkman	6/26/55	C.
23	Mrs Charles W. Grant	"	C.	58	Herbert H. Dunkman	"	C.
24	David M Grant	"	C.	59	Mrs. Gerald E Maynard Jr.	"	C.
25	Harry A. Johnson Jr.	"	C.	60	Gerald E Maynard Jr.	"	C.
26	Mrs. Harry A. Johnson, Jr.	"	C.	61	Mrs J H Seabrook		C.
27	Ray E Drenner	"	C.	62	Mrs James H Seabrook	"	C.
28	Mrs. Ray E. Drenner	"	C.	63	Miss Mary Anne Seabrook		C.
29	Percy B Whitenton	"	C.	64	James H. Seabrook Jr.	"	C.
30	Mrs Percy B Whitenton	"	C.	65	Mrs Edward Richmond		C.
31	J B Emerson	"	C.	66	Edward R. Richmond Jr.		C.
32	Mrs J. B. Emerson	"	C.	67	Edward R. Richmond Sr.		C.
33	Moody B Cunningham	"	C.	68	Mrs. Steve Fransioli Jr.		C.
34	Mrs. Moody B. Cunningham		C.	69	Mrs Floyd Dixon	"	C.
35	Mrs Ramon(?) Stidham	"	C.	70	Joanne Dixon		C.

No.	Name	Date	Manner
71	Irene Colby	6/26/55	c.
72	Clarence Colby Jr.	"	c.
73	Margaret H. Colby (Mrs. C.)	"	c.
74	Gladace Colby	"	c.
75	Troy Emerson	"	c.
76	Mr. Nat Dunn	"	c.
77	Mrs. Nat Dunn	"	c.
78	Natalie Dunn	"	c.
79	Jerry Dunn	"	c.
80	Ima Campbell	"	c.
81	Mrs Ben M Carpenter	"	c.
82	Ben M Carpenter	"	c.
83	Mrs. W. K. Martak	"	c.
84	Peggy Martak	"	c.
85	W. K. Martak	"	c.
86	Earl Montgomery	"	c.
87	Ruth Y. Montgomery (Mrs. Earl)		c.
88	John E. Montgomery	"	c.
x 89	R. Michael Montgomery		x
90	Mrs. Reeves D. Ingram		c.
91	Reeves D. Ingram	"	c.
92	Helen G. French (Mrs. Ned M.)		c.
93	Ned M. French	"	c.
94	Nick French	"	c.
95	Marian A. Drake	"	c.
96	Robert J. Drake	"	c.
97	Ida Arnette (Mrs. James B.)	"	c.
98	James B. Arnette	"	v.
99	R. M. Weaver	"	c.
100	Jean H. Weaver	"	c.
101	Mrs. George Darnes		c.
102	George Darnes	"	c.
103	Mrs R. T. Holt	"	c.
104	Dr. R. T. Holt	"	c.
105	~~Miss Patricia Court~~	"	

this 140

No.	Name	Date	Manner
106	~~Mrs Norman L. Bacy~~ ~~" " I. Court~~	6/26/55	
107	~~Mrs. Stanley C. Metcalf~~		
108	Mrs. O. F. Gibson	"	c
109	O. F. Gibson	"	c
110	Jeffrey Gibson	"	c
111	Nelson D. Wilson	"	c
x 112	Jeannie Wilson	"	x
113	Alliene Wilson	"	c
114	Mrs. Roy W. Barron	"	c
115	Roy W. Barron	"	c
116	Sandra Jean Barron		c
117	Mrs H. H. Holloway	"	c
118	Mrs John Brown	"	c
119	Virginia C. Grumbles	"	c
120	W. H. Grumbles	"	c
121	[illegible]	"	c
122	Emmett [illegible]	"	x
123	Mrs. J. F. Bigger, Jr.	"	c
124	Dr. J. F. Bigger Jr.	"	c
125	Miss Judy Garner	"	c
126	Ned Randolph Garner	"	c
127	Christine S. Garner (Mrs N. R.)		c
x 128	Ned R. Garner Jr.	"	x
129	Dain S. Riley	"	c
130	Mrs. Dain S. Riley	"	c
131	Helen E. Felts	"	c
132	Ernest J. Felts	"	c
133	Mrs. John W. Joost	"	c
134	Mrs. [illegible]	"	c
135	Frank W. Prichard	"	c
136	[illegible] Prichard	"	c
137	Lessie L. Speed	"	c
138	Maurice Speed	"	
139	Mrs. C. R. McDaniel	"	
140	Mr & Mrs Frank W. Fisher	"	

140½ $105

No.	Name	Date	Manner
141	Harry J. Moyer Jr.	6/26/55	c.
142	Mrs. H. L. Stanley	"	c.
143	V. D. Stanley	"	c.
144	Mrs. Jac H. Gates	"	c.
145	Martha F. Gates	"	c.
146	Jac H Gates	"	c.
147	Mrs. Sabra G. Pepper	"	c.
148	Elizabeth Templeton, (Mrs. W. E.)		c.
149	L Haskell Gass	"	c.
150	Ruby S. Gass	"	c.
151	J. L. Alston M.D.		c.
152	Mrs. James L. Alston Jr.		c.
153	Mrs. John A. [illegible]	"	c.
154	Mrs. Herschel Crowley Jr.		c.
155	Herschel Crowley Jr.	"	c.
156	Olen H. Davis	"	c.
157	Mrs. Olen H. Davis	"	c.
158	L G Barnard	"	c.
159	Vera Loze Barnard		c.
160	J. M. Meadows	"	c.
161	Mrs. J. M. Meadows	"	c.
162	Hal Q. Meadows	"	c.
163	Mrs. Lorene McCallum	"	c.
164	Mrs. Ruby L. Wilson		c.
165	Mrs. Lillian H. Samuels		c.
166	Mrs. Edna Cockrell	"	c.
167	Essie Cockrell	"	c.
168	Mrs. W. K. Bell	"	c.
169	Warren K. Bell	"	c.
170	Mrs. John Ricker Jr.		c.
171	H. Mither	"	c.
172	Mrs. Stella Wallace		c.
173	Jack H Wallace		c.
174	Mrs. T. Wade Smith		c.
175	T. Wade Smith	"	c.

No.	Name	Date	Manner
176	Mrs. Lee R. Hull	6/26/55	c.
177	Mrs. Jessie T. Rhodes	"	c.
178	Mrs. Kelley L. Rhodes	"	c.
179	Mr. Kelley L. Rhodes	"	c.
180	Mr. Earl H. Smith	"	c.
181	Mrs. Earl H. Smith	"	c.
182	Mr. Frank B. Liddell		c.
183	Mrs. Frank B. Liddell		c.
184	Mrs. Hugh F. Carey (Annie Belle Barney)		c.
185	Hugh F. Carey	"	c.
186	William C. Samuels	"	c.
187	Mrs. Jack P. Byrne	"	c.
188	Paul Byrne	"	c.
189	Jack P. Byrne	"	c.
190	[illegible]		
191	Mrs. Charles H. Sullivan		c.
192	Mr. Charles H. Sullivan		c.
193	Mrs. Mattie C. Thomas		c.
194	Agnes Thomas	"	c.
195	W. T. Stevenson	"	c.
196	Mrs. [illegible] Welch	"	c.
197	C. N. Clay Jr.	"	c.
198	Mrs. C. N. Clay Jr.	"	c.
199	C. N. Clay III	"	c.
200	C. G. Knight	"	c.
201	Dr. T. R. Harris	"	c.
202	[illegible]	"	c.
203	Mr. & Mrs. V. Hugo Akin	"	c.
204			c.
205	Mr. Lynwood H. Akin	"	c.
206	Mrs. E. C. Finley	"	c.
207	Mr. Wilfred E. Stevens	"	c.
208	Mrs. W. E. Stevens		c.
209	Beverly D. Stevens	"	c.
210	Mrs. Robert E. [illegible]	"	c.
211	Mrs. R. W. Caruthers	"	c.
212	Mrs. Jean Jaggers	"	c.

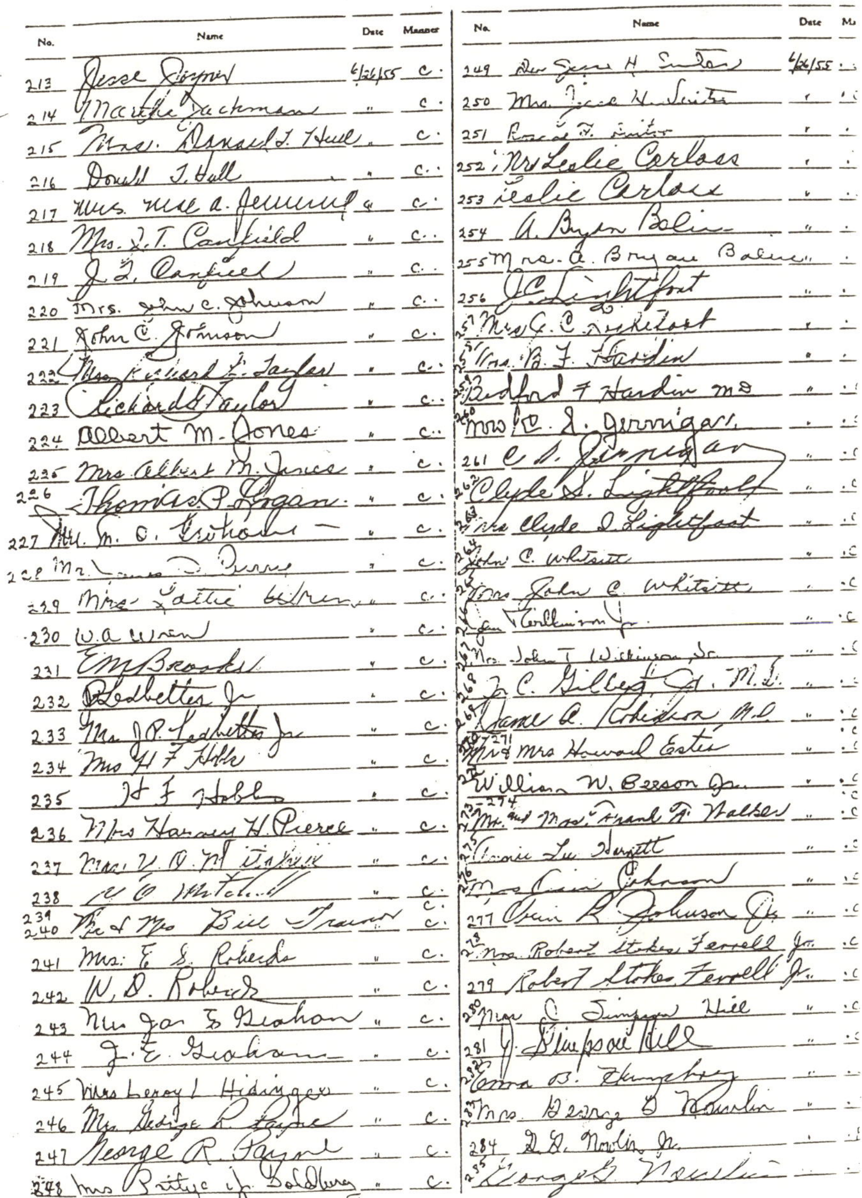

No.	Name	Date	Manner
213	Jesse Joyner	6/26/55	c.
214	Martha Jackman	"	c.
215	Mrs. Donald I. Hull	"	c.
216	Donald I. Hull	"	c.
217	Mrs. [illegible] A. Jennings	"	c.
218	Mrs. J. T. Canfield	"	c.
219	J. T. Canfield	"	c.
220	Mrs. John C. Johnson	"	c.
221	John C. Johnson	"	c.
222	Mrs. Richard L. Taylor	"	c.
223	Richard L. Taylor	"	c.
224	Albert M. Jones	"	c.
225	Mrs. Albert M. Jones	"	c.
226	Thomas P. Logan	"	c.
227	Mrs. M. O. Graham	"	c.
228	Mrs. James D. [illegible]	"	c.
229	Mrs. Lattie Wren	"	c.
230	W. A. Wren	"	c.
231	E. M. Brooks	"	c.
232	J. P. Ledbetter Jr.	"	c.
233	Mrs. J. P. Ledbetter Jr.	"	c.
234	Mrs. H. F. Hobbs	"	c.
235	H. F. Hobbs	"	c.
236	Mrs. Harvey H. Pierce	"	c.
237	Mrs. V. O. Mitchell	"	c.
238	V. O. Mitchell	"	c.
239, 240	Mr. & Mrs. Bill Traver	"	c., c.
241	Mrs. E. S. Roberts	"	c.
242	W. D. Roberts	"	c.
243	Mrs. Jas. E. Graham	"	c.
244	J. E. Graham	"	c.
245	Mrs. Leroy L. Hidinger	"	c.
246	Mrs. George R. Payne	"	c.
247	George R. Payne	"	c.
248	Mrs. [illegible] Goldberg	"	c.
249	Dr. Jesse H. Suiter	6/26/55	c.
250	Mrs. Jesse H. Suiter	"	c.
251	[illegible] F. Suiter	"	c.
252	Mrs. Leslie Carloss	"	c.
253	Leslie Carloss	"	c.
254	A. Bryan Bolin	"	c.
255	Mrs. A. Bryan Bolin	"	c.
256	J. C. Lightfoot	"	c.
257	Mrs. J. C. Lightfoot	"	c.
258	Mrs. B. F. Hardin	"	c.
259	Bedford F. Hardin M.D.	"	c.
260	Mrs. C. S. Jernigan	"	c.
261	C. S. Jernigan	"	c.
262	Clyde S. Lightfoot	"	c.
263	Mrs. Clyde S. Lightfoot	"	c.
264	John C. Whitsitt	"	c.
265	Mrs. John C. Whitsitt	"	c.
266	John Wilkinson Jr.	"	c.
267	Mrs. John T. Wilkinson Jr.	"	c.
268	J. C. Gilbert Jr. M.D.	"	c.
269	Dame A. Robinson M.D.	"	c.
270, 271	Mr. & Mrs. Howard Estes	"	c., c.
272	William W. Besson Jr.	"	c.
273–274	Mr. and Mrs. Frank F. Walker	"	c., c.
275	[illegible] Lee Hewitt	"	c.
276	Mrs. Orin Johnson	"	c.
277	Orin R. Johnson Jr.	"	c.
278	Mrs. Robert Stokes Ferrell Jr.	"	c.
279	Robert Stokes Ferrell Jr.	"	c.
280	Mrs. J. Simpson Hill	"	c.
281	J. Simpson Hill	"	c.
282	Emma B. Humphrey	"	c.
283	Mrs. George D. Nowlin	"	c.
284	G. D. Nowlin Jr.	"	c.
285	George D. Nowlin	"	c.

No.	Name	Date	Manner
286	Charles J. Creath [illegible]	6-6-55	
287	Mrs. John R. Frazier Jr.	"	c.
288	John R. Frazier Jr.	"	c.
289	Mrs. J. Porter McClean	"	c.
290	Mr. J. Porter McClean	"	c.
291	James E. Henderson	"	c.
292	Mrs. Charles R. Tate		c.
293	Charles R. Tate		c.
294	Mrs. Edward J. Verret		c.
295	[illegible]	"	c.
296	Mrs. Russell E. [illegible]		c.
297	Hubert C. Straupe Sr.		c.
298	Mrs. Hubert C. Straupe	"	c.
299	H. Clark Straupe Jr.	"	c.
300	J. Porter McClean Jr.	"	c.
301	Mrs. Charles A. McVean		c.
302	Charles A. McVean	"	c.
303	Mrs. James M. Doyle	"	c.
304	James M. Doyle	"	c.
305	James M. Doyle Jr.	"	c.
306	Mrs. J. C. Martin	"	v.
307	Dr. John C. Vantine	"	c.
308	Floyd Harvey	"	c.
309	Mrs. Floyd Harvey	"	c.
310	J. Earle Ruffin	"	c.
311	Mrs. James Earle Ruffin		c.
312	Mrs. Howard A. Boone		c.
313	Howard A. Boone	"	c.
314	Howard A. Boone Jr.		c.
315	Jody Norris	"	c.
316	[illegible] Norris	"	c.
317	R. H. Norris	"	c.
318	Mrs. R. H. Norris	"	c.
319	Mrs. Charles W. Baker	"	c.
320	Linda Carole Baker	"	c.

No.	Name	Date	Manner
321	Charles W. Baker	6/26/55	c.
322	Patricia Anne Emerson	"	c.
323	Susan Harker	"	c.
324	Mrs. F. E. Carpenter	"	c.
325	Mr. F. E. Carpenter	"	c.
326	Mrs. C. A. Birmingham		c.
327	C. A. Birmingham	"	c.
328	Mrs. J. H. O'Donnell Jr.	"	c.
329	Lynn O'Donnell	"	c.
330	Lalleta H. Newman	"	c.
331	J. H. O'Donnell Jr.	"	c.
332	Mrs. Samuel H. Mays		c.
333	Mrs. Everett C. Handorf	"	c.
334	Mrs. F. M. Rudolph		c.
335	Fred M. Rudolph Jr.	"	c.
336	Corinne Rudolph	"	c.
337	J. D. Murphy Sr.	7/3/55	c.
338	Mrs. J. D. Murphy Sr.	"	c.
339	Jeff D. Murphy Jr.	"	c.
340	Mrs. Early F. Mitchell		c.
341	Mrs. Jack B. Caskey	"	c.
342	Mrs. James D. Curry		c.
343	Mrs. Jack Kenner	"	c.
344	Mr. Jack Kenner	"	c.
345	Mrs. J. Clay Shelton Jr.		c.
346	J. Clay Shelton Jr.		c.
347	Mrs. Hunter K. Cochran	"	c.
348	Jack B. Caskey Sr.	"	c.
349	Jack B. Caskey Jr.	"	c.
350	Early Mitchell	"	c.
351	[illegible]	"	c.
352	Jesse M. Vineyard		c.
353	Horace F. [illegible]		c.
354	Mrs. James C. Ingram Jr.		c.
355	James C. Ingram Jr.		c.

No.	Name	Date	Manner
356	Mrs Laura Lee Parker	7/3/55	C.
357	Elizabeth Harwell (Mrs. H.F. Jr.)		C.
358	Mrs H.F. Harwell	"	C.
359	Lee McCormick Jr.	"	C.
360	Ellis McCormick (Mrs. Lee B.)		
361	[illegible]	"	C.
362	Martha Garrison	"	C.
x 363	Nancy McCormick	"	
364	Mrs A A Sippel	"	C.
365	[illegible]	"	C.
366	Andrew A. Sippel Jr	"	C.
x 367	Barbara Moore [illegible]		PF
368	Martha Ann Johnston (Mrs. Chas H)	"	C.
369	Chas H. Johnston	"	C.
370	[illegible] (Mrs. J. A. Jr.)		C.
371	J. Albert [illegible] Jr	"	C.
372	[illegible]		C.
373	Mrs. J.W. Pattman	"	C.
374	Mr W. C. Michel		C.
375	Mrs. W.C. Michel		C.
376	Mrs. W. E. Ragsdale	"	C.
377	Mrs. Lucille Harris	"	C.
378	C.P. Harris	"	C.
379	Mrs. C.P. Harris	"	C.
380	Eugenia Frances Harris	"	C.
381	[illegible] Ann Harris	"	C.
382	Floyd J. Barber	"	C.
383	Mrs. Floyd Barber	"	C.
384	Frances S Barber	"	C.
385	Floyd Johnson Barber Jr	"	C.
386	Mrs. John Huckabee	"	C.
387	C. Huckabee	"	C.
388	Robert Huckabee	"	
389	J.B. Emerson Jr	"	
390	[illegible]	"	
391	Margaret Hunch (Mrs Eric S.)	7/3/55	
392	Eric S Hunch	"	
393	Leland Helms	"	
394	Thelma Helms (Mrs Leland)	"	
395	Merle D. King	"	
396	Mrs Merle D. King	"	
397	Edward L. Carpenter	"	
398	Mrs Edward L. Carpenter	"	
399	Mrs. Frank P. Horton	"	
400	Frank P. Horton	"	
401	William Edward Horton	"	
402	Frank L. Horton	"	
403	Henry H Harry	"	
404	Mrs. Henry H. Harry	"	
405	Mrs. Robert M. Ford	"	
406	Robert Malcolm Ford	"	
407	Mrs. Hugh L. Cullen	"	
408	Hugh L. Cullen	"	
409	Mrs. Richard R. Kite	"	
410	Richard R. Kite	"	
411	Mrs. Harry S. Lowe	"	
412	Harriet Lowe	"	
413	Harry S Lowe	"	
414	Wm H.D. Jones	"	
415	Mrs. Wm H.D. Jones	"	
416	Jack L. Watson	6-19-55	
417	Mrs Jack L Watson	"	
418	Mrs Jack Wright	7/3/55	
419	Jack Wright	"	
420	Mrs Dinsley Carlis	"	
421	Christina Curry	"	
422	Herman M. Baker	"	
423	Mrs. Herman M. Baker	"	
424	John H. Baker	"	
425	Wilfred L. Stevens Jr.	"	

No.	Name	Date	Manner	No.	Name	Date	Manner
426	Mrs. Edward F. Kadlec	7/3/55	c.	461	Guy N. Copeland	7/4/55	c.
427	Edward F. Kadlec	"	c.	462	Guy Nelson Copeland, Jr.	"	c.
428	Mrs R. E. Stratton	.	c.	463	Elizabeth McMillan (Mrs C H)		c.
429	Richard E. Stratton		c.	464	[illegible] H. McMillon	"	c.
430	Mrs. Lawrence S. [illegible]		c.	465	David P. West	"	c.
431	[illegible]	"	v.	466	Mrs. Kathryn West	.	c.
432	William B. [illegible]	"	c.	467	Miss Anne West	"	c.
433	Mrs Edgar H [illegible]		c.	468	David West Jr		c.
434	Mrs. Armistead F. Clay	"	c.	(469)	see 6/67 – [illegible] [illegible] West		
435	Armistead F. Clay	–	c.	470	E. O. Edwards	"	c.
436	Mrs Forrest Dowling		c.	471	Mrs. E. O. Edwards		c.
437	Forrest Dowling	.	c.	472	Elaine Edwards	"	c.
(438)	see 6/64 Mrs C. E. Martin [illegible]	[illegible]		473	F. Jennings Loza Jr.		c.
439	Walter Scott	.	c.	474	J W Wash		c.
440	Mrs. Walter Scott	.	c.	475	Mrs. J. W. Wash	"	c.
441	Mr. L. G. Bone	.	c.	(476)	see 390 Mrs. Gordon A. Miles	.	c.
442	Mrs. L. G. Bone		c.	477	Mrs. W. L. Mason	"	c.
443	Mr T. Jeff Hammond	.	c.	478	Evelyn Kay Mason		c.
444	Mrs T. Jeff Hammond	.	c.	479	[illegible] Lee Mason		c.
445	F. M. Graham		c.	480	Annie Mae Wooten	.	c.
446	Mrs F. M. Graham	.	c.	481	Jesse D. Wooten		c.
447	Mac Graham	.	c.	482	Velma McPhetters (W.B.)	.	v.
448	Jane Graham		c.	483	Mrs James M. Francis ([illegible])		c.
449	Mrs G. E. Westbrook	.	c.	484	James M. Francis		c.
450	A. J. [illegible]	"	c.	485	Mrs. Chas. G. Cunningham		
451	Martha McCool		c.	486	Chas G Cunningham	.	c.
452	Mrs Ralph A. McCool	"	c.	487	Joe E. McKinney		c.
453	Ralph A McCool	.	c.	488	Mrs Joe E. McKinney	.	c.
454	Steve Francisik III.		c.	489	Dr Chas W Campbell	.	c.
455	Jane Aycock Francisik		c.	490	Mrs Chas. W Campbell		c.
456	Dr. B. H. Binn	.	c.	491	Mr. Wm H Walker	.	v.
457	Mrs. B. H. Binn	.	c.	492	Mrs. Wm H Walker		v.
458	Lynn Miles	"	c.	493	Robbie E Walker		v.
459	Gordon A. Miles		c.	494	William B. McPhetters		c.
460	Mrs. Guy N. Copeland	.	c.	495	Peggy Anderson	"	c.

No.	Name	Date	Manner
496	Jesse A. Anderson	7/3/55	c.
497	Mrs. Jesse A. Anderson	"	c.
x 498	Eugenia Lenoir Dowling	"	x
499	Mrs. Ralph Kyte Jr.	"	c.
500	Paul B. Yarbrough	7/10/55	c.
501	Mrs. Paul B. Yarbrough		c.
502	Martha E. Farnsley	"	c.
503	James L. Waller	"	c.
504	Jean Waller (Mrs. James L.)	"	c.
505	Mrs. Vernon A. Alexander		c.
506	Mrs. Horton G. DuBard		c.
507	~~Horton G. DuBard M.D.~~		c.
508	~~Joy~~ & Keith Weisinger		c.
509	Joy Weisinger	"	c.
510	Hunter H. Cochran	"	c.
511	Mrs. James Harris	"	c.
512	J. H. Harris	"	c.
513	Wm. Carl Cannon Sr.	"	c.
514	Robert S. Condra	"	c.
515	Mrs. Robert S. Condra		c.
516	William F. Bracken	"	c.
517	Ruth C. Bracken (Mrs. Wm. F.)		c.
518	Mrs. J. P. McClean Jr.		c.
519	James E. Hamer Sr.	"	c.
520	Mrs. James E. Hamer	"	c.
521	Mrs. Willie [illegible]	"	c.
522	Paul Bressel	"	c.
523	Myra Bressel	"	c.
524	Malcolm T. Jones	"	c.
525	Pauline T. Jones	"	c.
526	L. M. Blaylock Jr.	"	c.
527	David Blaylock		B
528	[illegible] Blaylock	"	c.
529	Fred F. Munson Jr.	"	B
530	Mrs. Fred F. Munson Jr.	"	V

No.	Name	Date	M.
531	Mrs. Simmie L. Land	7/10/55	"
532	S. R. Land	"	"
533	Mrs. David L. Hamilton		"
534	David L. Hamilton	"	c
535	Lenore P. Robinson	"	"
x 536	Charles McVicar	"	x c
537	John V. Welch	"	"
538	Mrs. John V. Welch	"	"
539	Jas. F. Duncan Jr.	"	"
540	Mrs. J. F. Duncan Jr.	"	"
541	Mrs. J. A. Summers	"	"
542	Sylvia Annette Summers	"	"
543	J. A. Summers	"	"
544	Eloise A. Tate	"	"
545	John M. Beckham	"	"
546	Mrs. John M. Beckham	"	"
547	Nancy Beckham	"	"
548	Mrs. B. C. Adams	"	"
549	B. C. Adams	"	"
x 550	Fay Stanley (not a charter member joined 1956)		x E
551	Tom Henderson	"	"
552	Mrs. E. J. Phelan	"	"
553	H. C. Roberts	"	"
554	Mrs. H. C. Roberts	"	"
555	Charles F. Hunt	"	"
556	Mrs. Chas. F. Hunt	"	"
557	R. E. McIntosh	"	"
558	Mrs. R. E. McIntosh	"	"
559	Marilyn McIntosh	"	"
560	Gene McIntosh	"	"
561	Mrs. Wm. T. Lawson Jr.	"	"
562	William T. Lawson Jr.	"	"
563	Mrs. Guy Cantrell	"	"
564	Guy Cantrell	"	"
565	Barbara Cantrell	"	"

No.	Name	Date	Manner
566	Elva Sue Lawson	7/10/55	C.
67	[illegible] Cantrell	"	C.
68	Mrs. Livingston Peyton		C.
69	Livingston Peyton	"	C.
70	Gerald F. Meadows	"	C.
71	William H. Schneider	"	B.
72	Mrs William H. Schneider		C.
73	Mrs G. W. Carter		C.
74	David Kelley		C.
75	Mrs. Robt. Reed Flinn		C.
76	Robert Reed Flinn, Jr.		C.
77	Eugene H. Surles		C.
78	Gerald T. Owens		C.
79	Mrs Gerald T. Owens		C.
80	Charley C. Owen		C.
81	Mrs Eugene H. Surles		C.
82	Harry J. Wright		C.
83	Mrs. Wilbert R. Scates		C.
84	Wilbert R. Scates		C.
85	James A. [illegible]	"	C.
86	[illegible]	7/12/55	C.
87	George D. Holt Jr.		C.
88	Mrs George D. Holt Jr.		C.
89	Kenneth Canfield		C.
90	Creighton Allen Cockrell		C.
91	Mrs. H. E. Waller III		C.
92	Mrs Kinsman E. Ford	7/13/55	C.
93	Mrs. Russ Bramblet		C.
94	Russ Bramblet	"	C.
95	Mrs Alfred W. Lenz		C.
96	Alfred W. Lenz	"	C.
97	Jennifer Ruth [illegible]		C.
98	A. W. Beasley, Jr		C.
99	F. E. Wilkins		C.
600	Mrs. F. E. Wilkins	"	C.

No.	Name	Date	Manner
601	Edwin F. Lindsey	7/15/55	C.
602	Mrs Edwin Lindsey	"	C.
603	Ronnie Lindsey		C.
604	Rudye Davis		C.
605	Mrs Blanche Lazicola		B.
606	Mrs W. A. Yancey		C.
607	William L. Yancey		C.
608	William H. Yancey		C.
609	Jack Henry		C.
610	Mrs Carl B. Maxwell		C. No
611	Carl B Maxwell		C. No
612	Mrs Joe Crasier		C.
613	Mrs Malcolm Baker		C.
614	Mrs. Frank Nebhut	3/	C. No
615	Miss Lynn Nebhut		C. No.
616	Ann Fisher		C.
617	Betty Fisher		C.
~~618~~	~~Roy P. Perkins~~		
~~619~~	~~Mrs Roy P. Perkins~~		
618	Annie Ninn Miller		C.
619	Sadie A. Miller		C.
620	C. B. Bland		C.
621	Mrs. C. B. Bland		C.
622	Charlie Bland Jr.		C.
623	Robert Coleman Bland		C.
624	Anne F. Blackwell		C.
625	Peggy N. K. Mackie	7-22-55	
626	Robert T. Mackie		
627	F. I. Nebhut	8/ /55	
628	Frank Nebhut Jr.		
629	Mrs. Louis J. Bauer	8-4-55	
630	E. C. Barrick		
631	John L. Murphey	7-27-55	No
632	Mrs John L. Murphey		No.
633	John L. Murphey		No.

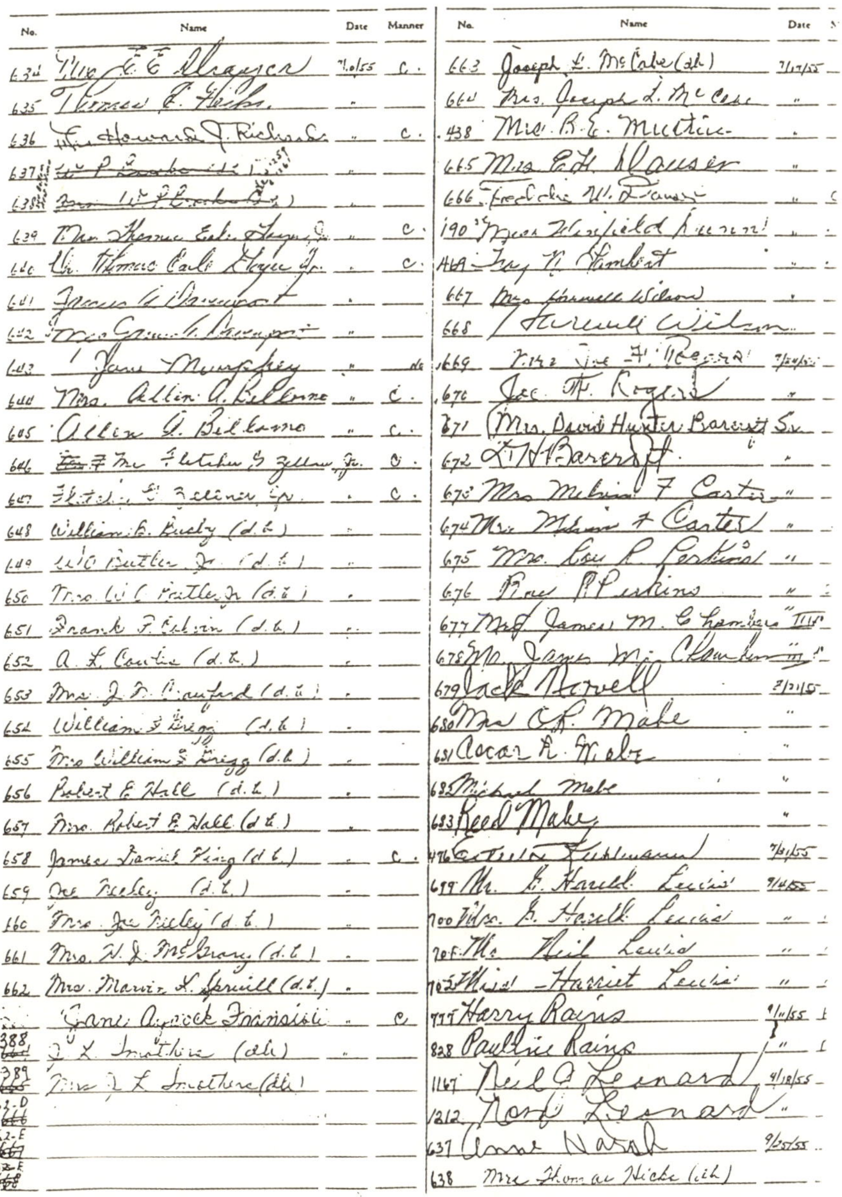

No.	Name	Date	Manner
634	Mrs. E. E. Strayer(?)	7/10/55	C.
635	Thomas E. Hicks.	"	
636	Mr. Howard J. Richardson	"	C.
637	[illegible]		
638	[illegible]		
639	Mrs. Thomas Earle Hoyle(?) Jr.	"	C.
640	Mr. Thomas Earle Hoyle Jr.	"	C.
641	James W. Davenport	"	
642	Mrs. Grace(?) W. Davenport	"	
643	Jane Murphey	"	
644	Mrs. Allen A. Bellamo(?)	"	C.
645	Allen A. Bellamo(?)	"	C.
646	Mrs. Fletcher G. Zellner, Jr.		C.
647	Fletcher G. Zellner, Jr.		C.
648	William E. Busby (d.t.)	"	
649	W. C. Butler Jr. (d.t.)	"	
650	Mrs. W. C. Butler Jr. (d.t.)	"	
651	Frank F. Colvin (d.t.)	"	
652	A. L. Coutie (d.t.)	"	
653	Mrs. J. T. Crawford (d.t.)	"	
654	William E. Gregg (d.t.)	"	
655	Mrs. William E. Gregg (d.t.)	"	
656	Robert E. Hall (d.t.)	"	
657	Mrs. Robert E. Hall (d.t.)	"	
658	James Daniel King (d.t.)	"	C.
659	Joe Kelley (d.t.)	"	
660	Mrs. Joe Kelley (d.t.)	"	
661	Mrs. W. J. McGrory (d.t.)	"	
662	Mrs. Marvin L. Spruill (d.t.)	"	
[illegible]	Jane Aycock Fransisli(?)	"	C
388	J. L. Smathers (dh)	"	
389	Mrs. J. L. Smathers (dh)		
662-D			
662-E			
662-F			

No.	Name	Date
663	Joseph L. McCabe (dh)	7/17/55
664	Mrs. Joseph L. McCabe	"
438	Mrs. B. E. Muthiu(?)	"
665	Mrs. E. H. Hauser	"
666	Frederic W. Hauser	"
190	Miss Winfield Pearson(?)	"
469	Fay N. Lambert	"
667	Mrs. Harrell Wilson	"
668	Harrell Wilson	
669	Mrs. Joe F. Rogers	7/24/55
670	Joe F. Rogers	"
671	Mrs. David Hunter Barcroft Sr.	
672	D. H. Barcroft Jr.	"
673	Mrs. Melvin F. Carter	"
674	Mr. Melvin F. Carter	"
675	Mrs. Roy P. Perkins	"
676	Roy P. Perkins	"
677	Mrs. James M. Chambers III	"
678	Mr. James M. Chambers III	"
679	Jack Novell	8/21/55
680	Mrs. O. R. Mabe	"
681	Oscar R. Mabe	"
682	Michael Mabe	"
683	Reed Mabe	"
476	Estella Kuhlmann	7/31/55
699	Mr. E. Harold Lewis	9/4/55
700	Mrs. E. Harold Lewis	"
701	Mr. Neil Lewis	"
702	Miss Harriet Lewis	"
777	Harry Rains	9/11/55
828	Pauline Rains	"
1167	Neil A. Leonard	4/18/55
1212	Nora Leonard	"
637	Anne Nash	9/25/55
638	Mrs. Thomas Hicks (dh)	

CHARTER MEMBERS–1955

Adams, B. C.
Adams, Mrs. B. C.
Akers, Mrs. Lawrence S.
Akin, Lynwood
Akin, V. Hugo
Akin, Mrs. V. Hugo
Alexander, Jim
Alexander, V. A.
Alexander, Mrs. V. A.
Alston, Dr. James L., Jr.
Alston, Mrs. James L., Jr.
Anderson, Jesse
Anderson, Mrs. Jesse
Anderson, Peggy (Carr)
Arnette, James B.
Arnette, Mrs. James B.
Baker, Charles W.
Baker, Mrs. Charles W.
Baker, Herman M.
Baker, Mrs. Herman M.
Baker, John H.
Baker, Linda (Merritt)
Baker, Mrs. Malcolm
Barcroft, David Hunter
Barcroft, Mrs. David Hunter, Sr.
Barnard, L. G.
Barnard, Mrs. L. G.
Barron, Roy W.
Barron, Mrs. Roy W.
Barron, Sandra (Stanton)
Barwick, E. C.
Bass, Mrs. Norman
Beasley, A. W., Jr
Beeson, Billy
Bell, Warren K.
Bell, Mrs. Warren K.
Bellomo, A. A.
Bellomo, Mrs. A. A.
Bigger, Dr. J. F.
Bigger, Mrs. J. F.
Billings, Earle
Billings, Mrs. Earle
Birmingham, C. A.
Birmingham, Mrs. C. A.
Blackwell, Mrs. Anne G.
Bland, Charles B., Jr.
Bland, Charles B., Sr.
Bland, Mrs. Charles B., Sr.
Bland, Robert C.
Blaylock, David
Blaylock, L. M.
Blaylock, Mrs. L. M.
Boensch, Paul
Boensch, Mrs. Paul
Bolin, A. Bryan
Bolin, Mrs. A. Bryan
Bone, L. G.
Bone, Mrs. L. G. (Yetive)
Boone, Dr. Howard
Boone, Mrs. Howard
Boone, Howard A., Jr.
Bracken, William F.
Bracken, Mrs. William F.
Bramlett, Russ
Bramlett, Mrs. Russ
Brooks, Ed M.
Brown, Mrs. John
Busby, William B.
Butler, William O.
Butler, Mrs. William O.
Byrne, Jack P.
Byrne, Mrs. Jack P.
Byrne, Paul
Campbell, Dr. Charles
Campbell, Mrs. Charles
Campbell, Tom
Canfield, James T.
Canfield, Mrs. James T.
Canfield, Kenneth
Cannon, W. Carl
Cantrell, Barbara (Schaffler)
Cantrell, Guy
Cantrell, Mrs. Guy (Lawson)
Cantrell, William Allen
Carey, Hugh
Carey, Mrs. Hugh
Carloss, Leslie, Sr.
Carloss, Mrs. Leslie, Sr.
Carpenter, Ben
Carpenter, Mrs. Ben
Carpenter, Ed L.
Carpenter, Mrs. Ed L.
Carpenter, F. E.
Carpenter, Mrs. F. E.
Carter, Melvin F.
Carter, Mrs. Melvin F.
Carter, Mrs. G. W.
Caruthers, Mrs. Roger
Caskey, Jack
Caskey, Mrs. Jack
Caskey, Jack, Jr.
Clay, Armistead
Clay, Mrs. Armistead
Clay, James N., III
Clay, James N., Jr.
Clay, Mrs. James N., Jr.
Cochran,. Hunter
Cochran, Mrs. Hunter
Cockrell, Creighton Allen
Cockrell, Ellis
Cockrell, Mrs. Ellis
Colby, Clarence

Colby, Mrs. Clarence
Colby, Clarence, Jr.
Colby, Irene
Colvin, Frank P., Jr.
Condra, Robert S.
Condra, Mrs. Robert S.
Conolly, L. A.
Conolly, Mrs. L. A.
Copeland, Guy
Copeland, Mrs. Guy
Copeland, Nelson
Cowles, A. L.
Craford, Mrs. J. N.
Creath, Charles J.
Crofford, Dr. Oscar, Sr.
Crofford, Mrs. Oscar, Sr.
Crosier, Mrs. J. W.
Crowley, Herschel
Crowley, Mrs. Herschel
Cullen, Hugh L.
Cullen, Mrs. Hugh L.
Cunningham, Charles
Cunningham, Mrs. Charles
Cunningham, Moody
Cunningham, Mrs. Moody
Curry, James D.
Curry, Mrs. James D.
Curry, Miss Christine
Danser, Freddie W.
Danser, Mrs. E. F.
Darms, George
Darms, Mrs. George
Davenport, Howard L.
Davenport, Mrs. Howard L.
Davenport, James
Davenport, Mrs. James
Davie, S. W.
Davie, Mrs S. W.
Davis, Olen H.
Davis, Mrs. Olen H.
DeZonia, Barry
DeZonia, Mrs. Barry
DeZonia, H. F.
DeZonia, Mrs. H. F.
DeZonia, Robert
Dixon, Joanne (McDowell)
Dixon, Mrs. Floyd
Dowling, Forrest
Dowling, Mrs. Forrest
Doyle, James M.
Doyle, Mrs. James M.
Doyle, Jimmy
Drake, Jennifer
Drake, Robert J.
Drake, Mrs. Robert
Drenner, Ray
Drenner, Mrs. Ray
Drenner, William E.
Drenner, Mrs. William E.
DuBard, Dr. H. G.
DuBard, Mrs. H. G.
Duncan, James F.
Duncan, Mrs. James F.
Dunkman, Herbert
Dunkman, Mrs. Herbert
Dunn, Dr. Winfield
Dunn, Mrs. Winfield
Dunn, Jerry
Dunn, Nat P.
Dunn, Mrs. Nat P.
Dunn, Natalie (Latham)
Earles, Dennis
Earles, Mrs. Dennis
Edwards, E. O.
Edwards, Mrs. E. O.
Edwards, Elaine (Koenig)
Emerson, J. B.
Emerson, Mrs. J. B.
Emerson, Patricia (Thompson)
Estes, Howard
Estes, Mrs. Howard
Fain, Bascom N.
Fain, Mrs. Bascom N.
Felts, Ernest
Felts, Mrs. Ernest
Ferrell, Robert S.
Ferrell, Mrs. Robert S.
Finley, Mrs. E. C. (Walker)
Fisher, Ann
Fisher, Frank
Fisher, Mrs. Frank
Fisher, Robert
Flinn, Robert Reed, Jr.
Flinn, Mrs. Robert Reed, Jr.
Fones, W. H. D.
Fones, Mrs. W. H. D.
Ford, Mrs. K. D.
Ford, Robert
Ford, Mrs. Robert
Francis, James M.
Fransioli, Jane (Browndyke)
Fransioli, Steve, III
Fransioli, Mrs. Steve, Jr.
Frazier, John R.
Frazier, Mrs. John R.
French, Ned M.
French, Mrs. Ned M.
French, Taylor "Nick"
Fulmer, Albert, Jr.
Fulmer, Mrs. Albert, Jr.
Garber, Susan (Ozier)
Garner, Judith (Carroll)
Garner, Mrs. N. R.
Garner, Ned R.
Garrison, Martha
Gass, Haskell
Gass, Mrs. Haskell
Gates, Jac
Gates, Mrs. Jac
Gates, Martha (Brown)

Gibson, Jeffry
Gibson, O. F.
Gibson, Mrs. O. F.
Gilbert, J. C., Jr
Ginn, Dr. B. H.
Ginn, Mrs. B. H.
Goins, James H.
Goins, Mrs. James H.
Goldberg, Mrs. Harry
Goyer, Dr. T. E.
Goyer, Mrs. T. E.
Goza, H. Jennings, Jr.
Graham, Fred M.
Graham, Mrs. Fred M.
Graham, J. E.
Graham, Mrs. J. E.
Graham, Jane (Hubbell)
Graham, Mac (Fred Jr.)
Graham, Mrs. M. O.
Grant, David
Grant, Mrs. Charles W.
Gregg, William S.
Gregg, Mrs. William S.
Grumbles, William H.
Grumbles, Mrs. William H.
Hall, Ernest W.
Hall, Mrs. Ernest W.
Hall, Robert E.
Hall, Mrs. Robert E.
Hamilton, David L.
Hamilton, Mrs. David L.
Hammond, T. Jeff
Hammond, Mrs. T. Jeff
Handorf, E. C.
Handorf, Mrs. E. C.
Hargett, Annie Lee
Harmer, James E.
Harmer, Mrs. James E.
Harris, C. P.
Harris, Mrs. C. P.
Harris, Dr. T. R.
Harris, Eugenia F.
Harris, Judith Ann
Harris, Teddy Tatum
Harry, Henry H.
Harry, Mrs. Henry H.
Harsh, Anne
Harvey, Floyd
Harvey, Mrs. Floyd
Harwell, Horace F.
Harwell, Mrs. H. F.
Harwell, Mrs. H. F., Jr.
Helms, Leland
Helms, Mrs. Leland
Henderson, James E.
Henderson, Mrs. Charles
Henderson, Tom
Henrich, Erie S.
Henrich, Mrs. Erie S.
Henry, Jack
Hidinger, Mrs. Leroy
Hill, Carolyn B.
Hill, J. Simpson
Hill, Mrs. J. Simpson
Hobbs, H. F.
Hobbs, Mrs. H. F.
Holloway, Mrs. H. H.
Holt, George D., Jr.
Holt, Mrs. George D., Jr.
Holt, Dr. Robert T.
Holt, Mrs. Robert T.
Hornsby, Martha
Horton, Frank Lawson
Horton, Frank P.
Horton, Mrs. Frank P.
Horton, William Edward
Huckabee, J. C.
Huckabee, Mrs. J. C.
Hull, Donald T.
Hull, Mrs. Donald T.
Hull, Mrs. Lee R.
Humphrey, Emma
Hunt, Charles F.
Hunt, Mrs. Charles F.
Hunter, Mrs. Willie
Ingram, James C., Jr.
Ingram, Mrs. James C., Jr..
Ingram, Reeves
Ingram, Mrs. Reeves
Jackman, Martha L.
Jennings, Mrs. Mae
Jernigan, C. S.
Jernigan, Mrs. C. S.
Joest, Mrs. John W.
Johnson, Harry A., Jr.
Johnson, Mrs. Harry A., Jr.
Johnson, John C.
Johnson, Mrs. John C.
Johnson, Orin L.
Johnson, Mrs. Orin L.
Johnston, Charles
Johnston, Mrs. Charles
Jones, Dr. A. M.
Jones, Mrs. A. M.
Jones, Malcom T.
Jones, Mrs. Malcom T.
Joyner, Jesse M.
Joyner, Mrs. Jesse M.
Kadlec, Edward F.
Kadlec, Mrs. Edward F.
Kelley, David
Kelley, Keith
Kelley, Mrs. Keith
Kenner, Jack
Kenner, Mrs. Jack
King, James Daniel
King, Merle D.
King, Mrs. Merle D.
Kite, Mrs. R. R.
Kite, R. R.
Knight, C. P.
Kuhlman, Estelle
Kyte, Mrs. Ralph
Lambert, Troy Neal
Land, T. L.
Land, Mrs. T. L.
Lawson, Sue (Hauck)

Lawson, William V., Jr.
Lawson, Mrs. William V., Jr.
Ledbetter, J. P.
Ledbetter, Mrs. J. P.
Lenz, A. W.
Lenz, Mrs. A. W.
Leonard, Neil J.
Leonard, Mrs. Neil J.
Lewis, G. Harold
Lewis, Mrs. G. Harold
Lewis, Harriet
Lewis, Neil
Liddell, Frank
Liddell, Mrs. Frank
Lightfoot, Clyde S.
Lightfoot, Mrs. Clyde S.
Lindsey, Dr. Edwin L.
Lindsey, Mrs. Edwin L.
Lindsey, Ronnie
Logan, Thomas P.
Lopiocolo, Mrs. Blanche
Lowe, Harriet (Mansfield)
Lowe, Harry S.
Lowe, Mrs. Harry S.
Mabe, Michael
Mabe, Oscar R.
Mabe, Mrs. Oscar R.
Mabe, Reed
Mankin, Dr. John C.
Mankin, Mrs. John C.
Martak, Patsy
Martak, W. K.
Martak, Mrs. W. K.
Maxwell, Carl B.
Maxwell, Mrs. Carl B.
Maynard, Gerald
Maynard, Mrs. Gerald
Mays, Harvey J.
Mays, Sam H.
Mays, Mrs. Sam H.
McCabe, Joseph L.
McCabe, Mrs. Joseph L.
McCallum, Mrs. Lorene
McClean, J. Porter
McClean, Mrs. J. Porter
McClean, Porter, Jr.
McClean, Mrs. Porter, Jr.
McCool, Martha (Young)
McCool, Ralph
McCool, Mrs. Ralph
McCormick, Lee
McCormick, Mrs. Lee
McCormick, Lee, Jr.
McDaniel, C. R.
McDaniel, Mrs. C. R.
McGrory, Mrs. H. J.
McIntosh, Marilyn (Draughon)
McIntosh, R. E.
McIntosh, Mrs. R. E.
McKinney, Joe
McKinney, Mrs. Joe (Kelly)
McKnight, Mrs. William
McKnight, William
McMillan, C. H.
McMillan, Mrs. C. H.
McPhatter, William B.
McPhatter, Mrs. William B.
McVean, Charles A.
McVean, Mrs. Charles A.
McVean, Charles D.
Meadows, Gerald
Meadows, Hal
Meadows, Marion
Meadows, Mrs. Marion
Mieher, W. C.
Mieher, Mrs. W. C.
Miles, Gordon
Miles, Mrs. Gordon
Miles, Lynn
Miller, Annie Wynn
Miller, Sadie A.
Mitchell, Early
Mitchell, Mrs. Early
Mitchell, Y. O.
Mitchell, Mrs. Y. O.
Montgomery, Earl
Montgomery, Mrs. Earl
Montgomery, John
Munson, Fred, Jr.
Munson, Mrs. Fred, Jr.
Murphy, J. D.
Murphy, Mrs. J. D.
Mustin, Mrs. R. E.
Nason, Evelyn Kay (Baker)
Nason, Hays Len
Nason, Mrs. W. L.
Neeley, Joe P.
Neeley, Mrs. Joe P.
Newman, Mrs. LaVilla
Noel, D. A.
Noel, Mrs. D. A.
Noel, Patricia
Norris, Judith
Norris, R. H
Norris, Mrs. R. H.
Norris, Virginia
Norvell, Jack
Nowlin, George
Nowlin, Mrs. George
O'Donnell, J. H.
O'Donnell, Mrs. J. H.
O'Donnell, Lynn (Roberts)
Owens, Charles
Owens, Gerald
Owens, Mrs. Gerald
Parker, Laura Lee (Ritz)
Parsons, John
Parsons, Mrs. John
Pattinson, Jeans
Pattinson, Mrs. Jeans
Payne, George R.

Payne, Mrs. George R.
Pennebaker, William B.
Pepper, Mrs. Sabra
Perkins, Roy R.
Perkins, Mrs. Roy R.
Peyton, Livingston
Peyton, Mrs. Livingston
Phelan, Mrs. E. J.
Pickens, John M.
Pickens, Mrs. John M.
Pickens, Nancy (Higgason)
Pickering, H. F.
Pickering, Mrs. H. F.
Pierce, Mrs. Harvey
Prichard, Dr. Frank
Prichard, Mrs. Frank
Prichard, Phil
Ragsdale, Mrs. W. E.
Rains, Harry
Rains, Pauline
Reeves, Russell
Reeves, Mrs. Russell
Reid, Sam
Reid, Mrs. Sam
Rhodes, Kelley
Rhodes, Mrs. Kelley
Rhodes, Mrs. Jesse T.
Richards, Mrs. H. J.
Richmond, Ed, Jr.
Richmond, Ed, Sr.
Richmond, Mrs. Ed, Sr.
Ricker, John B.
Ricker, Mrs. John B.
Ridolphi, Corinne (Nichols)
Ridolphi, Fred
Ridolphi, Mrs. Fred
Ridolphi, Fred M., Jr.
Riley, Dain S.
Riley, Mrs. Dain S.
Roberds, Mrs. E. S.
Roberds, William D.
Roberts, Dr. H. C.
Roberts, Mrs. H. C.
Robinson, Dr. James A.
Robinson, Mrs. Leonese P.
Rogers, Joe F.
Rogers, Mrs. Joe F.
Ruffin, J. E.
Ruffin, Mrs. J. E.
Samuels, Mrs. Lillian H.
Samuels, W. C., Jr.
Sarber, Frances (Shearer)
Sarber, L. John, Jr.
Sarber, Lloyd
Sarber, Mrs. Lloyd
Scates, Wilbert
Scates, Mrs. Wilbert
Schneider, W .H.
Schneider, Mrs. W. H.
Scott, Walter
Scott, Mrs. Walter (Pearl)
Seabrook, J. H., Jr.
Seabrook, J. H., Sr.
Seabrook, Mrs. J. H., Sr.
Seabrook, Mary Ann
Seabrook, Mrs. L. H.
Shelton, H. Clay
Shelton, Mrs. H. Clay
Shroyer, Mrs. E. E.
Sippel, Andrew A., Jr.
Sippel, Mrs. A. A.
Sippel, Thomas
Smith, Earl W.
Smith, Mrs. Earl W.
Smith, T. Wade
Smith, Mrs. T. Wade
Smothers, J. L.
Smothers, Mrs. J. L.
Speed, B. M.
Speed, Mrs. B. M.
Spruill, Mrs. Marvin L.
Stanley, C. P.
Stanley, Mrs. C. P.
Stanley, C. P., Jr.
Stanley, Mrs. C. P., Jr.
Stanley, David
Stanley, Mrs. David
Stanley, Mrs. R. G.
Stephenson, W. F.
Stevener, Beverly
Stevener, Robert
Stevener, W. E.
Stevener, Mrs. W. E.
Stevener, Wilfred, Jr.
Stidham, Mrs. Ramon
Stirewalt, Martha
Stratton, R. E.
Stratton, Mrs. R. E.
Stroupe, H. C.
Stroupe, Mrs. H. C.
Stroupe, H. Clarke
Suitor, Dr. Jesse H.
Suitor, Mrs. Jesse H.
Suitor, Roscoe "Rusty"
Sullivan, C. H.
Sullivan, Mrs. C. H.
Summers, Jake A.
Summers, Mrs. Jake A.
Summers, Sylvia (Williams)
Surles, Eugene
Surles, Mrs. Eugene (Bays)
Tate, Charles R.
Tate, Mrs. Charles R.
Tate, Eloise (Foster)
Taylor, Richard G.
Taylor, Mrs. Richard G.
Templeton, Dr. W. J.
Templeton, Mrs. W. J.
Tenent, Ed
Tenent, Mrs. Ed
Thomas, Agnes
Thomas, Mrs. F. R.
Thomas, Mrs. Mattie

Trainor, William T.
Trainor, Mrs. William T.
Verret, Mrs. E. J.
Vineyard, Jesse M.
Walker, Frank
Walker, Mrs. Frank
Walker, Robbie
Walker, William H.
Walker, Mrs. William H.
Walker, Zetta
Wallace, Jack
Wallace, Mrs. Jack (Stella)
Waller, James L.
Waller, Mrs. James L.
Waller, Mrs. Harlin E., III
Wash, J. W.
Wash, Mrs. J. W.
Watson, Jack
Watson, Mrs. Jack
Weaver, Russell
Weaver, Mrs. Russell
Weisinger, Keith
Weisinger, Mrs. Keith
Welch, Mrs. Ben
Welch, John
Welch, Mrs. John
Wellons, T. E.
Wellons, Mrs. T. E.
West, Ann
West, David
West, Mrs. David
West, David, Jr.
Westbrook, A. J.
Westbrook Mrs. A. J.
Whitenton, Percy
Whitenton, Mrs. Percy
Whitsitt, John
Whitsitt, Mrs. John
Wilkinson, John T.
Wilkinson, Mrs. John T.
Wilson, Harwell
Wilson, Mrs. Harwell
Wilson, Mrs. Ruby
Wilson, Nelson
Wilson, Mrs. Nelson
Wooten, J. D.
Wooten, Mrs. J. D.
Wren, W. Albert
Wren, Mrs. W. Albert
Wright, Jack
Wright, Mrs. Jack
Wright, Harry, Jr.
Yancey, William A.
Yancey, Mrs. William A.
Yancey, William Sims
Yarbrough, Paul
Yarbrough, Mrs. Paul
Zellner, Fletcher
Zellner, Mrs. Fletcher

Annual Net Membership and Budget

1956: 876	$193,422
1957: 1,119	$165,635
1958: 1,316	$555,505
1959: 1,413	$235,181
1960: 1,489	$414,613
1961: 1,579	$358,848
1962: 1,684	$358,806
1963: 1,893	$463,027
1964: 1,941	$408,082
1965: 2,091	$421,410
1966: 2,275	$366,701
1967: 2,501	$400,265
1968: 2,615	$441,800
1969: 2,592	$554,144

Membership and budget totals are from the *Memphis Annual Conference Journals*.

✣ ✣ ✣

LAY DELEGATES TO ANNUAL CONFERENCES

1956: Dr. W. J. Templeton
Fred Ridolphi

1957: Dr. W. J. Templeton
W. K. Martak

1958: Dr. W. J. Templeton
W. K. Martak

1959: Dr. W. J. Templeton
Dr. Howard Boone

1960: George Atkinson
Ed Thorne

1961: Bert Ferguson
Jesse Vineyard

1962: J. H. Seabrook Sr.
H. L. Davenport
Dr. William Lovejoy

1963: Dr. Shed Caffey
William H. D. Fones
Jack Renshaw

1964: J. H. Seabrook Jr.
James Briggs
John Parsons
John Whitsitt

1965: John Tole
Charles R. Tate
Paul McQuiston
Clay Shelton

1966: Jesse Anderson
Bert Ferguson
Dwight Koenig
Lee McCormick

1967: Jack Renshaw
D. A. Noel
H. C. Ramsey Jr.
George T. Roberts

1968: Sam Mays
Earle Billings
Ben Carpenter
Burns Landess
Henry Hottum
Harold Benson

1969: William Cazy Smith
Morris Liming
Henry Foster
Orin Johnson
C. W. Hoover Jr.
Dan Farrar

First Board of Trustees

Howard L. Davenport
Chairman

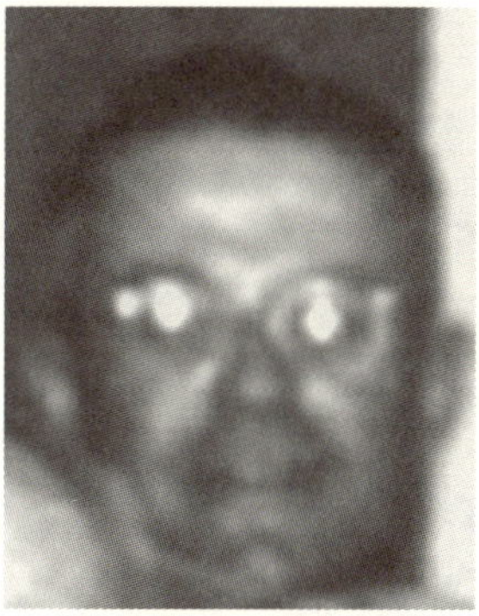
James Canfield

C. R. McDaniel

John A. Parsons

Dr. W. J.Templeton

Ed H. Tenent

First Architect and Building Committee

Everett Handorf
Chairman

Harry A. Johnson Jr.

Lee McCormick

Ministers
of
Christ United Methodist Church

Dr. Charles W. Grant
Senior Minister
1955–1969

Rev. B. L. Gaddie
1956–1957

Rev. Marshall Morris
1958–1963

Rev. Howard Rash
1963–1988

Rev. Charles H. Lynn
1967–1969

QUARTERLY CONFERENCES

The report of the Pastoral Relations Committee to the Quarterly Conference on March 20, 1956, gives a definitive overview of the work of the Official Board, the operating budget, the building fund, and the general attitude of this congregation and its leadership nearing the end of the first year of the church's existence.

Christ Methodist Church
4370 Poplar Avenue
Memphis, Tennessee
March 20, 1956

Charles W. Grant
Minister

Bishop W. T. Watkins
The Methodist Church
Louisville, Kentucky

Dr. J. E. Underwood, District Superintendent
The Methodist Headquarters
Memphis, Tennessee

Dear Brethren:

As Pastoral Relations Committee and as members of the Quarterly Conference of Christ Methodist Church, Memphis, Tennessee, we desire to report on the activities of our Church and to express our sincere appreciation to God and to you for the many blessings we have received, making it possible for us to achieve our present status and to accomplish the results outlined below:

Our first service was held on June 19, 1955 and our church was officially organized on June 26, 1955 and a Board of Stewards elected. At that time approximately 600 persons had indicated they would become members of Christ Methodist Church. That number has grown steadily and rapidly and, as of March 12, 1956, we have a total of 801 active and consecrated members.

Also, on June 26, 1955 a Commission on Education was elected and a Sunday school organized. As of today our Sunday school has an enrollment of 600 with an average attendance of 390.

A Woman's Society of Christian Service was organized immediately following the organization of the Church, with a membership of 144 which has grown rapidly to a total of 225 members, with eleven Circles and a Wesleyan Service Guild.

A Methodist Men's Club was organized during July 1955 with 107 men attending the first meeting, and with a Charter Membership of 215. This Men's Club is cooperating actively in the work of the Church, and is working diligently through Visitation Evangelism to increase our membership. Each week some 20 or more teams of two each make calls on prospective members, and are doing a magnificent work for God and our Church.

A fine musical program has been carried on in our Church since its inception through our Sanctuary Choir. Recently a Minister of Music and an Organist have been employed, and in addition to the Sanctuary Choir two or three Youth Choirs will be trained.

A Boy Scout Troop was organized and is actively carrying on its work, and it now has 23 members of the Troop. We have an active Methodist Youth Fellowship with an average attendance of 75 each Sunday afternoon. During last August a daily Vacation Bible School was held with 71 boys and girls enrolled.

The women of the Church have organized several prayer groups, and a prayer group meets each weekday morning, Monday through Friday.

Financially, we have been blessed also and our people have given generously and sacrificially. Many have moved into the Tithing Group, while others have advanced still further and are giving 15 percent, 20 percent and up to 25 percent of their income to the work of the Church and to advance the Kingdom of God here on earth.

In August of 1955 we employed Fred Alexander of Fred Alexander & Associates to conduct our Budget Pledge Campaign and our Building Fund Campaign. On his recommendations, we began our campaign in September and during two weeks of that month we solicited pledges from members for the remaining nine months of the Conference Year for our Budget; and also for a five months' Building Fund. Then in January 1956, we again made calls on our members and solicited pledges for our Building Fund to run for a period of three years. The results of the two campaigns and our financial picture can be seen from the following data taken from our records:

	Pledges	**Payments on Pledges**	**Balance Due**
Five Months' Building Fund Pledge	$ 38,264.22	$ 33,191.31	$ 5,072.91
Three-year Building Fund Pledge	$ 376,898.60	$ 26,372.25	$ 350,526.31
Gift from Church Extension (Conf.)	$ 50,000.00	$ 24,000.00	$26,000.00

Payments Made without Pledging	$ 21,872.70	$ 21,872.70	$ 0.00
Total Pledges to Budget Account	$487,035.52	$ 32,225.53	$ 16,645.42
Pledges to Budget Account	$ 48,870.95	$ 32,225.53	$ 16,645.42
Payments Made without Pledging	$ 7,209.31	$ 7,209.31	$ 0.00
Loose Collection	$ 2,189.41	$ 2,189.41	$ 0.00
Total Pledges to Budget Account	$ 58,269.40	$ 41,623.98	$ 16,645.42
Grand Total All Pledges & Collections as of January 31, 1956	$545,304.92	$147,060.24	$398,244.68

During the month of February 1956, collections on the Building Fund amounted to $11,283.03 and on the Budget account $4,481.23, which amounts added to the collections shown above make a total of $162,824.50 paid into Christ Methodist Church for the first nine months of its existence.

Payment in full has been made on the 6.4 acres at 4488 Poplar Avenue, which was purchased at a cost of $95,000.00 for our Church home. A small Chapel has been erected on our property at 4370 Poplar at a cost of $8,655 and has been paid for in full from our Budget Account. A Parsonage located at 4227 Belle Meade Cove has been purchased for $33,000 and is now being redecorated and furniture is being purchased. Financing of the Parsonage and the property at 4370 Poplar is being handled through our Budget Account, so that all the Building Fund Pledges can be used for our permanent Church home. Architects were employed immediately after the church was organized and the architect, Walk Jones Jr., has been busily at work on plans and specifications for our future home. A small scale model of our proposed Sanctuary and our Educational Buildings has been prepared and submitted to our Official Board, and members of the Church and has been approved. Work on our first unit should begin early in June, but in the meantime we plan our official groundbreaking for Easter Sunday afternoon.

Our membership is enthusiastic and is working, and we believe that God has been directing our efforts and has given us results and blessings far beyond our hopes and dreams. One of our greatest blessings has been the wise, consecrated ministry of our beloved minister, Dr. Charles W. Grant, who has given us leadership in all fields that could not have been surpassed. We want to express our sincere thanks and appreciation for your wisdom in selecting him to lead us in our great undertaking, and we are confident that he was the right man and that he is the man to continue the great work he has begun.

Officially, we the members of the Pastoral Relations Committee and members of the Quarterly Conference request that Dr. Grant be returned to us, and that he be permitted to remain with us for the foreseeable future, certainly until our building program can be completed. In addition, we request that an associate pastor be assigned to us beginning with the new conference year, and that Dr. Grant be permitted to select or at least make recommendation for that associate so that our work can continue to go forward in every way.

Again, in conclusion, we want to express our deep appreciation to our bishop and our district superintendent for their vision, sympathetic understanding, and cooperation. As we build with brick and stone, we dedicate ourselves and our Church to spiritual values, to the promotion of the program of the Methodist Church, to the extension and development of the Kingdom to the salvation of men's souls, to the Conquest of the World for our Lord and Savior, Jesus Christ.

Respectfully and sincerely yours,
Pastoral Relations Committee, Christ Methodist Church

James H. Seabrook
Howard L. Davenport
John A. Parsons
C. A. Cunningham
Edgar H. Tenent

✣ ✣ ✣

Dr. Charles W. Grant presented the attached plan for naming the buildings planned for the newly acquired property at Poplar Avenue and Grove Park Road. This plan was never enacted. The only name that survived was that of the first building, the Fellowship Hall. Its name was changed to the Rash Building about thirty-five years later.

The major worth of this paper is contained in the last two paragraphs. Dr. Grant's stated "High Purpose" for Christ Methodist Church was that each member embrace the passion and dedication of the statement. Dr. Grant followed the 1956 statement above by another statement in 1958 that expressed the church's primary purpose.

> Be it resolved that from now on we call our educational Building *B* The Aldersgate Building and when educational Building C is erected, it will be called The Oxford Building. The purpose of this is as follows: While every church truly born of God has a divine mission, we feel that Christ Methodist Church had a singular and unique birth and it is incumbent upon us and all succeeding generations to put forth a strong, true, well-balanced Gospel. The ideals of this will be continually held before the succeeding generations by properly naming these buildings. The name of the first building erected, the Fellowship Hall, of course, bespeaks Christian communion or fellowship. Here we will have our dinners, wedding receptions and other church activities that bespeak and generate fellowship. The second, the Aldersgate Building, will remind all informed Methodists of John Wesley's heartwarming experience at Aldersgate. It should keep before us the ideal of evangelism. The third building to be built will be the Sanctuary.
>
> The fourth to be built, but the third educational unit, completing the court, will be the Oxford Building. The Oxford Building should remind us of Wesley's Oxford days. We know,

of course, that Methodism was born on a college campus, hence the importance of Christian education—education that is pedagogically, sound and true to the scripture, which will meet the needs of our people. Of course, the sanctuary bespeaks worship and thus we have within the court: evangelism, education, fellowship and divine worship.

At a later date, when adequate inspiration comes, we shall seek and find a fitting name for the social activities building.

Meanwhile, may we remind ourselves of the words of Dr. Rufus Jones, the distinguished Quaker philosopher who summarized Methodism with great clarity: "One of the most dynamic things the modern world has seen was that same evangelical movement in the days when it moved, with its original high caloric. It came like a vernal equinox into the morally dull arid static life of the 18th century. It turned water into wine, it brought prodigals home, it raised life out of death. It produced miracles of transformation. But the most remarkable thing about it was the freshly inspired social impulse, which it produced. It transformed persons, it stopped the slave trade, it freed slaves. It made its converts uncomfortable over wrong social conditions. It sent missionaries to create hospitals and to conquer ignorance in almost every land on the globe. It was always as much outward as it was inward, though its creative spring was assured a birth of new life from the central source of life."

This is the high purpose of Christ Methodist church. It should be our passion and each member is urged to make such dedication as may be required to produce the high caloric needed for such an hour as this.

The Church's primary ministry is to supply a continuous vision of the first principles by which alone men may live. That is to say, if we put other principles first, people perish first, then the church decays next. The church must keep this vision—first things first—before itself and the world. When men forget this, as they frequently do, life is rooted in the supersensual and they become lost in greed, ambition, lust and envy. And so we take seriously the warning of T. S. Eliot:

The church must be forever building, for it is forever
Decaying, within and attached without;
For this is the law of life; and you must remember that
While there is time of prosperity
The people will neglect the Temple, and in time of
Adversity they will decry it.

The strength of the church comes not from favorable social conditions, acceptability of men, high tides of prosperity—but from God.

Prayerfully,
Charles W. Grant

Quarterly Conference, May 7, 1956.

THE FIRST–FOURTH QUARTERLY CONFERENCE HELD IN THE LITTLE CHAPEL

May 7, 1956

1. Howard L. Davenport
2. Carey Stanley Sr
3. Earl Montgomery
4. James H. Seabrook
5. Samuel H. Mays
6. Dr. J. E. Underwood, District Superintendent
7. Dr. Charles Grant
8. Haskell Gass
9. Everett Handorf
10. Charles McVean
11. Ned French
12. Bill Meadows
13. William Martak
14. Henry Harry
15. Jim Duncan
16. Leland Helms
17. Charles Tate
18. Dr. Horton DuBard
19. Robert Drake
20. Jack Byrne
21. Jeff Bigger
22. Bill Drenner
23. Fred Ridolphi
24. unidentified
25. Edgar Tenent
26. unidentified
27. Harry A. Johnson Jr
28. unidentified
29. Early Mitchell
30. Richard Stratton
31. unidentified
32. Jesse Joyner
33. James T. Canfield
34. C. P. Harris
35. L. A. Conolly
36. Lee McCormick
37. Clarence Colby
38. unidentified
39. Lloyd Sarber
40. Porter McClean
41. Dr. Howard Boone
42. Hugh Carey
43. Charles Johnston
44. unidentified
45. Dr. Robert T. Holt
46. Earle Billings
47. Herbert Dunkman
48. Jac Gates
49. Roy Barron
50. James Doyle
51. John Whitsitt
52. Keith Kelley
53. unidentified
54. unidentified
55. Percy Whitenton
56. unidentified
57. Paul Yarbrough
58. unidentified
59. Jeans Pattinson
60. unidentified
61. J. B. Emerson
62. unidentified
63. unidentified
64. Ralph McCool
65. Jesse Anderson
66. Ernest Felts
67. James Clay Jr
68. Dr. W. J. Templeton
69. Dennis Earle
70. Jack Caskey
71. W. C. Mieher
72. unidentified
73. unidentified
74. J. Marion Meadows
75. Jesse Vineyard
76. D. A. Noel

✣ ✣ ✣

Dear Brethren,

The time of decision is at hand.

We approach this hour in a spirit of humility, gratitude and confidence, that by His grace and with the power of the Holy Spirit we shall be equal to the issues that confront us.

Most of us will ask within our hearts, "How much shall I give—what shall be the measure of my gift?" There are three tests we can use to arrive at our decision. If the amount that we decide upon survives these standards, there is no doubt that victory shall be ours, and certainly His commendation, "Well done, thou good and faithful servant" shall be our reward.

The first test is faith. Let us give and pledge in faith. Faith that He will maintain us in a position to fulfill our commitment—faith that His boundless blessings shall continue to be ours. One of the essential elements of the Christian is his faith.

The second test is sacrifice. As we look upon the cross, we are shocked with the realization that His love for us was so great that He gave not five percent—not ten percent—He gave His all—one hundred percent. What more can a man give? In view of His sacrificial example, it would seem that if we are to be worthy of the name "Christian," our gift must bear the element of sacrifice.

The third test is that our gift meet the Lord's approval. When we are convinced by the Holy Spirit that He approves, we have reached a proper amount. If in doubt, let us pray. Prayer will bring the sunrise of God's will to us in a very clear way. His peace will come to our hearts.

My wife and I have made our pledge, and we tried to apply these tests when we made our decision. We sincerely recommend this to you, our brethren, for your consideration.

Yours fraternally,
James H. Seabrook
Chairman of Official Board

✣ ✣ ✣

The following two pages list the people who signed bonds to guarantee the payment of funds used to finance the first building program. In addition to the two bond issues, fifty members signed notes payable to First Tennessee Bank in the amount of ten thousand dollars each. All of this was necessary because this new congregation did not have sufficient giving history to justify the loans needed to build the Fellowship Hall, the Grant Building, and the sanctuary.

Those who signed the notes at First Tennessee Bank were much the same as those who guaranteed the two bond issues. Without these guarantees, the establishment of Christ Methodist Church would have come to a standstill. Thanks be to God the congregation paid its pledges and no guarantor was called upon to redeem the bonds or the note.

ZIEGLER ORIGINAL $250,000.00

Charles W. Grant	$ 5,000.00	Henry Harry	$ 5,000.00
E. H. Tenent	$10,000.00	Deane A. Noel	$ 2,500.00
E. C. Handorf	$ 2,500.00	Horton G. DuBard	$ 5,000.00
Howard L. Davenport	$10,000.00	J. Porter McClean	$ 3,000.00
James H. Seabrook	$10,000.00	W. A. Wren	$ 3,000.00
J. A. Parsons	$10,000.00	H. F. DeZonia	$ 2,500.00
Lee B. McCormick	$10,000.00	Roy W. Barron	$ 3,000.00
C. R. McDaniel	$10,000.00	H. F. Harwell	$ 2,500.00
W. J. Templeton	$10,000.00	P. B. Whitenton	$ 3,000.00
H. C. Shelton Jr.	$10,000.00	Lloyd J. Sarber	$10,000.00
Jesse A. Anderson	$10,000.00	Jack P. Byrne	$ 7,500.00
Howard A. Boone	$10,000.00	R. H. Weaver	$ 7,500.00
William H. Grumbles	$10,000.00	Harry A. Johnson Jr.	$ 5,000.00
W. K. Martak	$ 5,000.00	Richard G. Taylor	$10,000.00
Hugh F. Carey	$ 5,000.00	Frank I. Nebhut	$ 3,000.00
Sam B. Reid	$ 5,000.00	Ned H. French	$ 2,500.00
D. K. Kelley	$ 5,000.00	C. P. Harris	$ 7,500.00
R. H. Norris	$ 5,000.00	C. P. Knight	$ 4,000.00
J. H. Gass	$ 3,000.00	R. R. Kite	$ 5,000.00
J. C. Huckabee	$ 2,500.00	Charles A. McVean	$ 2,500.00
Frank N. Prichard	$ 5,000.00	Henry C. Roberts	$10,000.00
Clarence Colby	$ 5,000.00	James M. Francis	$ 5,000.00
Samuel H. Mays	$ 2,500.00	Paul Yarbrough	$10,000.00
Charles R. Tate	$ 2,500.00	Earle H. Billings	$10,000.00
William H. D. Fones	$ 2,500.00	Dain S. Riley	$10,000.00
Earl Montgomery	$10,000.00	J. H. Gates	$ 5,000.00
Russell Reeves	$10,000.00	Ben M. Carpenter	$ 5,000.00
J. N. Clay Jr.	$ 5,000.00	Ralph A. McCool	$ 2,500.00
Jesse Joyner	$10,000.00	N. J. Leonard	$ 5,000.00
J. Marion Meadows	$ 5,000.00	Dennis Earles	$ 3,000.00
J. B. Emerson	$ 5,000.00	Jesse H. Vineyard	$ 2,500.00
F. M. Ridolphi	$ 5,000.00	J. B. Caskey	$ 5,000.00
L. W. Helms	$ 5,000.00	E. H. Tenent Sr.	$10,000.00

Ziegler Series B Bonds $150,000.00

Howard L. Davenport	$10,000.00	Richard G. Taylor	$10,000.00
C. P. Stanley	$10,000.00	J. H. Gates	$ 5,000.00
J. B. Caskey	$ 5,000.00	John H. Tole	$ 2,500.00
C. R. McDaniel	$10,000.00	Henry Harry	$ 5,000.00
George T. Roberts	$ 5,000.00	F. M. Ridolphi	$ 5,000.00
Alfred W. Lenz	$ 5,000.00	R. E. Stratton	$ 2,500.00
James H. Seabrook	$10,000.00	Howard A. Boone	$10,000.00
J. A. Parsons	$10,000.00	W. J. Templeton	$10,000.00
Charles W. Grant	$ 5,000.00	John C. Whitsitt	$ 2,500.00
Frank W. Prichard	$ 5,000.00	Sam E. Dunn Jr.	$ 2,000.00
Edward R. Richmond	$ 2,000.00	Robert J. Drake	$ 2,500.00
Roy W. Barron	$ 3,000.00	Donald T. Hull	$ 2,000.00
Earle N. Billings	$ 3,000.00	R. H. Norris	$ 2,500.00
Charles A. McVean	$ 3,000.00	W. K. Martak	$ 5,000.00
Jack P. Byrne	$ 7,500.00	Archie Hoss	$ 2,000.00
Deane A. Noel	$ 2,500.00	Early Mitchell	$ 5,000.00
H. G. DuBard	$ 5,000.00	William E. Drenner	$ 2,500.00
Harry A. Johnson Jr.	$ 2,500.00	Russell Reeves	$10,000.00
Ned H. French	$ 2,500.00		

REPORTS

The reports that follow give a hint of the surefooted and steady leadership in developing the firm foundation that took broad and optimistic vision to accomplish. Meetings were long; some lasting until after midnight. There was always a great deal of discussion and varied opinions on how to accomplish the goals. The goals themselves had to be defined and agreed upon.

The great thing about these people with such diverse and often conflicting opinions was that when a vote was taken, after these thorough discussions, every leader and the congregation put their shoulder to the wheel and made it happen. The reason the goals were accomplished was that all were convinced that this overwhelming project was indeed the will of God and that He would bless their every effort. Time has proven them to be right in their assumptions that were undergirded with prayer.

Official Board Meeting Minutes

Monday, February 3, 1958

The regular monthly meeting of the Official Board of Christ Methodist Church was called to order by Chairman Howard L. Davenport at 7:55 P.M., Monday, February 3, 1958, in the Chapel at 4370 Poplar Ave.

Mr. Tom Loberg presented an interesting and thought-provoking devotional and, at its conclusion, led the meeting in prayer.

The Secretary called the roll, noting 70 Stewards, Mrs. Clarence Colby, Mrs. Percy Whitenton and Dr. Grant present.

The Minutes of the January meeting were read and approved.

Mr. Robert Norris, Chairman of the Commission on Membership and Evangelism, read the report of his group, which is attached hereto. He highlighted one item from his report which he asked the Board to think about, and that was the advisability of having a meeting every month or six weeks on Sunday afternoon for new members of the Church. He did not recommend any action at this time, however.

Mr. Harry Johnson, reporting for the Commission on Education, stated they already have about 25 paid registrations for the weekday kindergarten to begin in September. Mrs. Charles McVean and Mrs. A. A. Sippel are the teachers and they are eminently qualified. The kindergarten will be entirely self-supporting and the tuition is $12.50 per month. As a matter of information, Mr. Johnson mentioned that they have been approached as to the possibility of having a first grade school in 1959, adding a second grade in 1960.

Mr. James Seabrook read a portion of a letter from the Board of Missions complimenting the work of our Brewsters, and stating we should be proud to have them representing us. He gave some figures on the number of patients handled at Christ Hospital in Borneo since its opening. He added that $4,300 had been received against the $6,000 needed for their support, leaving a balance of $1,700 to be subscribed. He called attention to our home missions project, Scenic Hills Methodist Church, and asked everyone to remember them in his prayers.

Mr. George Roberts read the report of the Commission on Stewardship and Finance dated January 30. Upon motion by Lloyd Sarber, which was duly seconded and unanimously carried the report was adopted and is attached to these Minutes.

Although the Building Committee had no report, Chairman Davenport commented that the contractors probably would finish with their work on February 8, then the Furnishings Committee would need two or three weeks to finish their decorating. It was his opinion the earliest we could hope to get in the new building would be either February 23 or March 2.

The Goodwill Committee reported they had received notice of one sick call in the hospital and this had been taken care of. Mr. Marion Meadows, chairman of the House Committee, stated that a custodian had been employed and began work last Saturday. He asked if anyone had any extra tools they would like to donate to the church, to please let him know.

Chairman Davenport mentioned the fact that the developers of the area had agreed to provide parking space for some 280 cars across the street from the first unit, the space to be covered with four inches of Camden gravel with the proper parking space marked for each car. He expressed his appreciation for their efforts in this direction. Mr. Jeans Pattinson, on behalf of Mr. John Parsons who has been working with the developers on this matter, read a letter from them which is attached to these Minutes, setting out expenses incurred by them in providing this parking area free of charge to the church. Chairman Davenport called attention to the fact that we had been requested to get signatures to a petition which the developers need to present to the Zoning Commission in order that they may get a five and one-half acre tract running to the end of the church's property on the east side of Grove Park Road zoned commercial. He solicited the support of those stewards who had not already signed the petition. He added that the church would have perpetual parking rights to some acres of off-street parking.

Mrs. Margaret Colby, president of the WSCS, reported that group had voted to sponsor a Girl Scout troop at the church and had elected Mrs. Wm. G. Farquhar as vice president, replacing Mrs. J. V. Cowan, who has moved out of town. She stated some few small items still had to be purchased, but all of the equipment for the kitchen was about completed. Facilities in the Fellowship Hall for serving about 200 people will be available.

Chairman Davenport urged more stewards and their families to attend the Sunday night services.

Mr. Davenport then read a letter from Mr. Bert Ferguson, who is in charge of the stewardship phase of the Commission on Stewardship and Finance, to the effect that at the March meeting of the Board, his group would ask that each steward become a tither. This letter is attached to and forms a part of these Minutes.

Dr. Grant in his report emphasized the importance of tithing, especially to a building program such as we are undertaking, and expressed his appreciation to the Commission for their energetic plans in this direction. The good work being done by Mr. Barry DeZonia and Mrs. Ethel Whitenton since their addition to the Church staff was praised by Dr. Grant. He stated there were many areas which, for the moment, we may have to forego, among them the Children's and Youth Choirs. He said Mr. Cianciola was aware of the fact that February 27 would be our last Sunday in the Plaza and again expressed his thanks to their staff for their wonderful cooperation. He thanked the Publicity Committee for their splendid work and the cooperation received from radio, television and newspaper organizations. He mentioned that a number of items had been given as memorials, among them the lectern, baptismal font, the brass cross and the pulpit Bible.

The Pastor's training for membership class will begin on March 8. Children taking the course will be received into the church on Palm Sunday.

Dr. Grant called on Mrs. Whitenton for a report of her activities and she stated that during January some 200 calls had been made on prospective members and others.

Mr. Harry Johnson stated that a diagram of the first floor of the building would be prepared and distributed and urged the members of the Board to familiarize themselves with it so that when people asked information as to the location of classrooms, they could be given the proper directions.

Mr. Seabrook suggested that although Mr. Cianciola had been notified of our plans to vacate the Plaza, the Resolutions Committee prepare a suitable a resolution to him and his staff, thanking them for the many courtesies extended to us during the time we held services there.

Dr. Horton DuBard expressed his appreciation to Harry Johnson, the Commission on Education and others who have spent so much time and energy in working towards occupying the new unit.

There being no further business to come before the meeting, same was adjourned at 9:10 P.M. with a prayer by Dr. Grant.

Respectfully submitted,

Earle Billings
Secretary

Official Board Meeting
Christ Methodist Church

Monday, March 3, 1958

The regular monthly meeting of the Official Board of Christ Methodist Church was called to order in the Fellowship Hall at 4488 Poplar at 7:45 P.M., Monday, March 3, 1958, Chairman Howard Davenport presiding.

Dr. W. J. Templeton opened the meeting with a very interesting devotional and prayer.

The Secretary called the roll, noting 67 Stewards present.

The Minutes of the preceding meeting were approved as read.

Chairman Bob Norris of the Commission on Membership and Evangelism presented the report for his group, which is attached and forms a part of these Minutes. He told of plans for a reception for new members of the Church on Sunday, March 16, at which the Chairman of the Board and the Chairmen of the other Commissions and Dr. Grant would give short resumes of the responsibilities of their groups. Afterwards, refreshments would be served and the building officially opened for inspection. He mentioned his Commission had voted to send two men to Washington, D.C. on July 3–6 to attend the meeting of the Methodist Committee on Evangelism.

Harry Johnson reported that attendance in the church school last Sunday was 651, our largest to date, and gave a breakdown of this figure:

Youth Division	4370 Poplar	102
Men's Bible Class	Room 302	34
Ladies' Class	Choir Room	16
Sr. Adult Class meeting for the first time Mrs. Grant, teacher	Conference Room	11
Aldersgate Class		110
Young Adult		over 40

He asked everyone to talk to their friends about the Day Kindergarten. They have 40 paid registrations to date and have room for 100.

Chairman James Seabrook gave a report on Scenic Hills Methodist Church, which we are helping support. They have a membership of about 100, mostly young people, with prospects for the future of being one of the best Methodist Churches in this area. They have about completed financing for their first building, consisting of a small chapel with adjoining Sunday school rooms, to take care of 150–225 people.

Chairman Caskey presented the report of the Commission on Stewardship and Finance, which was adopted and is attached hereto. He then asked Mr. Bert Ferguson to explain the program planned for Stewardship cultivation in Christ Methodist Church. Mr. Ferguson stated that the Official Board in any church was the guiding force and his group felt that before we could approach the membership of the church, we should have the active backing of the members of the Board on the matter of stewardship. Cards having spaces to check for (1) *Proportionate Giver* (2) *Tither* (3) *Prayerfully consider Tithing* were passed to those present and they were asked to return them. A report of the results will be made at the next meeting of the Board.

Mr. Everett Handorf, Chairman of the Architects' Committee, turned over to the Church building plans and other data and stated there were some matters to be checked out with the subcontractors. He mentioned a number of change orders that had been agreed with the Building Committee and the subcontractors. He thanked all of the people who had worked so closely and cooperatively with his group and stated there were no unfinished contracts and there only remained the final close out of the building. Chairman Davenport, on behalf of all present, thanked Mr. Handorf and his committee for the excellent work they had done.

Mr. Ned French, chairman of attendance for the Board, reported that the lowest percent of attendance was in October with 61 percent and the highest in July with 78 percent. Ten months' average to date was 69 percent. Several stewards have not missed a meeting.

Chairman Davenport complimented Bill Meadows and his Ushers Committee on their fine work in handling the huge crowd at our opening Sunday in the new building. Mr. Meadows thanked all those who had helped at the Plaza and here and proposed to alternate the members of his committee monthly. He also proposed using the young people to usher at night. This was approved.

The Goodwill Committee reported one call referred to them during the month, and this was dispatched promptly.

Suggestions were made that we try to get two policemen to direct traffic on Sundays, get the city to paint walkways and to erect a *No Parking* sign for Dr. Grant. Jesse Vineyard agreed to handle this with Mr. Huntzicker. A suggestion was also made to light the building whenever activities are held.

Mr. Charles Johnston stated that a number of suggestions had been made with regard to insurance and they were being considered. In the meantime, the building is adequately covered.

Mr. Bill Fones presented a resolution to be sent to Mr. Cianciola, expressing the Church's appreciation for the many courtesies extended to us during our stay at the Plaza Theater. The resolution was duly adopted and the Secretary instructed to transmit it to Mr. Cianciola. This has been done and a copy is attached to these Minutes.

Mr. Richard Taylor reported for the Scouts, stating they were planning a trip to Camp Currier in the near future. He also mentioned the baseball diamond and asked suggestions as to the removal of the backstop since trees had been planted on the present diamond. Mr. Jim Clay agreed to assist in getting a truck with a hoist to move the poles of the backstop, which are set in cement.

Mr. Carey Stanley reported $30,077.99 had been spent for furnishings with some $95.00 worth of miscellaneous items yet to be purchased. This is 5172.99 above the arbitrary figure of $30,000.00 set for furnishings for the new building. He stated some $1,772 in memorials had been pledged and when these are paid they can be applied against the above figure. He thanked Messrs. Earl Montgomery and Lloyd Sarber for their excellent cooperation and for their services in securing material for the church at below wholesale costs. He said he wanted the Board to know how well Mr. Barry DeZonia had cooperated in working out details in connection with furnishing the building and then stated the Furnishings Committee was turning the building over to the Trustees furnished as requested.

Upon motion duly made and carried, it was agreed to order clamps for the chairs in the Fellowship Hall to make them steadier at a cost of about $75.

Official Board Meeting Minutes

Monday, April 7, 1958

The regular monthly meeting of the Official Board of Christ Methodist Church was called to order at 7:40 P.M., Monday, April 7, 1958 in the Fellowship Hall at 4488 Poplar, Memphis, Tennessee, Chairman Howard L. Davenport presiding.

Mr. John Tole presented an inspirational devotional on Being Happy, after which he led the meeting in prayer.

The Secretary called the roll and read the Minutes of the preceding meeting which were approved, as were those of the Special Meeting on March 23.

Mr. Harry Johnson, reporting for the Commission on Education, cited an average attendance over a five-Sunday period last year of 468 compared with 577 for this year. He called attention to the Leadership Training School in Room 301 on the subject of *Understanding Children*. The course is to be taught by Mrs. Richard Taylor and workers with children and parents of children through the sixth grade are invited to attend. He also mentioned a committee working on youth activities and one under the chairmanship of Bill Fones on Family Life; the latter is planning a family picnic to be held at the church on May 4.

Chairman Jack Caskey presented the report of the Finance Commission together with financial statements for the month of March. Both were approved and are attached to these Minutes.

Mr. Bert Ferguson gave a brief report on the stewardship program, stating that 60 out of 95 stewards had signed tithing commitments, after which Mr. C. R. McDaniel gave a personal testimony on tithing and what it meant to him.

Mr. Edgar Tenent presented some figures to the Board to show our present indebtedness in the light of suggestions made by some that we construct the sanctuary next. Considerable discussion ensued. Mr. Jack Caskey observed that any discussion on building was premature at this time until we could determine what the cost of operating the first unit would be.

Mr. Bob Norris presented the report of the Commission on Membership and Evangelism, which was duly adopted and is attached to these Minutes.

Mr. Marion Meadows, Chairman of the House Committee, reported that at present we have two custodians and one maid, that the two men have been working about 55 hours a week and the maid 45, and that it may be necessary to employ additional help in the future.

Mr. Richard Taylor presented a proposal for Mr. Jimmy Westerfield for a baseball team for 13–15 year-old boys, outlining the need for uniforms at a cost of $150. After some discussion of this matter, Mr. Howard Boone made a motion that the uniforms and equipment be financed in some way outside of the church budget. The motion carried.

Mrs. Margaret Colby stated that the WSCS had held their first luncheon in the Fellowship Hall and that they would hold their annual election of officers in May.

Chairman Davenport mentioned the Family of the Year program being conducted by *Together* magazine and stated that the Howard Boone Family had been nominated from Christ Methodist Church. Upon motion by Bill Fones, seconded by Harry Johnson and unanimously carried, the nomination of the Boone family was approved.

Chairman Davenport also mentioned that Dr. Grant would be out of town on Sunday, April 13, but had arranged for visiting ministers for the morning and evening services.

The question of holding two services was brought up for discussion and this matter was thoroughly explored. A motion to hold two services for a trial period was made by Mr. Clay Shelton and duly seconded. After additional discussion, a motion to table by Mr. Lee McCormick was seconded and carried.

The following committee to nominate officers for the Board was appointed by Chairman Davenport:

C. R. McDaniel, Chairman;

Robert Holt	Charles McVean
Clarence Colby	John Tole

There being no further business to come before the meeting, it was adjourned with prayer by Mr. Seabrook at 9:30 P.M.
Respectfully submitted.

MINUTES OF COMMISSION ON STEWARDSHIP AND FINANCE

The Commission on Stewardship and Finance of Christ Methodist Church met Thursday, September 4, 1958 at 7:45 P.M. with 18 present and Chairman Jack Caskey presiding. The meeting was opened with a short prayer by James Seabrook, after which the quarterly and monthly finance statement of the church's operations were distributed and discussed. Copies of same are hereto attached and made a part of these minutes.

The church kindergarten, whose recent inception has met with tremendous success, was submitted for discussion, specifically as to the method of accounting and disbursing of funds. The Pastor explained that the Commission on Education is directly responsible for the operation of the kindergarten, and the wisdom of comingling the school funds with the finance program of the church was debated. Upon a motion by Al Lenz, seconded by Russell Reeves, it was decided that Mr. D. A. Noel would set up the books for the school, the teachers, Mrs. Sippel and Mrs. McVean, would make the entries to the books, and Mrs. Ford, the financial secretary of the church, would disburse the money upon instructions from the teachers. This situation to be reviewed later and revised if found necessary. This motion was carried unanimously.

Dr. Grant submitted to the committee a six-month financial report on the kitchen activities. A copy of this report is hereto attached and made a part of these minutes. It was disclosed that total expenses of serving of the meals amounted to $5893.18, total income derived from those servings $3144.67, inventory on hand $263.43, making a net loss of $2391.02. Particular note was made of the fact that total expenses included Mrs. Dunn's salary, and that the kitchen had served MYF groups, Men's Club, WSCS and fellowship dinners. Eleven fellowship dinners were served during this period at a cost of $1281.48 with an income of $1659.75 derived therefrom, making a net income from this source around $378.27. The committee was reminded that at the beginning of the fellowship dinners it was decided that if the church could break even on the food cost alone, and bear the salaries as an overhead, that the kitchen activities overall would have been considered a great success. In view of these results and after many observations, pro and con, it was moved by Gerald Owens to increase the charge for adults from $.75 to $1.00, to charge children of school age (i.e. from 6 to 18) $.50, and to admit children under six without charge. These changes are to become effective at the next fellowship dinner, September 17, 1958. The motion was seconded by Ed Richmond and the vote tallied, with 10 voting affirmatively, five voting negatively, and three not voting.

Dr. Grant then informed us of the Worldwide Communion the first Sunday in October, and also discussed the need of a hymnal holder to place on the back of chairs in the Sanctuary. It was suggested that the latter be referred to the House Committee.

Report to the Official Board
Official Board Minutes

Monday, March 2, 1959

The regular monthly meeting of the Official Board of Christ Methodist Church met Monday, March 2, 1959, at 4488 Poplar Avenue, Memphis, Tennessee, Chairman Howard L. Davenport presiding.

The meeting was opened with prayer by Mr. Clarence Colby, after which the Secretary called the roll.

The reading of the Minutes of the preceding meeting was dispensed with.

Upon motion by Mr. Harry Johnson, seconded by Mr. Bill Fones and unanimously carried, the establishment of a First Grade class at Christ Methodist

Church was approved, starting in September 1959. Fee is to be $250 for the year, per child, plus $90 per year for lunches.

Chairman Caskey read the report of the Finance Commission, which is attached to and forms a part of these Minutes. Individual action was requested on the following items:

1. Mr. Ed Tenent read the agreement that the Building Finance Committee proposed to enter into with Leader Federal (copy of which is attached), whereby the Church would borrow $500,000 at an interest rate of 5.7 percent with a two-point discount. Upon motion by Mr. Tenent, seconded by Mr. Caskey, it was unanimously agreed to accept the Leader Federal proposal;

2. Upon motion by Mr. Caskey, seconded by Mr. Charles McVean and unanimously carried, the appointment of a permanent Campaign Committee was approved;

3. On motion by Mr. Caskey, seconded by Mr. Earl Montgomery, and unanimously passed, Mrs. Frank Walker's employment as Executive Secretary of the Campaign Committee was approved at a salary of $1.50 per hour for the approximately 15 to 20 hours a week she would work;

4. Mr. Noel Gilbert was employed to work with the Junior and Youth Choirs, on a trial basis, at a salary of $150 per month;

5. The placing of an order for the steel for Unit B by the Architects and Building Committee was approved on motion by Mr. Caskey. The action was unanimous. A meeting of the above committee was called for Thursday night at 7:30 P.M. in the Conference Room.

In response to a request by Mr. Jack Caskey, Mr. Bill Meadows agreed to assist in carrying the Sunday collections to the bank for deposit.

Mr. Fred Alexander reported on the Fund Campaign as follows:

Total Prospects	595
Total Turndowns	149
	446
Not Worked	80
Pledged $495,000	336
Estimated from 80 unworked cards	30,000
Total	$525,000

He stated that we could not afford to fail in this campaign because:

1. The progress of the Church would be set back a number of years;
2. The esprit de corps would be hurt, perhaps irreparably;
3. Methodism generally in Memphis would be hurt;
4. Christ's cause in this community would be damaged;
5. The name of Christ could not be held quite as high due to our failure in this Church.

Mr. Alexander stated that there were two things that could be done: First, submit this matter to the Board or to a representative group from the congregation; second, present the matter to the entire congregation at 10:45 on Sunday morning.

Davenport stated that while Dr. Grant was reluctant to present the matter to the congregation during the worship service, the matter was of such extreme importance that he had agreed to go along with this method.

✣ ✣ ✣

May 6, 1963
Members of the Quarterly Conference:

Two cows, standing in a field chewing their cud saw a milk truck speeding toward the city. The sign on the panels read: *Pasteurized, homogenized, Vitamin D added.* One cow turned to the other and said, "Makes you feel kind of inadequate, doesn't it?"

Something of that same spirit may be present when a Methodist minister reads the 28 specific areas of responsibility [1960 *Discipline*, p.352] assigned the pastor in the local church. It may inspire as well as demoralize a man to be reminded periodically of the high purposes with which he first requested the privilege of joining the ranks of the traveling preachers.

To adequately describe the work of the year will require the excessive use of superlatives.

The various Commission chairmen will present in detail the accomplishments of the year. In a thumbnail sketch, let me say, I think that this will prove to be our best year since the inception of the church in almost every area. I am sure it will be true in the area of new members received, at least by the time of annual conference. With the exception of the first year, during which 900 members were received and, of course, it is not right to use that for a norm, we will receive a greater number into membership this year than any other single year since our organization. So the same may be said about church school attendance, church school enrollment, total amount received in cash for both building and budget, the aggregate attendance at divine worship services and perhaps in other areas. My thanks to my co-workers on the staff, the lay leadership of the church, and the membership-at-large who have cooperated in order to make such a report possible.

We are a happy church not only because of our achievements but also because of the high goals we set for ourselves. I think all of us are thrilled that at this time we are finalizing the preparation for the actual construction of our Sanctuary. Another thing that thrills us is the unanimous consent to reach out and extend our program of missions, by agreeing to give full support to three couples rather than two. The imminent European theologian Emil Brunner said, "The church exists by mission as a fire exists by burning." If and when and as we forget others, here and abroad, if and when we have no evangelistic zeal, then it is like refusing to put more coals on the flame and the fire goes out. We have no reason to exist. We Christians live for others.

In addition to the areas of responsibility mentioned in the opening paragraph, your pastor, like every other pastor of the Methodist Church, has District and Conference as well as civic responsibilities. He is serving on the District Committee of the Wesley Foundation, as vice chairman of the District Committee of the Wesley House, as a member of the District Committee on Ministerial Training and Qualifications, the Conference Committee on Missions and as Chairmen of the Conference Committee on Urban Life, all of which I greatly enjoy and all of which is highly important yet requires some time and strength. In addition, numerous television appearances, by invitation, particularly on the Memphis Round Table and the Minister of the Week on another station, together with having served for quite some time as a director for Memphis Boys Town, on the Memphis Committee on Alcoholism, United Cerebral Palsy, and United Tennessee League.

More thrilling and challenging experiences are in store for us as will be divulged by the various chairmen in this meeting and the meetings to follow. During these intensely busy days when so many first-magnitude decisions must needs be made, as your pastor, I rededicate myself to the proposition that a vitally spiritual ministry is not only the key to success but the only key that will open the hearts of the people and make possible a vibrant program which will meet the needs of the people about us and be commensurate with both our magnificent building program and our unprecedented opportunity. Your prayers and cooperation to assist me in the realization of this ever-receding goal will be appreciated.

Cordially,
Charles W. Grant

✣ ✣ ✣

MEMPHIS ANNUAL CONFERENCE HELD AT CHRIST METHODIST CHURCH

Memphis, Tennessee 1965

You will be able to see the very simple needs involved in the preparation and costs of the Annual Conference in 1965, as compared to the conference held at Christ Church in 1986, 1991, and 1996.

The records of the 1986 and 1991 conferences can be found in Volume III, which covers the tenure of Dr. Maxie D. Dunnam. The 1996 conference is covered in Volume IV, during the tenure of Dr. Bill Bouknight.

Convenient Locations for Accommodations for Memphis Annual Conference

Admiral Benbow Inn
4720 Summer Avenue—Tel. 682-4601
(all are double beds)

Single	$7.00
1 double bed, 2 persons	$10.00
2 double beds, 1–4 persons	$12.00

Holiday Inn
4941 Summer Avenue—Tel. 683-2411

1 double bed, 1 person	$6.00
1 double bed, 2 persons	$9.00
2 double beds, 2 persons	$10.00

($2.00 for each additional person)

Parkview Hotel
1914 Poplar Avenue—Tel. 274-7860

Single	$6.00 (e.p.)
Twins or double	$10.00 per day (e.p.)

Britling's Cafeteria
Laurelwood Shopping Center (across street)

Knickerbocker Restaurant
4699 Poplar Avenue

Dobbs Snack Bar
474 S. Perkins Ext.

Dobbs House Inn
4726 Poplar Avenue

Kress's Hearth
Laurelwood Shopping Center (lunch bar)

Embers Restaurant
3881 Park Avenue

Shoney's
Eastgate Shopping Center
(White Station Road at Poplar Avenue)

Carousel
688 S. Mendenhall Rd. (So. off Poplar)

International Pancake House
567 S. Perkins Ext. (So. off Poplar)

✣ ✣ ✣

The letter written in 1968 to the General Board of Christian Concerns transmitting the resolution of the Official Board of Christ Methodist Church in Memphis, Tennessee, is included in this history to point out that disagreements with the General Conference are not a new phenomenon.

The answer to the Christ Church resolution from the General Board of Christian Social Concerns is also included to show the value of the opportunity to understand such actions and the reasoning behind the actions.

The beliefs and thought processes within the local church are as diverse as those of the General Conference. Since John Wesley birthed this church it has thrived on its diversity, has accomplished great things, and can continue to do so if we are committed to listening and attempting to understand the thoughts of others.

May God bless the privilege we have to express our opinions and listen to those of others.

✣ ✣ ✣

Resolution Concerning Unrest in the Church and in the World

WHEREAS, because of action taken at the General Conference in Dallas, together with positions and stands made elsewhere, we find a considerable number of our members are disturbed to the point that action from the leaders of our church to guide the way toward a better Christian understanding should be undertaken and

WHEREAS, investigation has revealed that Report No. 17, on The Rule Of Law And The Right Of Dissent, made to the General Conference in Dallas recently was adopted by a slim majority of the delegates present, and that such passage and its interpretation has caused much concern; and

WHEREAS, a thorough reading of Report No. 17 will recognize that it is capable of misinterpretation in that it can and is being used to say that we approve of riots and civil disobedience, and

WHEREAS, our people are further disturbed over the action of the Board of Missions in withdrawing Ten Million Dollars ($10,000,000.00) from the First National City Bank in New York because the bank lends money to the Union of South Africa and

WHEREAS, the question of clergymen counseling on war and like subjects has created concern:

NOW, THEREFORE, in order to make the position of the Christ Methodist Church clear on such issues,

BE IT RESOLVED:

1. That we stand for the necessity of a society rooted in law and of citizenry who respect the law. We recognize the right to dissent in a nonviolent manner. We do not approve of civil disobedience. We live in a democracy where proper redress for all wrongs, misdoings, injustices, unfair customs, and unjust laws may be had by the simplest citizen by petition, appearance, protest and vote. We believe that civil disobedience inevitably leads to riots, riots to revolution, revolution to anarchy and the downfall of government. We respectfully believe it is better to live in a democracy as we know it with the right of redress provided by law and the ballot box than to see our government fall which would mean our churches falling also, for we know that churches do not occupy the prominent place in the lives and beings of the peoples of countries under dictatorships.
2. That we are opposed to the withdrawal of funds in New York as such withdrawals amount to an economic boycott. Likewise, church members who fail to make a pledge or fail to pay their pledges when made because they disagree with some action of the church are boycotting the church. We disapprove of both of these.
3. That clergymen and others in counseling and ministering to persons on matters of conscience should be mindful of that right and the serious responsibility attached thereto. Certainly on matters that are spiritual and religious, their counsel should be sought and respected. We do not believe the clergy or laity should ever counsel anyone in such a way as to lead that individual to be disloyal to his country. America has traditionally been a nation of separation of church and state. This we believe ought to continue for breakdown on this would ultimately lead to national churches whose very existence depends on the government in power.

Having set forth our position on the above matters, we now recommend to the Official Board of Christ Methodist Church

1. That we confess our sins and ask forgiveness for them;
2. That our first love and loyalty is for Christ and His church. The church is the bride of Christ and he who strikes at the heart of the church, strikes at the heart of God. We believe that a divided church is not within the will of God, but a united church has endless power to do His will;
3. That we recognize that injustices and inequities do exist in all phases of life and that we deplore this fact. We dedicate ourselves as a church to strive to eliminate them for all our citizens;
4. That we have deep concern for the impoverished and underprivileged of Memphis and resolve to assist them in every way possible;

5. That we tithe our income toward undergirding our church and rendering a greater service to mankind through the wholehearted support of the many splendid programs of our church and particularly our home and foreign missions, as well as our work in the "inner city." Having set forth our position, we authorize the sending of a copy of this report to the district superintendent, the bishop, the Commission on Missions, and the Commission on Social Concern of the United Methodist Church.

✣ ✣ ✣

BOARD OF CHRISTIAN SOCIAL CONCERN OF THE UNITED METHODIST CHURCH

Mr. E. R. Richmond, Chairman
Mr. Harry C. Brahm, Secretary

The Official Board
Christ Methodist Church
4488 Poplar Avenue
Memphis, Tennessee 38117

Dear Brothers Richmond and Brahm:

I have been asked by Dr. A. Dudley Ward, General Secretary of this Board, to acknowledge receipt of the Resolution of the Official Board of Christ Methodist Church entitled Resolution Concerning Unrest in the Church and in the World.

I want to express appreciation on behalf of the General Board of Christian Social Concerns, its membership and its staff, for your bringing this resolution to our attention. I presume you are aware that the Southeastern Jurisdictional Conference has challenged this particular General Conference resolution, to which your resolution refers, on the grounds of constitutionality. The Judicial Council of The United Methodist Church will be hearing this matter argued at its next meeting in Denver on November 8–9. The General Board of Christian Social Concerns will be arguing on that occasion that the General Conference resolution is not unconstitutional. The theological base for the General Board argument will be that the Christian's loyalty must be first to God and that God alone is to be given absolute obedience by men of faith. Any requirement of absolute obedience to the State and to its laws is a form of idolatry. For this reason, a duty of civil disobedience is always within the realm of possibility for a Christian, even in the best forms of government that humans have devised.

If you care to have a copy of this statement as prepared by this Board, please let me know and I will see that it is sent to you.

A great deal of criticism and unrest has been evidenced in the membership of The United Methodist Church in relation to the General Conference resolution entitled The Rule of Law and the Right of Dissent. The Civil Disobedience section, in particular, has caused criticism, question, and unrest. Part of the reason is due to a misunderstanding. Many people today are linking riots with civil disobedience. Your Official Board resolution does this, although you do not necessarily equate them. The General Conference, however, provides no aid and comfort for rioters. The civil disobedience approved by the General Conference in extreme cases only, must always be "nonviolent." The dilemma we see, however, is that involved whenever you take a position which flatly and absolutely opposes any form of civil disobedience upon any possible occasion whatsoever. This can only be justified, in a Christian point of view, it seems to me, if one assumes that the laws of our country are always justifiable, or are always justifiably administered. As I say, this commits, in our view, the sin of statolatry, which is simply a specialized form of idolatry and condemned by all ethical religion.

Does the official Board of Christ Methodist Church condemn all economic boycotts upon all occasions no matter what? Have the members of your Official Board thought through the question of Christian responsibility for ethical use of economic resources? The members of the General Board of Christian Social Concerns have studied this matter with some care over a period of months, and would be in a position to call to your attention some of the relevant study materials that are currently applicable to this discussion.

Most important of all, the General Conference resolution on The Rule of Law and the Right of Dissent has precipitated a great deal of study and discussion throughout the Church on these highly important matters of law, order, and justice. When these studies and discussions are carried out in the spirit of prayer and seeking as is evidenced in the statement of the Official Board of Christ Methodist Church, we will all be learning from one another, and surely this is one of the fruits of obedience to Christ.

Thank you again for sharing with us your resolution. I enclose for your information a publication of the Board of Missions on this subject, based on an essay by Judge William H. Maness of Jacksonville, Florida, a Methodist layman.

Grover C. Bagby
Associate General Secretary

✣ ✣ ✣

Opportunity

My opportunity! Dear Lord, I do not ask
That Thou shouldst give me some high work of Thine,
Some noble calling, or some wondrous task—
Give me a little hand to hold in mine.

I do not ask that I should ever stand
Among the wise, the worthy or the great;
I only ask that, softly, hand in hand,
A child and I may enter at Thy gate.
Give me a little child to point the way
Over the strange, sweet paths that lead to Thee.

Give me a little voice to teach to pray;
Give me two shining eyes Thy face to see
The only crown I ask, dear Lord, to wear
Is this—that I may teach a little child
How beautiful, O how divinely fair
Is Thy dear face, so loving, sweet and mild.
I do not need to ask for more than this.
My opportunity? 'Tis standing at my door;
What sorrow if this blessing I should miss
A little child! Why should I ask for more?

—Author Unknown

THE CHURCH SCHOOL

This section of the history of the church covers the educational committees, the teaching departments, the directors of Christian Education, and other facets of our continuously evolving educational programs.

THE ORGANIZATION OF THE CHURCH SCHOOL FOR CHRIST METHODIST CHURCH

The Steering Committee, created to organize Christ Methodist Church, was limited to three men from each of the five churches. Harry A. Johnson (age thirty-three in 1954) was invited to attend most of their meetings. In about January or February 1955, he was invited to attend the meeting being held at the Leader Federal Building across Poplar from East High School. Lee McCormick was presiding. After some other items of business, Lee said the committee had agreed that they wanted Harry to organize the church school. He handed Harry a key to the house they had taken from First Methodist. Harry drove out there the next morning and almost lost his desire to be a part of this new undertaking. A huge oak tree about three or four feet in diameter was lying across the dirt (mud) driveway. The old house was wooden with paint peeling on the outside and with rough lumber interior walls with wallpaper falling off them, and the house was filthy and small.

Harry managed to find some men who would cut up the tree and haul it away for the firewood. Bill Martak worked for Southern Cotton Oil Company and managed to get several truckloads of roofing shingle ends and they spread them over the mud driveway and made it at least possible to drive up to the house.

Immediately after being given the job, Harry asked all of the representatives of the five churches on the Steering Committee to get the names of all leaders and teachers in their church schools who expected to come to the new church. He talked to these people on the phone, then in person, and began to find out who the best-qualified leaders were from each church. He decided that Mrs. Leland (Thelma) Helms could do the job as Children's Division Superintendent; Sam Mays, Youth Division Superintendent; Pete Emerson, Adult Division Superintendent; Ella McVean, Nursery; Clarcy Sippel, Kindergarten; Mrs. Jack (Martha) Wright, Primary Department; Helen Kite, Intermediate Department; and Mrs. E. L. Carpenter, Junior Department. They began to fill in with the needed teachers and workers and set up training schools for all of them (required). Leland Helms and H. Clay Shelton were secretary and treasurer.

Harry started looking for places to put Sunday school classes. The Steering Committee had negotiated a lease with Augustine Cianciola for the Plaza Theater. They used the theater office for the secretary and treasurer and placed one adult class in each corner of the theater proper (four in all). It became a problem as to how to divide the adult classes since everyone would begin on the same Sunday. Harry tried general age groupings and then tried to find the right teacher for each class. An amusing thing happened. John Parsons was president of Memphis Bank and Trust Company. He did many things for Christ Methodist and he and Harry became good friends. John called Harry early in the planning stages and asked him to come by his office on Union. He did. John was twenty or twenty-five years older than Harry was, but looking him in the eyes he said that people their age needed to stay young, and he shared that he played tennis with his son, Frank, regularly. This indication that they were the same age didn't help Harry's attitude toward him very much. John had been teaching the young adult class at St. John's for many years. The reason he wanted to see Harry was to tell him he wanted to teach the young adults in the new church. John was well read, well prepared, and a great Sunday school teacher, but each member of his class from St. John's said one of the reasons they were coming to the new church was to do everything new, including a new perspective from a new teacher. So, Harry had to look John in the eyes and tell him he was assigned to teach an older adult class. He didn't like it very much at the time, but he did an outstanding job and all those in his class dearly loved him.

There was room in each wing on either side of the movie screen for a class of thirty or forty. They needed to get Augustine Cianciola to agree to move a great deal of equipment on Saturdays so they could use it on Sunday. There was enough room in the theater lobby for the intermediate class, and the theater cry room offered the perfect place for the nursery. Children's division classes were set up in the cottage in the dining room, each bedroom, and in the living room. Dr. Grant's office was in the southeast corner room, which had been the breakfast room. Harry had talked to the management of the Sunshine Home across the street and all the stores in the Plaza Shopping Center about useable space with no luck.

Harry asked the new teachers and many others to help, and they cleaned up the cottage and made it at least useable. All the happenings to this point had been done without any expenditure of funds, but now they needed chairs, tables, and literature. He made up a list of student literature, teacher literature, and other materials along with an estimated cost. He got competitive prices on metal chairs for adult and youth and oak chairs and tables for children meeting in the cottage. All of this furniture had to be compatible with the estimated future needs of the church.

They had to have about 150 metal folding chairs for the theater which had to be unfolded and set up early on Sunday morning and folded and stored behind the screen after church. Penny and Harry lived at 3416 Walnut Grove Road at the time, only a block from the theater. He walked up each Sunday morning about an hour-and-a-half before Sunday school, set up the chairs, and stayed after church as

Children's Sunday school in the little cottage.

long as it took to fold up and store them. They needed a pulpit to use at the theater, which Harry purchased; it too had to be brought out and set up each Sunday.

In addition to the oak chairs and tables for the children at the cottage, they needed metal folding chairs for the M.Y.F. meetings on Sunday nights and for Wednesday night preaching services on the lawn (preaching from a front porch pulpit, which also had to be purchased). These metal chairs were also used for all communion and committee meetings held in the living room. The bishop gave the church permission to have a larger Board of Stewards than the membership justified mainly because most of the leadership of the churches came to Christ Church. They used the chairs for crowded board meetings in the cottage. Everyone came to all meetings although they lasted an inordinately long time.

It was confirmed in about April (his appointment to take effect June 1) that Dr. Charles Grant would be the minister, coming from Madison Heights where he had been for two years and was the choice of the Steering Committee. He turned out to be the perfect choice for this assignment.

The first Sunday, they had all the Sunday school meet in the theater for instructions about where they would be meeting and how they would conduct matters. Harry introduced Dr. Grant, and he got upset, saying that no ordained minister of the Methodist Church needed an introduction to his congregation, including him. Harry was also one of the five members of the Nominating Committee that set up the first organization of the church and stayed on that Nominating Committee for about six years.

Intermediate Sunday school in the lobby of the Plaza Theater, with Mrs. Richard (Helen) Kite teaching.

During this nominating process Sam Mays called Harry and wanted to have lunch at Bill and Jim's Restaurant on Madison Avenue. Harry met with him and he brought William H. D. Fones (now Chief Justice of the Tennessee State Supreme Court). He and Bill were close friends, and Sam thought that Bill would make a good chairman of the Commission on Education. Harry came to agree, and he and Bill worked closely together for the next two years. He contributed greatly to the success of the church school.

Harry set up training classes for the teachers and they had many meetings before the first Sunday. On that first Sunday in June 1955, they had 105 church school teachers and workers and over 600 in attendance at Sunday school. They had about 100 at M.Y.F. on Sunday nights, and mothers took turns bringing sandwiches and cold drinks for the M.Y.F. meetings. In that first year they also set up a Cub Scout pack and a Scout troop. As Harry remembers, Richard Taylor and David Stanley did a tremendous job with the Scout program.

Penny Johnson had helped in the kindergarten and nursery before but never as a children's teacher. Ruth Montgomery prevailed upon her to come out to the cottage and just be a helper in her second grade class. The second or third Sunday, Ruth locked herself out of her house and left her car keys inside. Penny was a teacher whether she wanted to be or not. She ran back and forth, asking Martha Johnston what to do. She became a regular second grade teacher, then a fifth grade teacher, and then superintendent of the Primary Department.

In 1955–56, women wore hats and gloves. One Sunday in July 1955, Penny wore a white straw hat. She took it off to teach the children and hung it on the light beside the medicine cabinet in the bathroom of the cottage. Someone came in, used the bathroom, turned on the light, and it burned up Penny's hat. A week later she was telling some people about it, and Ed Carpenter said, "That's covered by your insurance," and promptly replaced the hat.

The lawn in front of the cottage, along with the metal chairs, was also used for Men's Club. Bill Grumbles was the first president. All these services and meetings on the lawn were fine during the summer of 1955, but winter was coming. It was decided to build a temporary wooden building beside the cottage to hold all the meetings that had been held on the lawn and crowded into the living and dining rooms of the cottage. It performed its purpose beautifully.

They had square dances for young adults in this building, but Dr. Grant insisted they call them folk games. Everyone brought card tables for meals they had within the building. Dr. Grant insisted they were *utility* tables, not card tables.

They had teacher training classes from the beginning of the church. These were held in Harry's house on Sunday during the Sunday school hour. They got up early on Sunday morning. Harry walked to the theater to set up for Sunday school and church. Penny fixed breakfast, got their children, Harry (then six) and Janet (two) dressed, and put a pot of coffee and cups out. She left the front door open, the teachers came, held their class, and left. Penny took Janet to the theater and Harry to the cottage. She taught her class, loaded up her car with children, gave them to their parents at the theater, joined her husband, Harry, and they attended church together. Penny says Harry was always doing something and very seldom sat with her. The theater proved to be a real sanctuary for everyone. Some of the most moving services Harry ever attended were held there.

Jesse Anderson was the volunteer choir director. The choir sat on the front rows. When it came time to sing, Jesse stood up behind the choir facing the front of the theater. The choir turned around and he directed their singing. George Muns, Ph.D., was the first paid choir director. He was very talented and the choir performed a rendition of the "Battle Hymn of the Republic" that Harry still remembers with tears in his eyes.

A few weeks after that first Sunday, Harry asked Everett Handorf where he went during Sunday school. He said he left Charlie, his son, at the cottage and met some friends at the barbeque joint at the corner of Poplar and Colonial—the building is still there—David Barcroft's formal shop just moved out of it in 1988. Harry went there the next Sunday and Everett Handorf, "Strat" Stratton, and Bob Drake were having coffee.

After a little talking they agreed to start a men's Bible class if Harry would find a place for them to meet. The first place he got was the basement of Walgreens; mice were there but no coffee. Harry talked to the manager of Baker's Shoe Store, and he agreed to come and open up just for them. Stores weren't open and again there was no coffee. The next stop was Britling's Cafeteria, who agreed to open early and furnish free coffee. The men's Bible class was well on its way. They had some outstanding teachers such as Tom Loberg, who had attended a Lutheran seminary. The men's class was, from the beginning, a very outspoken discussion group. They had two great parties each year and for many years had from fifty to sixty in attendance every Sunday.

Everett Handorf was the chairman of the first architects and Building Committee. Lee McCormick and Harry were on that committee and there were two others that Harry doesn't recall. Walk Jones was the architect and Ed Thorne and Jim Adams (church members) were part of that firm. After Harry's experience with large adult classes, he insisted that no class hold more than 50 people (100 to 150 on roll). After many hours trying to project the needs of the church school, Harry suggested that there be three buildings to accommodate Sunday school that would support a church membership of six thousand. They recommended that the Fellowship Hall building be first. This would provide offices, a sanctuary, and Sunday school rooms. The Sunday school rooms were all built with a partition to provide two classrooms until another building could be built; the second church school building was to be what became the Grant Building; the third was to be a three-story classroom building to be built across the north side of the courtyard. Mr. Jim Canfield was selected as the contractor of the Fellowship Hall. He was a member of the church, and his grandson lives next door to Penny and Harry now.

The masonry contractor built a small sample wall of several suggested choices of bricks. The best selection by all concerned were the bricks they have used for all the buildings. When Dr. Grant was told the name of the bricks, it sealed his choice—*mission pink*.

When the church was organized in June 1955, the only land they had title to was where the "little cottage" was and where the Marsonne Apartments are now (and they owed about twenty-five thousand dollars on that). A great effort was being made to obtain the additional land they needed to build the church. The Wallace family owned the property between the cottage and Cherry Road, where the soccer fields are now. The family wanted far more money than the property was worth and would not negotiate the sale. Hall Jones was in the process of developing Laurelwood Shopping Center. He needed a buffer between the shopping center and the Cherry Road residents. He offered the church the property where the sanctuary, Fellowship Hall, Grant Building, and Beaty Activities Building are for ninety-five thousand dollars, which was less than its value at the time, and in addition offered a permanent easement for parking on the shopping center's parking lot. This easement was/is worth much to the church, in land value, in cost of paving, and in cost of upkeep. In order to borrow the money to buy the land and to build the Fellowship Hall the church needed guarantors since they did not have other collateral.

About twenty-five people were asked to sign notes to First National Bank for ten thousand dollars each. Harry signed on the faith that the church would pay its debts. At the time, Harry was making four hundred dollars per month and it meant that if he and Penny had to pay off that note it would take the rest of their lives. They never were called on to pay it, only to pay their pledges to the church. The land on both sides of Cherry Road was obtained at a later date.

Mr. Howard Davenport, who was the second board chairman and a member of the Steering Committee, was a very gentle Christian gentleman. He and his wife Mary helped Penny in the second grade for several years. Howard was about six feet–five inches tall. You can imagine seeing him as he sat on one of the small second grade oak chairs patiently listening and talking to those little children.

Mr. Edgar Tenent, who was the first chairman of the Financial Committee, worked untiringly to see that money was available as needed. He personally guaranteed some interim and temporary loans and obtained long-term loans from sources not available in Memphis. He made one of his memorable statements after the Fellowship Hall was occupied and long discussions were taking place about which building should be built next. Some wanted the next building to be the church school building, some a gym/recreation building, and some the sanctuary. Edgar said, "The young people were indeed the future of the church, but they didn't and couldn't give the money it would take for the present needs and without a present there is no future." This being the case, he said that it was "imperative to build the sanctuary that the older members wanted."

The architects and Building Committee had a scale model of architect Hall Jones's idea of what the church buildings should be like and showed it in the lobby of the Plaza Theater, where they were holding Sunday morning services and where the most people could see it. It had a separate freestanding bell tower. Almost everyone pictured the new church as looking similar to Second Presbyterian Church, so the freestanding bell tower concept was rejected overwhelmingly. The present sanctuary was the next concept.

Mrs. Alice Gibson could be used as maybe the number one example of good and faithful lifetime service to the church. She taught in the children's division for over thirty years, never taking time off for long vacations or sickness. She also sang in the choir with the same faithfulness and dedication all these years without asking for or receiving recognition.

Especially during the first year and for the first four years, many meetings lasted for hours, many until after midnight. This could have led to lost tempers and disunity, but it never did. Dr. Grant and Harry had worked together ever since Dr. Grant came to Memphis. They understood each other. They disagreed wholeheartedly at times but once the decision was made, they both supported the decision. Dr. Grant told Harry many times, when he couldn't attend a meeting, to vote for him "affirmatively for those things that were right and against those things that were wrong."

Once Lee McCormick, on behalf of the Steering Committee, handed Harry the key to the "little cottage" they never reversed any decision he made concerning either people or money. The money was always supplied for the needs. Harry has no estimate of the number of hours of work and its monetary value or the items of value given by many people before and after the formation of the church.

The teachers were initially told that they were to teach two years, then take the third year to attend training schools and adult Sunday school classes to enhance their skill and rejuvenate their spirits and their place in other aspects of church life. This worked for several years. It meant that a continual program of teacher recruiting had to be implemented and maintained week in and week out.

The special report by the Commission on Education given to the Feasibility Study Committee chaired by Jesse Anderson in 1967 shows the amount of work and research that was invested in the projects and planning for the future of the church in its early years. These volunteers gave untold numbers of hours and days to their church and did multiple jobs which would be a credit to paid consultants.

Jim Briggs, chairman of the Commission on Education at the time of this report, set up personal appointments with the outstanding congregations in Memphis. Jim personally interviewed the leader at Bellevue Baptist Church, First Baptist Church, and Lindenwood Christian Church. He set up appointments for Gene Williams to interview the leader at Mullins Methodist Church and for Harry Brahm to interview those at Second Presbyterian Church. These interviews are in the volume of minutes for 1967, pages 60–78.

✣ ✣ ✣

SPECIAL REPORT OF COMMISSION ON EDUCATION FEASIBILITY

Statisical Information

1. Average Sunday school attendance, past three years:

1964–1965	760.8
1965–1966	736.8
1966–1967 (9 months)	*818.5

*Average would be slightly lower if the months of June, July, and August were included as these are historically light attendance months.

2. M.Y.F. (evening) Average Attendance:

1964–1965	75.6
1965–1966	95.6
1966–1967 (9 months)	95.8

3. Average Sunday school Attendance Increase, Past Seven Years:

1959–1960	584.6
1966–1967	818.5
Average Attendance Increase	233.9
Percent Increase	40.0

4. M.Y.F. (evening) Average Attendance Increase, Past Seven Years

1959–1960	63.0
1966–1967	95.8
Average Attendance Increase	32.8
Percent Increase	52.1

5. Comparison of Church and Sunday school Average Attendance for the Year Ending May 31, 1967:

Church	986
Sunday school	782
% S. S. Attendance to Church Attendance	79.3

6. See Charts number I and II, pp. 2 and 3, of the 1967 Minutes of the Official Board found in bound volume of minutes in the CUMC archives for growth trends in membership and attendance from 1959 to the present.

PROJECTED CLASSROOM NEEDS, NEXT TEN YEARS

Current Classroom Needs

Class	No. of Classes	Classes Needed	Classrooms Needed
Crib–2-year-old	5	6	1
3-year-old	2	3	1
4 and 5-year-old	3	4	1
1st and 2nd Grade	3	4	1

11th Grade	1 (cottage)	1	1
12th Grade	1 (cottage)	1	1
Susanna	1 (parlor)	1	1
Additional Classrooms Currently Needed		7	

Estimate of Classroom Needs Based on Anticipated Growth, Next Ten Years

Church membership has increased at a fairly steady rate of 150 per year for the past few years. If this trend continues, as it very possibly could, the membership would be at about 4,000 at the end of the next ten-year period. The current enrollment is slightly over 2,500; add to this figure a projection of 1,500 net new members over the next ten-year period.

Assuming the church attendance can be maintained at roughly 40 percent of the membership, as in fiscal year 1966–1967, attendance at the end of this period will be, on the average, 1,600 per Sunday.

Assuming Sunday school attendance can be maintained at approximately 75 percent of church attendance (79 percent in 1966–1967), the Sunday school attendance at the end of this period will be, on the average, 1,200 per Sunday.

This estimate appears to be in line with the historical growth in Sunday school attendance. For the five-year period ending August 31, 1966, the average weekly attendance increased at a rate of 22 percent. Projecting this same rate of growth for the next ten years, Sunday school attendance will be at an average of 1,191 per Sunday based on the current average attendance of approximately 800.

Based on the projected average weekly Sunday school attendance in ten years of 1,200, the net increase in attendance for the same period will be 400 per Sunday. Applying a rule-of-thumb attendance measure of 30 members per class, the projected additional classroom needs based on growth during the next ten years, is roughly 13 (400 x 30). Add to this the current classroom needs 7, it appears that a minimum of 20 classrooms should be included in the building expansion program.

✣ ✣ ✣

Projected Recreational and Activities Needs

Justification for a Recreational Program

I. The church is interested in the whole man and has affirmed this interest through providing:
   - A. Hospitals to provide for the sick,
   - B. Homes to provide comfortable living for the aged,
   - C. Schools to educate the uneducated,
   - D. Special teachers and classes to train the mentally retarded,
   - E. Counseling to assist socially troubled individuals and
   - F. other special programs.

II. The church is interested in the whole family and the brotherhood of man and has affirmed this interest through providing for and encouraging participation in:
   A. Retreats,
   B. Family dinners and picnics,
   C. Sunday school and other group parties, and
   D. Other activities which further fellowship among families and individuals.

III. The church is concerned about the increase in juvenile delinquency and has taken steps to counteract this trend by:
   A. Supporting active H.Y.F. groups and encouraging participation in:
      1. Retreats,
      2. Social activities,
      3. City, district, and conference-wide activities, and
      4. Athletic programs, etc.
   B. Youth choirs,
   C. Scouting programs, and
   D. Other youth programs.

IV. The church is aware of its responsibility as good stewards of its money. Maximum utilization of expensive church grounds and buildings is the only reasonable justification for building expansion.

V. The church is aware of its need to attract more people to its facilities and, in turn to Christ. The goals of the church cannot be achieved if growth is limited because of a lack of adequate facilities and programs.

Recreational Objectives

I. Health Development Objective
   A. The manner in which a person spends his leisure time determines in great measure, whether his physical, mental, emotional and spiritual health are of high quality.
   B. A range of activities exist to enhance one's health.

Youth basketball team, 1957.

C. Activities exist that enables one to relax, escape from tensions, forget problems, thereby contributing to a healthier personality.

II. The Human Relations Objective

A. Recreational programs develop many individual qualities which make for better adjustment such as courage, justice, patience, tolerance, fairness and honesty.

III. Civic Development Objective

A. Recreation contributes in many ways to the development of any community.

B. Recreation unites people.

C. Recreation builds morale.

D. Recreation fights crime.

E. Recreation makes the community more prosperous by better health standards.

Upper-left: *1960 youth baseball team.* **Upper right:** *1958 youth baseball team.* **Above:** *1960 youth baseball trip to St. Louis for a Cardinals' game. Adult coaches Barry Carter, George Darms, Harry Johnson, Earl Billings, and Marshall Morris.*

IV. Self Development Objective
   A. Recreation helps one reach his fullest potential.
   B. Recreation allows for growth:
      1. Mentally.
      2. Competitively.
      3. Physically.

Recreational Needs for Christ Methodist Church

The athletic programs now provided by Christ Methodist Church are confined essentially to outdoor sports, such as baseball and volleyball. Our basketball teams must use facilities of other churches on a when-available basis.

Although these programs represent an attempt to provide recreational activities for our membership, they are, by and large, aimed at the teenage male group. In addition, several programs are directed to citywide competitive events, which precludes the participation of many youngsters.

The majority of recreational activities provided by the city and other churches are of the type and organization whereby youngsters are dropped off by the parents and picked up by the parents an hour or two later. Ideally, church recreational and activities programs should be of such diversification and organization so as to provide activities for the whole family. The parents can remain at the facility with their youngsters because there is also something of interest for them, either individually or as a family group. (Barry Robinson, *A Congregation's Attempt to Find and Meet its Community's Needs*, unpublished, First Cumberland Presbyterian Church, Chattanooga, Tenn., May 15, 1966.)

It is the sincere belief of the Commission on Education that the goals of the church can be best served by providing facilities that will attract people to it. Only by contact with the spiritual life which permeates its every activity, can these people be drawn closer to a Christian life. A recreational and activities building appears to be the only physical facility lacking at Christ Methodist Church with which it can more effectively achieve these goals.

Summary

Christ Methodist Church has very attractive physical facilities that are reasonably adequate to provide for the spiritual needs of its present membership and attendance. There are, however, two critical areas of need, which can be corrected only through a building expansion program. These are (1) a lack of adequate Sunday school classrooms which are needed immediately and (2) the lack of recreational facilities which provide activities for the entire Church membership.

RECOMMENDATION

Based on the aforementioned information, the Commission on Education respectfully recommends that the following facilities be included in the plans for a building expansion program:

1. A minimum of 20 classrooms—at least two of these rooms should be comparatively larger than the other 18 in order to handle assemblies, other larger meetings, and to accommodate scouting activities. These two larger rooms should have exterior entrances and exits and adequate, lockable storage facilities to store the scouting equipment. Recommend consultation with the Scout Committee to ascertain special requirements.

2. A college-size gymnasium—this recommendation needs little qualification from the standpoint of maximum utilization of the building. Additional utilization can be attained, however, by the inclusion of a floor finish, which would accommodate roller-skating with specially outfitted skates. Also, pull-out bleachers which would seat at least 250 spectators would greatly enhance participation and use of the space and would offer Christ Church the opportunity to host district- and conference-wide competitive events.

3. Hobbycraft facilities—inclusion of storage facilities and, possibly, collapsible partitions, may make it feasible to utilize certain classrooms for this activity. Crafts to be considered are ceramics, sewing, basketweaving, and so on.

4. A woodworking shop—this facility, because of its highly specialized equipment, the dust problem, and the noise created by the equipment, not to mention the dangerous aspects, would necessitate a separate, acoustically finished, ventilated room.

5. A swimming pool—this facility is probably on par with the gymnasium, in terms of maximum utilization of the building. Although the construction of a swimming pool would be expensive, it is believed the normal maintenance costs would be provided for through the charging of admissions and/or membership cards. This would provide Christ Church members, and others, with an outstanding recreational and healthy activity that is not now available except at certain private clubs.

6. Handball courts—this facility should be included, if at all feasible; however, from the standpoint of cost and maximum utilization of the building, it is considered to be difficult to justify.

7. A bowling alley—this facility should be included, if at all feasible; however, from the standpoint of cost, maximum utilization of the building, and the noise factor, it is difficult to justify. Also, private bowling facilities are easily accessible to Church members.

8. A snack bar—it is believed this facility would receive heavy traffic, especially from the youth. This could be a self-supporting facility, offering a

variety of cold drinks, sandwiches, plate lunches, and so on. It would, of course, require a paid manager.

9. Lounge(s)—at least one nice-sized, pleasantly finished lounge should be provided.

10. Offices—adequate office space for a recreation director and his staff is definitely needed.

11. Storage space—in addition to the storage space for the scouting program, adequate storage facilities are necessary for athletic equipment for the gymnasium and the outside playgrounds.

12. A recreation director—although this recommendation does not involve a building requirement, it must be included in the plans for a successful recreation program. A full-time, highly competent recreation director, once the facilities are provided, is as important as the facilities themselves, in order for the church to realize maximum benefits from the application of its funds.

VI. Alternatives—realizing that certain economies must be considered in any large building program, the following alternatives are offered:

First Alternative:	delete the bowling alley.
Second Alternative:	delete the bowling alley and the handball courts.
Third Alternative:	delete the bowling alley, the handball courts, and the woodworking shop.
Fourth Alternative:	delete the above and reduce the size of the gymnasium to a regulation-size basketball court.
Fifth Alternative:	in addition to the above, delete the swimming pool.

COMMISSION ON EDUCATION MEETING MINUTES

September 26, 1967

The September Meeting of the Commission on Education was held at Christ Methodist Church on Tuesday night, September 26, 1967, at 7:30 P.M.

The meeting was opened with prayer by Gene Williams.

Mr. Ed Richmond Sr. reported the Official Board had voted to buy the Roundtree property west of the church property. The official action will not be completed until Dr. Flatt returns from Europe to sign the official contract. He also showed the Commission on Education some preliminary drawings by Ed Thorne of the new proposed recreation/educational building. The whole commission enjoyed seeing these drawings.

Chairman Jim Hillis stated that the study and recommendations for the new building had been completed by the Commission on Education Subcommittee and had been given to Chairman Jesse Anderson. Jim also reported that he had asked Andy Sippel, chairman of the Advisory Committee, to work with all of the adult superintendents in setting up a training school for prospective teachers in our church. This training school would last 10 weeks and be held during the Sunday school hour. It is hoped this will give us a backlog of teachers to draw from.

Chairman Hillis also reported that Christian Education Sunday was an outstanding success, with a total 1079 present that Sunday. The goal was 1050. This was a record attendance. Jim wanted the minutes to show his and the entire Commission on Education appreciation to Paul McQuiston and his committee for their fine job.

Mrs. Harry Brahm announced that the date of the youth revival would be June 23–28, 1958.

Danny Farrar announced the senior highs would have a weekend retreat at Grenada Lake Mississippi, October 13–15. It will be led by Reed Gilbert of Lambuth College.

Mrs. Robert Condra (General Secretary) turned in reports for July, August and September These reports are a part of the official minutes of each month.

John Rhodes announced that the Lamplighters Class would act as host for the Kingswood Class for the Sunday night service on October 8.

Harry Brahm reported that a Scout Court of Honor was held September 25 and the church had two Eagle Scouts, Al Best and Chris Carpenter.

Bill Crump reported that our missionary, John Studstill, would be with us Sunday and Monday, October 1 and 2. He will speak to various groups and functions on these two days.

Bill also reported the Lamplighter Class is in need of a teacher. Jac Gates has agreed to teach the class a few Sundays on a trial basis.

Bill mentioned the Fall School of Religion, and the need for all interested persons to sign up for classes.

A District Leadership School will be held at St. Luke's, October 8–12. (Copy attached)

A new Children's Church will begin the first of October. It will meet in the Chapel each Sunday during the 10:45 service, ages six through ten.

Meeting closed with a prayer by Bill Crump.

Respectfully submitted,
/s/ Gene Williams
Secretary, Commission on Education

✣ ✣ ✣

Christ Methodist Church
4488 Poplar Avenue
Memphis, Tennessee

January 1, 1956

Charles W. Grant
B. L. Gaddie
Ministers

Dear Fellow Worker,

The Commission on Education has planned a Leadership School for the Children's Division to begin Sunday morning, January 13, 1957, from 9:30–10:20 A.M., continuing for ten Sundays.

This School is being held for the teachers who were unable to attend the District Training School last fall. It will be held in the home of Mr. Harry Johnson Jr., 3416 Walnut Grove Road.

The course to be taught is *Teaching Older Children*. The textbook is *Guiding Children in Christian Growth*, by Dr. Mary Alice Jones (price $1) and the manual for your age group. Mrs. Robert A. Clark will be the instructor.

May we urge you to attend each of these sessions.

Cordially,
Charles W. Grant, Pastor
Harry Johnson Jr., Church School Superintendent
Mrs. V. Hugo Akin, Secretary, Leadership Training

✣ ✣ ✣

Christ Methodist Church
4488 Poplar Avenue
Memphis, Tennessee

October 10, 1956

Charles W. Grant
B. L. Gaddie
Ministers

Dear ———,

Thank you for your splendid service to Christ Methodist Church School. Now that our rotation system has been set up and as you look back upon your past activities, I am sure you rejoice in your rich experience. Please remember in your daily prayers not only the pupils you formerly served but also the present splendid staff. This will enable you to continue to do good and also sustain your interest in the Church School.

Within the next year there will be a number of opportunities for you to take a Leadership Training course. May I urge you to avail yourself of every such opportunity? Such a course taught by an experienced instructor will not only better prepare you to serve in the future but will keep alive in you the desire.

Isn't it thrilling to be a part of such a major and glorious undertaking as Christ Methodist Church, especially in the training of our children where the future seems to be so full of promise!

Gratefully and prayerfully,
Harry A. Johnson Jr.
Chairman, Commission on Education
Charles W. Grant
Minister

✣ ✣ ✣

	Average Attendance			Present Sq. Ft. Space			
	1955	1956	1957	Now	Need	1957	Person
2–3-year-old Nursery	34	40	55	448	1,400	1,925	35
4–5-year-old Kindergarten	36	43	55	381	505	1,925	35
1–3 Grade Primary	41	75	125	795	2,250	3,750	30
4–6 Grade Junior	42	63	95	1,500	1,890	2,850	30
7–9 Grade Intermediate	35	55	91		770	1,274	14

High School Senior	11	16	24	160	240	10
College			20	150	200	10
Aldersgate	46	44	42	440	420	10
Fellowship	73	66	56	660	560	10
Bible		14	25	140	250	10

The above are average attendances—not maximum attendances.

✣ ✣ ✣

It is difficult for adults to have more than one class in a single room and practically impossible for children, with or without dividing screens.

The older youth class is now being organized and will meet in the cry room at the theater.

We need about three more adult classes. The above figures do not reflect the potential, only the facts about the adult classes.

The space by "sq. ft" does not reflect the complete need. Number and accessibility of rooms outside and to toilets are major considerations. If the space is in too many or too few rooms, the teacher problem is multiplied.

The above clearly shows an urgent need for space, but it is my recommendation that no money be spent or additions made at 4370 Poplar. We have the finest workers in our Church School that could be found anywhere, and I know they will continue to do an outstanding job under increasingly difficult circumstances if they can see relief in time to properly take care of an ever-increasing membership.

Sincerely,
Harry A. Johnson Jr.
Church School Superintendent

✣ ✣ ✣

THE MEN'S BIBLE CLASS

Memories and Brief History

In the beginning. Almost everyone was attending Sunday school except Everett Handorf and a few other men. Harry Johnson finally found them in the old Bar-B-Q joint on the corner of Poplar and Colonial. There were R. E. "Strat" Stratton and Bob Drake having coffee after dropping their children off at Sunday school. Including a few other things, Harry threatened to tell their wives, who were busy working in the Sunday school, if they didn't help him start a Men's Bible Class. They agreed to help if Harry would find a place for them to meet. He scoured that part of Memphis for months looking for such a space. He arranged with Walgreens for the group to meet in the basement of the store next to the Plaza Theater. This was nice but there was no coffee, so Harry had to find another place. The manager of Baker's Shoe Store agreed to open up especially for the class (stores didn't open at all on Sunday in those days), but they only had ten places to sit, so that didn't last too long either. Finally, the Britling's Cafeteria manager hit their "hot button" by offering to open up and furnish a pot of coffee. The Men's Bible Class was officially underway.

Our fearless leaders. From the very beginning this class was, and still is, a very frank, outspoken discussion group. They demanded outstanding teachers such as Tom Loberg, the governor of the state of Tennessee, the president of the University of Tennessee, and many other well known and distinguished teachers—but none more distinguished than those who teach us today.

On the move. The class started meeting in the southeast corner room on the third floor of the Fellowship Hall as soon as it was completed. The average attendance grew to about sixty in that room. The next stop was the southwest corner room on the second floor of the Grant Building, which is now the Day School library. They then migrated to the ground floor of Fellowship Hall and shared the room with "Bible" Smith and the Day School. She and the children left notes for them, and they helped them. From there, the class moved to room 327 Dunnam as soon as that building was finished.

Celebration. The class typically had two big parties each year, usually at the Parkview Hotel or Anderton's Restaurant. That all changed when Roy and Louise Perkins started having their famous Bar-B-Q dinners at their home. People would join the class just to be invited to those dinners. A tradition for many years was the College Christmas Breakfast. Everett Handorf appointed Harry, as chairman, and Dr. "Slick" Templeton to organize those breakfasts. George Atkinson volunteered to get the food and oversee "Effie", the cook in the church kitchen, and the preparation. He purchased country hams, bacon, sausage, and everything a breakfast lover could ask for. All of the college students were invited and getting them all together was a real pleasure, not to even mention the breakfast. The class held the breakfast for many years and only quit when James Loftin, as youth director, came up with a better program for the youth.

CHRIST METHODIST DAY SCHOOL HISTORY

In 1957 Mrs. Pansy Trenor contacted Harry Johnson about using Christ Church's name and facilities for establishment of a day school nursery and kindergarten.

She had a fine reputation in this area, but, after much discussion, Dr. Grant and Harry decided we needed a day school, but that it should be a ministry of Christ Church and not a for-profit school. We interviewed several people. Our final choice was a great one. Mrs. Charles (Ella) McVean became the first director of the Day School and did an outstanding job for nine years.

Beginning in 1958

Seventy-five students were enrolled in three classes that year. The faculty included two full-time teachers, Mrs. Charles McVean and Mrs. A. A. Sippel. Mrs. James Curry was hired as a teacher trainee, and a full-time maid was found. The tuition was established at $12.50 per month per student.

From the beginning, high standards have been maintained. As was stated by Mr. Johnson, this Day School was set up to provide the finest kindergarten program conducted by thoroughly qualified Christian teachers. And so it has continued through the years.

Mrs. McVean was named the director of the Day School in 1958 and oversaw the first fifteen years of its growth and development. Through her many years of tireless effort and her dedication to high standards, Christ Methodist became established as one of the finest institutions providing a Christian education in our city.

In 1960, the need for expansion was recognized. Thus, first grade and a program for four year olds were added. From 1961 through 1965, one section of one new grade was added through the sixth grade. Christ Methodist graduated its first class of sixth graders on May 17, 1966.

In 1985, there were 239 students enrolled and the first open house was held in 1987.

✣ ✣ ✣

September 8, 1958
Report to the Official Board
Christ Methodist Church

Mr. Chairman:

The Commission on Education wishes to report that it is thoroughly prepared for the new Church School year beginning October 1.

The rotation system is working superbly in the Children's Division and we are sure it will do the same in the other divisions in the near future. There is a need for a few workers in several departments, but as a whole, we are going into the new year better prepared to do a finer teaching job in all divisions than ever before.

Mr. Bledsoe, the Church School Superintendent, will give you the details of the fine job that is now being done in the Youth Division.

Included is a report on the Kindergarten Day School, which I move the Board approve.

✣ ✣ ✣

Report on the Kindergarten Day School

Christ Methodist Church Kindergarten Day School was established by the Commission on Education to fill a need that exists within the congregation and the community. This has been done only after a thorough study of the need over a period of the last two years and favorable action of the Official Board.

We have enrolled about 75 pupils, divided into three classes. There are two morning classes and one afternoon class. Thirty-seven of the 75 are children of the members of Christ Methodist Church.

This Day School is set up to provide the finest Kindergarten program, conducted by thoroughly qualified Christian teachers. There will be 25 pupils in each of the morning classes and 25 in the afternoon class. There will be four employees, as follows.

Mrs. Charles McVean	Full-Time Teacher
Mrs. A. A. Sippel	Full-Time Teacher
One maid	Full-Time—morning and afternoons
Mrs. James D. Curry	Trainee Teacher, Mornings only.

The expenses of the school will be as follows:

Mrs. Charles McVean	Monthly salary, $300.00
Mrs. A. A.Sippel	Monthly salary, $300.00
Mrs. James D. Curry	Monthly salary, $ 80.00
Maid	Monthly salary, $ 80.00
Total Salaries	$760.00

Monthly expenses	
(Juice, supplies, and etc. estimated)	$100.00
Total Monthly Expenses	$860.00
Monthly Income 75 pupils @$12.50 each	$937.50

This will show an income of $77.50 per month over estimated expenses, which will take care of unforeseen expenses and begin to build an equipment replacement fund and for needed new equipment, which would be purchased at the end of the year, for use in future years by the Day School and Sunday school.

We have an additional fund of $750.00 from the $10.00 per pupil registration fee, which will also be used for the above purposes.

Mr. D. A. Noel, of the Church's Audit Committee, is setting up a bookkeeping system, which will be kept by the teachers and audited at the end of the school year by the Audit Committee. The teachers will collect the monthly fees from the parents and turn these funds over to the church's Financial Secretary for deposit each month. They will O.K. the bills for supplies monthly and give them to the financial secretary for payment. There will be only two or three suppliers to be paid each month.

The three teachers have agreed to one salary check each month, the maid to be paid weekly.

There has been the expression of a need for the establishment of a Day Grade School. A survey will be made among the Kindergarten pupils to see if this need is real, if so, plans will be made by the Commission on Education for a first grade beginning in September 1959 and presented to the Official Board for approval at an early date.

These schools are being established only to fill the needs of the congregation and the community, which we feel is our responsibility as a church. They will be established only on an economically self-sustaining basis, making great use of the outstanding physical facilities which we possess.

This is a function of the church and all facilities and funds will be used judiciously and prayerfully to the benefit of the church and its people.

MISSIONS

1956

Christ Methodist Church has two members on the General Board of Missions of the Methodist Church. Mr. James H. Seabrook and Mrs. Charles Henderson. Only 8.81 percent of all monies that go to the Board of Missions are used for missionary education, promotion, service administration, and some interdenominational cooperation. The balance, a whopping 91.19 percent, goes to the mission fields. James Seabrook was invited to attend the General Board of Missions meeting in India for the centennial celebration. William Drenner spent a full day at the Board of Missions headquarters in New York. As the Christ Church Missions chairman, his knowledge of operations and personnel will benefit Christ Church missions program immeasurably.

1956

Dr. Brewster visited Christ Church in September to help plan the mission to Sarawak, Borneo. Dr. and Mrs. Brewster will build Christ Hospital to care for medical needs and as a base to combine agricultural, educational, and spiritual works as spearheads of an essentially evangelistic mission designed by God to win an entire people to Christ.

Dr. Harold Brewster was born of missionary parents in Hengwha, China, received his M.D. from Boston University, interned at Queen's Hospital, Honolulu, and was a medical missionary at Union Hospital, Foochow, China, where he pioneered in tuberculosis treatment. In 1945–46 he studied at the Harvard School of Public Health and earned his master of public health degree. He served as medical secretary of the Board of Missions and visited hospitals and missionaries in Liberia, the Belgian Congo, Southern Rhodesia, the Transvaal, Portuguese East Africa, Angola, India, and Korea. No man could be better qualified to build and open Christ Hospital and mission in Borneo. His wife is the former Dorothy Davidson of Brockton, Massachusetts. In Borneo she taught English, conducted baby clinics, worked with Chinese women's groups, did hospital bookkeeping, led the choir, and reared four children, three girls and one boy.

In August 1958, Dr. and Mrs. Loreto Crisologo visited Christ Church in preparation to replace Dr. and Mrs. Brewster who will finish their two-year commitment in Borneo in mid-September. A letter from the Crisologos, Sarawak, Borneo, dated January 15, 1959, just arrived (April 6, 1959). Concerning Borneo:

It is so quiet and peaceful. I would like to underline the word 'peaceful' in contrast to the impression of the wild men and headhunters of Borneo. The people are simple but they are most sincere and friendly. On the night they gave us a dinner of welcome, each one who spoke seemed inspired and was grateful for our coming.

Just to give you a mild example of recent happenings: Lorie was operating on an emergency case of bleeding ectopic pregnancy when a winged cockroach landed at the center of the operating field—not to mention about a half-dozen smaller creatures that joined in the excitement under the bright lamp. Everybody expected a rough post-operative course, but the patient didn't show any sign of infection. The wound healed nicely in spite of everything. What an explosive tragedy this would have been to a state-side hospital management. Here we are quite resigned to helplessness. This old schoolhouse has been well inhabited long before a dream to make it a hospital was made. They have persisted and resisted eviction in spite of the repeated treatment and insults from the sprayers and flit brigade of the Hospital staff and employees of World Health Organization. However, we have greater hopes as soon as we get transferred to our new hospital.

1959

The Missionary Challenge printed in the church *Courier* on August 23, 1959:

The missionary challenge of the present day is the greatest in the history of the world. Before Jesus left the world, He commanded His disciples to go into all the world and preach the gospel to every creature. But previous to their going in the fulfillment of this great commission, the Master commanded His disciples to tarry for the baptism with the Holy Spirit. Following the fulfillment of the promise, in the coming of the Holy Ghost with His mighty baptism, the disciples went everywhere proclaiming the Gospel message. They went in the face of great opposition, persecution, and many became martyrs for the Gospel of Christ. Extraordinary measures must be taken to meet the present missionary challenge of the world. A thousand million people sit in darkness who have not heard the story of Christ's redeeming love for their lost souls. The need of the lost multitudes who sit in darkness spell out in large letters the words, "No man careth for my soul." The physical suffering in the pagan lands of the earth, as a result of ignorance, superstition and lack of medical aid, is appalling to contemplate. It is estimated that there are 20 million lepers in the world today and that perhaps 90 percent of these could be made symptom-free under proper medical treatment. That is only one small segment of the horrible blight on the bodies of men presenting a medical missionary challenge on a scale beyond anything the world has ever known. But the spiritual blight on the souls of men is far greater than the physical blight.

It is estimated by a United Nations study that the earth's population will increase from about two and one-half billion to six and one-half billion within the next 42 years. We must quicken our people in missionary endeavor and gird ourselves for the evangelization of thousands of millions that the kingdoms of this world may become the Kingdom of our Lord and Christ (from the *Herald*, August 1959).

Let us pray that our church will receive a greater baptism of the Holy Spirit than ever before and that our young people will feel a call from God to serve Him in whatever field they may choose.

1960

Excerpt from a letter written by Dr. Grant on April 11, 1960:

For our members, "Borneo" and "Southern Rhodesia" are household words. Having undertaken the full support of the Crisologos and the Heyers, our missionary load is heavy. It has been deemed wise this year to let our entire Easter offering go for the support of our own missionaries. As one reads of the miracles that are happening in Borneo and Southern Rhodesia, he is thrilled beyond words at the privilege of having some part in this great redemptive scheme.

1961

Excerpt from a letter to the district superintendent on May 1, 1961:

We have continued our support of four missionaries—two in Borneo and two in Southern Rhodesia. The support of these missionaries has been a bright spot in our Church life, and voluntary contributions from our membership at large has been sufficient to defray the entire cost. For the ensuing year our Church has unanimously voted to continue and in fact enlarge our missionary program. Twenty-eight percent of our budget for 1961–62 is "for others."

1961

Part of a letter sent to Rev. and Mrs. Edward Heyer in Southern Rhodesia, Africa, by Ralph Scherr, Chairman, Commission on Missions, July 27, 1961:

Dr. Grant tells us that you supervise about 30 schools and over 300 teachers. What a wonderful opportunity of service that is and how different it is from the activity of missionaries in years past. To have people who are eager for an education; to be able to select, train and oversee their teachers; to be permitted to give religious instruction in the elementary and secondary schools; to have the government pay a major portion of the cost; all of this is so different from the first work in the mission field. The Roman Catholics have long recognized that their parochial schools have been their best method of promoting their beliefs. In our church we are placing more and more emphasis on youth and adult education. Evidently the same trend is occurring in missionary work.

We are deeply concerned about the needs and yearnings of the uneducated and underprivileged people of the world. We are anxious to see their physical needs supplied, and we are just as anxious that the first knowledge that they obtain is the knowledge that Jesus taught. We are delighted to know that we have you as our representatives to accomplish this and we pray that God may bless your work.

September will be missionary emphasis month at Christ Methodist. We are always anxious to hear from you. We would be particularly happy to have a letter that we could share with the congregation at that time. Please send us pictures of your activities to be used at this time. Our knowledge of what is really happening in Africa and what the people are thinking is very limited so all news is welcome.

1961

From a letter to the congregation concerning support of our missionaries, written on October 24, 1961:

> Mr. and Mrs. Loreto Crisologo, in their mission of healing and evangelism in Christ Hospital, Sarawak, Borneo, are alleviating the suffering of thousands in the name of Jesus Christ. Rev. and Mrs. Edward L. Heyer, through their ministry of education and evangelism, are "feeding the multitudes" of Southern Rhodesia, Africa, and bringing to them a more abundant life.
>
> Did you know that you could support a missionary for a full period of time as follows?
>
> Day, $10.31; Week, $72.12; Half Week, $36.06; Month, $312.50
>
> Most of us cannot go, but we can send someone. The enclosed envelope can be used for your pledge or gift. Won't you join with us in Christ's Name, and tell the Gospel story to the "least of these" in Borneo and Rhodesia?

1962

Dr. and Mrs. Crisologo, our missionaries from Borneo, were in the United States on a sabbatical leave and visited at the Thanksgiving season, 1962, speaking at both the morning and evening worship services on Sunday. They also met with the diverse Sunday school classes including the children and youth of the Church. Each time missionaries come to visit, it is thrilling to hear of their work and to know that Christ Church is helping spread the Gospel.

1963

The church agreed to support Rev. and Mrs. Gravely as missionaries to Brazil in addition to the Crisologos in Borneo and the Heyers in Southern Rhodesia.

1964

Christ Church finished the building of the sanctuary this year and assumed the debt of over $1 million but continued to support the three missionary couples. The Commission on Missions was informed by the General Board of Missions that $9000–$9500 would be needed for each missionary couple in 1965 instead of the $7500 needed in 1964.

1965

The Commission discussed the need to increase the funds budgeted for local mission activity. The above in addition to the support of the Crisologos, the

Above: *Rev. & Mrs. Edward Heyer and family, Southern Rhodesia, Africa.* **Upper right:** *Dr. & Mrs. Loreto Crisologo.* **Lower right:** *Rev. & Mrs. Gravely, Brazil.*

Gravelys, and Louise Morris in Japan. Louise is a graduate of Lambuth, and Brownsville, Tennessee, is her hometown. The Heyers are on extended leave of the mission field in Southern Rhodesia. John Studstill was added to our missionaries list, going to the Belgian Congo, Africa.

1967

The General Board of Missions gave Christ Church a globe showing all current Methodist mission fields because this church ranks third in all of America in Methodism in its Advance Special giving.

1968

Following that, Keith Weisinger, Chairman, Commission on Missions, presented the Mission Commission's budget for approval to the Official Board on July 1, 1968. The budget included $5,000 for inner-city mission work. Dr. Grant announced that Elizabeth Poole, currently director of Bethlehem Center, would become our inner-city mission worker under the direction of Rev. Frank McRae. Mrs. Poole was charged with developing opportunities of Christian ministry for Christ Church members and with implementing social services in the inner city.

Mrs. Poole began work September 1, 1968. St. Mark United Methodist Church in the Hollywood/Hyde Park neighborhood, undergoing a racial transition from white to black, was chosen as a base of ministry because of the lack of social services in the area.

A listing of opportunities for volunteer service was prepared and shared with Christ Church groups who responded enthusiastically. Erroll Eckford was chosen as chairman of volunteer recruitment; Sugar Walker agreed to become the coordinator of volunteer services to the inner city.

Opha Hawkins was among the volunteers who answered the phone and manned the St. Mark office. Later, the Women's Society of Christian Service funded an answering service for the office.

Members of the Lamplighters Class responded with an interest in sponsoring basketball teams at our two Methodist neighborhood centers, Bethlehem Center and Wesley House. Jim Ellis, Ben Latimer, Erroll Eckford, Max Winn, and others coached and worked in this successful effort. Metropolitan Baptist Church next door to Bethlehem Center opened the doors of its gym for the teams to practice. These teams continued for some time, resulting in friendships among coaches and players and, in some instances, employment for the youth.

One of the earliest mission efforts was the establishment of a thrift store at St. Mark where families could select and purchase used clothing and household goods at reasonable prices. It was felt this was more helpful than giving away items that may or may not be needed or used by persons. Under the leadership of Joy Weisinger, president of the Women's Society of Christian Service, items of clothing and other goods were collected and prepared for sale. Later, other United Methodist churches made contributions to this ministry.

Cecil Woods assumed a leadership role in this venture. Keith Weisinger secured a cash register for the store. Among the many Christ Church volunteers were Jesse Joyner, Dot Kopacek, Ann Ross, and Virginia Hollon.

Additionally, the Women's Society of Christian Service circles contributed toys for a pre-Christmas sale at which parents were able to select toys to give their children as Christmas presents. Circles also collected gifts for the youth at the correctional schools at Jordonia (Nashville) and Pikeville.

Later, when the St. Mark Church property was sold, the contents of the thrift store were transferred to the newly opened branch of United Methodist Neighborhood Centers at Schoolfield United Methodist Church where a thrift store had been started. Later, Goodwill Industries opened a store in the Hollywood/Hyde Park area.

Led by Sugar Walker, another area of witness involved two schools. Volunteers tutored students at Hollywood and LaRose Schools. The Women's Society of Christian Service made contributions to the LaRose School clothes closet. They provided books for the *Reading Is Fundamental* program for many years. Volunteers at the schools included Helen Markwell, Dot Kennon, and Sugar Walker.

Sewing classes were begun. Some of the instructors were Virginia Hollon, Jean Thurman, and Mrs. E. O. Edwards at St. Mark and Pat Bigger at LeMoyne Gardens (Bethlehem Center area). Ben Birdwell was instrumental in securing sewing machines from the Singer Sewing Center for a sewing project at Harris Memorial United Methodist Church (Wesley House area).

Some Christ Church members provided transportation for senior citizens for doctor's visits. In at least one instance, this service resulted in a long-standing friendship as Betty Gully rendered many kindnesses to LeMoyne Gardens resident

Willie Mae Strong and her mother. Wilbur McClintock, Jesse Joyner, and others also participated in this ministry.

In an effort to strengthen the Bethlehem Center ministry to the families of youth at the correctional schools, Christ Church members made friendly home visits, sharing educational materials. Among these volunteers were Martha Anne Johnston, Helen Markwell, and Stella Beaty.

A wide range of activities took place across the city. Violet Pope worked with a group of young ladies at Wesley House. Wes Lawson provided transportation. Rubye Carlile utilized her secretarial skills to prepare church bulletins. Victor Smith and others served as mentors for young boys. Hank Shelton and other Key Club members helped spruce up St. Mark Church. Mildred Whitsitt served as a volunteer. Serving as Bethlehem Center Board president enabled Eloise Mays to provide insight and guidance.

When Christ Church decided to focus on an inner-city ministry, our neighborhood centers, Wesley House in north Memphis and Bethlehem Center in south Memphis, had been serving the needs of individuals in those areas for many years. Christ Church volunteers increased the areas of ministry to those youth and families. For example, a ministry to juvenile offenders involved Family Service counseling at Bethlehem Center; it also included arranging trips for families to visit the correctional schools. Another dimension of ministry was added when Christ Church volunteers visited in their homes. Also, gifts were provided for the youth by the Women's Society of Christian Service one Christmas. Another example of enhanced service came about when a volunteer provided transportation to a senior citizen who was a member of the Bethlehem Center "Golden Age" Club (probably the first senior citizens' group in Memphis).

In her first report (October 4, 1968) to Christ Church, Mrs. Poole had outlined her plan for this inner-city effort. In addition to matching Christ Church volunteers with an area of ministry, it was felt that the Hollywood/Hyde Park neighborhood could benefit from the development of a grassroots organization made up of neighborhood residents and representatives of the schools, churches and business in the area. The purpose of this organization was to focus on a need in the neighborhood and seek ways to alleviate or abolish that particular need and to implement the agreed upon approach to solving the problem.

After numerous personal contacts, such an organization came into being. Under the guidance of Cecil Woods, the Chelsea Communities Coordinating Committee (the Four Cs) was chartered as a nonprofit organization. This group utilized St. Mark Church as a base of operation. It considered the needs of the area and agreed to sponsor a much needed day care center, a major undertaking. Fortunately, St. Mark Church met most of the site requirements and was approved as a site. Initially, the funding for the center was provided by Christ Church and Christ Church individuals. Minnie Nelson was chosen as the director. Later, funding was provided as the center became part of the Community Day Care Association. Following the closing of St. Mark Church, the day care center merged with another center, becoming the Cypress Hooks-Dominick Center located at Cypress Middle School. This center has continued with Minnie Nelson as director. The Chelsea Communities Coordinating Committee qualified for and received federal funds for neighborhood projects.

1968

The Rev. and Mrs. Edward Heyer are returning to the mission fields after a hiatus. Christ Church will sponsor them as they go to serve in Sierra Leone, West Africa. The Heyers are in addition to the Crisologos in Borneo, the Gravelys in Brazil, and Elizabeth Poole as our inner city missionary.

✣ ✣ ✣

Christ Methodist Church
4370 Poplar Avenue
Memphis, Tennessee

CHARLES W. GRANT
B. L. GADDIE
Ministers
September 17, 1957
Memphis, Tennessee

Dear Member:

The new 24-bed, temporary Christ Hospital in Sarawak was opened in February. Already more than 1,000 have been treated there. Outpatient clinics have been set up, and more than 2,000 visits have been made by the traveling medical ministers.

Hundreds for the first time have heard the story of Jesus: have seen the visible fruits—healing—of the Christian faith. Old pagan beliefs are crumbling. These erstwhile headhunters are now receiving God's Word and becoming Christians. On Christmas Day 1949 the first Dyaks were baptized. Methodists now have 60 churches and 23 ordained pastors. Present membership is 6,000, with 11,000 preparatory members. Islam and Roman Catholicism are bidding for the Ibans. Christ Methodist Church must not fail the Ibans, the Brewsters or Christ!

We are beginning the second year of our support of the Brewsters. They have done incalculable good, and not all the good has been done in Borneo. They have done us good. Perhaps the greatest single blessing that has come to Christ Methodist Church, and there have been many, has been the privilege of supporting these medical missionaries.

Last year it cost $4,800 to give full support to the Brewsters. During the past nine years the cost of support has gradually increased. This year it is $6,000. The increase is understandable. We feel that without a moment's hesitation you will increase your support accordingly. Notice on the envelope the breakdown of the cost of support. Pray about this and check the amount you can give. This is the most vitally Christian call that issues from your church office. In fact, this call comes directly from Christ. We only pass the word along. It is our prayer that every member participate.

Sunday is "Brewsters' Day." Let us make it a day of triumph as we present our pledges and cash for the support of our missionaries for the next 12 months.

Cordially,
Charles W. Grant, Minister
James H. Seabrook, Chairman, Commission on Missions
W. J. Templeton, Co-Chairman, Commission on Missions
Harry A. Johnson Jr., Chairman, Commission on Education
R. H. Norris, Chairman, Commission on Membership and Evangelism
J. B. Caskey, Chairman, Commission on Stewardship and Finance
Mrs. Clarence Colby, President, Woman's Society of Christian Service
Jeans Pattinson, President, Methodist Men
H. L. Davenport, Chairman, Official Board
Howard A. Boone, Lay Leader

TRUSTEES

The copies of letters and documents from 1954 (when the Steering Committee for the establishment of Christ Methodist Church began to look for suitable property on which to build the new east Memphis church) through the early year of land acquisitions and building programs follow in chronological order.

There have been many discussions about the easements conveyed to Christ Methodist Church by Laurelwood Shopping Center in order to provide a proper buffer between the shopping center and the residential area to the west and north of the property.

The original letters and easement descriptions are among these documents as well as a letter in 1967, reflecting the change in the needs of both Christ Methodist Church and Laurelwood Shopping Center. The hour and days the stores are open have changed considerably over the years. The church membership is now at least ten times what it was in 1955. The size of funerals, weddings, and other weekday activities have skyrocketed over the years as well.

With the nearness of Laurelwood parking to the sanctuary, parking will always be a problem but we need to keep trying to solve it.

Reasons L. Hall Jones (President, Joyner Heard Realty Co.) Believes the Methodist Church Should Purchase the Southwest Corner of the Clark & Fay "Perkins Estate" Property

Size

This property would face approximately 357 feet on the north side of Poplar as measured along Poplar with a depth along its west line of 800 feet; along its east line at 945 feet; and a rear width measured at right angles to the west line of 320 feet.

The width of this property at 320 feet is approximately the size of a downtown city block in other words, the west side of Main Street from Madison to Monroe, which is occupied by Lerner's Vogue, Ellen's Hat Shop, Mednikow Jewelers, Grayson, Mary Jane Shoes, Butler's Shoes and the large Lowenstein store, is 313.50 feet.

Location

This site is ideal for a fine church. It is close to the center of the residential area in which live the high income people of Memphis with an established trend eastward for this group which undoubtedly in the foreseeable future will make this site the center of the area inhabited by the higher-income group. In addition, it will be highly accessible for middle-income families living north and south of the site.

Accessibility

Every part of the approximately 6.4 acres contained in this site will be easily and readily accessible from either Poplar Avenue or a new fully-improved 60-foot wide dedicated street, which will be put in adjacent to the east boundary line at the expense of the sellers of this property. This 60-foot street will offer easy access to Walnut Grove Road and areas north of Walnut Grove Road. It will also offer considerable parking apace.

Parking

This site being adjacent to a commercial shopping area will provide the church on Sundays and at the time of the church's peak parking demand, practically unlimited off-street parking facilities and will make a church built on this property, so far as Harry knows, the only church in Memphis with adequate off-street parking facilities.

Cost of Development

A minimum of four acres devoted exclusively to parking will be needed by the Church, mostly on Sundays when the stores are not open. It would seem economically unsound for the Church to buy four acres of ground, use it exclusively for parking purposes mostly only one day during the week and, besides paying the cost of the land acquisition, pay approximately $52,000 for paving and lighting the area when parking could be made available without cost to the Church on the adjacent commercial property. For the Church to have 6.4 acres of usable property for church buildings, recreational purposes, beautification, etc. and still have adequate parking, the Church would, if they do not buy this site, have to buy 10.4 acres in order to have 6.1 acres for church use other than parking.

Cost of Maintenance of Parking Areas

If the church develops its own off-street parking areas, it will also have the burden of the maintenance and cleaning of these areas. This would not be true if, under the terms of the proposed contract, parking rights were reserved on the adjacent property.

Price

The price at $124,000 is approximately $19,300 per acre but considering the four acres and more of parking which would be made available on the adjacent property, the church would have the use during the times when it needed it of more than ten acres of ground, which, in effect, would give the church use of more than 10 acres at a price of around $12,000 per acre.

Terms
The purchase at this site would not require all cash and reasonable terms can be arranged. If the First Methodist Church, which Harry believes owns a piece of property on the north side of Poplar between East and West Cherry Circle, became interested in the purchase of the Clark & Fay site, the sellers of the Clark & Fay property would lend The First Methodist Church its full purchase price of the property presently owned by the Church on Poplar: $30,800 for one year at 3 percent interest, this to allow the church to resell its presently owned property in an orderly manner at the highest price. Any profits could then be applied to further reduce the acquisition cost of the Clark & Fay site.

1. ***Architects.*** Recommend the employment of office to Walk C. Jones Jr., Architect, Memphis, Tennessee for the complete Architectural and Engineering service including preliminary study, overall layout, long-range plan, and detailed drawings and specifications for each phase of the project. Each unit of work to be a separate contract.

2. ***Discussion.*** *Units*
   a. Church School by stages with Assembly Hall.
   b. Sanctuary.
   c. Recreation/Dining Hall.
   d. Chapel.
   e. Methodist Kindergarten School.
   f. Athletic Field.
   g. Boy/Girl Scout Hut.
   h. Others—Pool, Organ, etc.

3. ***Type Architecture.*** Colonial or colonial modified for entire project. Treatment to consider adjacent buildings.

4. ***Landscape.*** Separate contract and special committee.

5. ***Parsonage.*** Special committee to select lot within reasonable distance to church and negotiate for plan and construction designed for Parsonage.

6. ***Sewers, Streets, Etc.*** Sewers, streets, grading, etc. is not in final stage for the location. This will be carried on by developers and final approval of Clark and Fay property.

7. ***Parking Facilities.*** Final deed for property to include parking ratio of five to one as required in new city planning code. Parking in lot immediately east of street to be named.

Committee Meeting
July 6, 1955

Signed,
E. C. Handorf
Lee McCormick
Harry A. Johnson Jr.
Jesse Anderson

Legal contract with Walk Jones referred to Jesse Vineyard.

✣ ✣ ✣

Architect and Building Committee Report

Church Board Meeting October 3, 1955

Contract for Temporary Chapel at 4370 Poplar completed on Friday 23 September, 1955 with contractors Morris Mills and Paul Ligon in office of Dennis Earles. Turnkey completed price of $8385 for building 30 feet by 70 feet and also enclosing side porch and connecting walkway, walk and items in specifications and plans. Performance bond executed by the Church through Legal and Insurance Committee. Work now in progress with completion date on or before November 1.

Architects Walk Jones Jr. and associates preliminary report for the main church plant reviewed by committee and other interested groups and approved for final draft. Design and plans moving along according to schedule.

Street plan on Grove Park Road now in City Engineering Department. Performance bond for street, sewers, etc. is between City and Hall Jones and associates. Recommend that trustees execute final contract regarding recording of plot and notation on parking facilities. Church of 1500 requires parking for 300 cars as outlined in city code.

Number assigned Church plant is 4488 Poplar.

Parsonage report acted on by committee and request for action if Board desires this committee to proceed.

This committee appreciates cooperation from a number of individuals and committees.

Everett C. Handorf

✣ ✣ ✣

WARRANTY DEED from Dolph Clark, Clarence Colby, H. L. Davenport, C. C. Evans, O. R. Mason, J. E. Perkins, C. P. Stanley Sr., A. H. Stovall and Jesse M.

Vineyard, Trustees of and for The First Methodist Church of Memphis, Tennessee, to Howard L. Davenport, Edgar H. Tenent, John A. Parsons, Dr. W. J. Templeton, James Canfield and C. R. McDaniel, Trustees of and for Christ Methodist Church of Memphis, Tennessee. Dated March 2, 1955, recorded in Book 3516, Page 440, Register's Office of Shelby County, Tennessee. Conveyed property described as follows:

> Part of Lot 3, William White Subdivision of the Perkins 160 acres more particularly described as follows:
>
> Beginning at a point in the present north line of Poplar Avenue 443.9 feet southeastwardly from the east line of Cherry Circle West; thence northwardly parallel with said east line 465.2 feet to a point, said point being the southwest corner of the parcel of land conveyed to Homer C. Smith et ux by Warranty Deed of record in Book 2790, Page 640 in the Register's Office, Shelby County, Tennessee; thence eastwardly along the south line of said Smith property 259.4 feet to the southeast corner of said Smith property; thence southwardly parallel with Cherry Circle West, 589.3 feet to a point in the present north line of Poplar Avenue, said point being 287.8 feet southeastward from the point of beginning, as measured along the north line of Poplar Avenue; thence northwestwardly along the present north line of Poplar Avenue 287.8 feet to the point of beginning.

WARRANTY DEED from Clyde L. Patton, J. Kimbrough Willey, Emmett E. Joyner and L. Hall Jones to James T. Canfield, Howard L. Davenport, C. R.

Little chapel.

McDaniel, J. A. Parsons, Dr. W. J. Templeton, and Edgar H. Tenent, Trustees for the Christ Methodist Church. Dated October 27, 1955, Recorded in Book 3585, Page 202, Register's Office of Shelby County, Tennessee. Conveyed property described as follows:

> Lot 1, Poplar-Perkins Subdivision, as shown on a map or plat of record in Flat Book 20, Page 26, in the Register's Office of Shelby County, Tennessee, more particularly described as follows:
>
> Beginning at a point in the northerly line of Poplar Avenue (as widened) 300.0 feet eastwardly from the easterly line of East Cherry Circle, said point being in the easterly line 0; William White's Cherry Circle Subdivision, 6.0 feet north of the old north line of Poplar Avenue (46.0 feet north of the center-line of Poplar Avenue); thence northwardly along the easterly line of William White's Cherry Circle Subdivision, 793.36 feet to a point, corner of Lot 3 of the Poplar-Perkins Subdivision; thence eastwardly along the southerly line of said Lot 3, 320 feet to a point in the westerly line of Grove Park Road, corner of said Lot 3; thence southwardly along said westerly line of Grove Park Road 897.27 feet to a point, the beginning of a curve of 30 foot radius; thence southwardly and westwardly along said curve 60.37 feet to a point in the northerly line of Poplar Avenue; thence westwardly along the northerly line of Poplar Avenue 306.59 feet to the point of beginning, and containing 6.37 acres.

Resolution

WHEREAS, Clyde L. Patton, Emmett E. Joyner, J. Kimbrough Willey and L. Hall Jones, the owners of Lot 3, of the Poplar-Perkins subdivision, desire to petition the planning Commission of the City of Memphis to have an additional approximate 400 feet of that Lot zoned commercial and have offered The Christ Methodist Church an easement for parking purposes of this additional acreage if same is zoned commercial provided the Church joins in and assists the owners of the land in securing the rezoning.

NOW, THEREFORE, BE IT RESOLVED BY THE BOARD OF STEWARDS OF THE CHRIST METHODIST CHURCH that the Church approve the plan for rezoning of the additional approximate 400 feet of Lot 3, of the Poplar-Perkins Subdivision, and do hereby authorize the Building Committee of the Church to take whatever steps it deems necessary to assist Clyde L. Patton, Emmett E. Joyner, J. Kimbrough Willey and L. Hall Jones in the securing of the rezoning of this parcel.

WARRANTY DEED from Katherine H. Gardner and husband, Robert Goodwyn Gardner, to James T. Canfield, Howard L. Davenport, C. R. McDaniel, J. A. Parsons, Dr. W. J. Templeton, and Edgar H. Tenent, Trustees of and for Christ Methodist Church. Dated February 13, 1956, recorded in Book 3632,

Page 340, Register's Office of Shelby County, Tennessee. Conveyed property described as follows:

> East 10 feet of Lot 12 and West 95 feet of Lot 13, Belle Meade Subdivision, of record in Plat Book 12, Page 26, of the Register's Office of said County, being more particularly described as follows:
>
> Beginning at a point in the south line of Belle Meade Cove 163.6, four feet eastwardly from the point of intersection of said south line with the east line of Belle Meade Lane; thence eastwardly with said south line of Belle Meade Cove 105 feet to a point 5 feet westwardly from the line dividing Lots 13 and 14 of said subdivision; thence southwardly parallel with said dividing line 200 feet to a point; thence westwardly 105 feet to a point 199.83 feet southwardly from the point of beginning; thence northwardly 199.83 feet to the point of beginning.

✣ ✣ ✣

QUARTERLY CONFERENCE MEETING MINUTES

February 19, 1956

The Quarterly Conference of Christ Methodist Church met pursuant to the notice of special meeting made in accordance with the *Discipline* of the Methodist Church, which notice was announced at the regular Sunday morning service on February 5, 1956, and February 12, 1956, at 8:30 o'clock P.M. on February 19, 1956, at the Little Cottage, 4370 Poplar Avenue, Memphis, Tennessee with Dr. Charles Grant, Pastor of Christ Methodist Church, presiding, and with the consent in writing of the district superintendent, which consent is attached hereto as part of the minutes of the meeting.

Mr. Sam Mays was unanimously elected Secretary of the meeting, after being nominated by Mr. Edgar Tenent.

Discussion was held concerning the purchase of a parsonage for the use of the pastor of Christ Methodist Church and an explanation of the contract to buy 4227 Belle Meade Cove, Memphis, made to the meeting by Mr. Edgar Tenent.

Upon motion of Mr. William Martak, seconded by Mr. Roy Barron and Dr. W. J. Templeton, the following resolution was adopted by a majority of the members present, which represent more than a quorum of the membership of the Quarterly Conference:

> Be it resolved by the Quarterly Conference of the Christ Methodist Church of Memphis, Tennessee that the contract between Katherine H. Gardner and husband, Robert Goodwyn Gardner and Christ Methodist Church relative to the sale of the property known as 4227 Belle Meade

Cove, Memphis, be and the same is hereby approved for the purchase price of Thirty Three Thousand ($33,000) Dollars.

Be it further resolved that the Christ Methodist Church borrow the sum of Twenty Three Thousand ($23,000) Dollars from Leader Federal Savings & Loan Association of Memphis to be repaid in monthly installments over, a period of twenty years, and bearing five (5%) percent interest, and to be secured by a deed of trust on the hereinafter described property for part of the purchase price and pay the remainder in cash at closing of sale.

Be it further resolved that the title to the following described property located in Memphis, County of Shelby, State of Tennessee, together with all improvements and appurtenances thereon, to wit:

East 10 feet of Lot 12 and West 95 feet of Lot 33, Belle Meade Subdivision, of record in Flat Book 12, Page 26, of Register's Office of Shelby County, Tennessee, having located thereon a house known as 4227 Belle Meade Cove be authorized to be conveyed to James T. Canfield, Howard L. Davenport, C. R. McDaniel, J. A. Parsons, Dr. W. J. Templeton and Edgar H. Tenent, as Trustees of and for Christ Methodist Church of Memphis, Tennessee, and their successors in office as such Trustees in accordance with the requirements of the *Discipline* of the Methodist Church.

✣ ✣ ✣

Minutes of Special Called Meeting of the Quarterly Conference

Christ Methodist Church
October 6, 1958

A Special Called Meeting of the Quarterly Conference of Christ Methodist Church was called to order at 8:00 P.M., October 6, 1958, in the Fellowship Hall at 4483 Poplar Avenue, Memphis, Tennessee, Dr. Charles W. Grant presiding.

Upon motion duly made and carried, Earle Billings was elected secretary of the Call Meeting.

Dr. Grant stated that written consent for the special session of the Quarterly Conference had been received from our district superintendent, Dr. John Horton, and that 10 days' notice of the meeting had been given. The regular Quarterly Conference will be held Monday night, December 1, 1958.

The purpose of the meeting was to make some decision as to our building procedure. Dr. Grant stated he was sure that many present had given much thought to this matter and invited remarks from the floor. Mr. Edgar Tenent read a statement, which follows:

Members of Christ Methodist Church and Friends:

Many of you are asking what building shall we build next—sanctuary or Building B, which is a church school building. We know that everyone would like to build a sanctuary in keeping with the Fellowship Hall, which we now occupy. There is only one reason why it cannot be built now: money. If there is some way of raising the additional amount required everyone would vote for building of the sanctuary next.

I want to give you something to think about before you decide which building we shall build.

1. It has been estimated by leading architects of this city that the cost of building and furnishing a sanctuary for seating 1,250 to 1,500 people will be a $1 million. Before we could proceed with the building it would be necessary to have architectural plans drawn. That would cost $60,000, of which 75 percent would have to be paid within 12 months. In order to borrow $1 million, you must have assets equal to twice the amount you wish to borrow. Our present assets consist of:

A Building	$450,000
Land	$150,000
4370 Poplar	$100,000
This makes a total of	$700,000

On this basis, we could borrow $350,000 provided the indebtedness is paid. We still owe $260,000 on our present building.

2. By building the sanctuary we would have to add an additional $10,000 to our present budget operation to cover insurance, help and utilities, also the payments on a $1 million loan would be $9,200 a month, which is more than our monthly collection on our building fund now.

3. There have been several large churches built and several building campaigns undertaken to build additional buildings and in every case there have been large contributions. When I speak of large, I mean $50,000 to $75,000 gifts. This we do not have in our church.

4. All these churches have memberships of 2,500 or over where our membership is around 1,300. You can readily see that if we should build a sanctuary that the debt per member would be twice as much as other large churches and should we have a recession it might be very difficult to make the payments on the principal.

5. No building & loan company or bank will loan us $1 million on a one-purpose building. The only way we can finance a sanctuary costing this much is through a bond issue. This is attested by the fact that First Baptist Church recently sold $600,000 in bonds at a four-point discount with interest ranging from 5 to 5.1 percent. Bellevue Baptist Church and quite a few other large churches have found it necessary also as the building & loan and bank would not finance a loan of this type. It is too large.

6. The yardstick used by insurance companies and loan companies is twice the budget. Of course, it is a safe rule and may be varied but not to the loan of a $1 million to build a sanctuary. We can build the church school building. It is estimated that this building would cost $375,000. The architect's plans have been paid for, which means we would owe only one and one-half percent of the cost which is approximately $5,000. This would be paid during the construction period. We are now collecting approximately $100,000 a year on our Building Fund. It is possible that we can sell 4370 Poplar for $100,000 and we can borrow approximately $200,000 from Leader Federal, which will be ample to build and furnish the building. Our payments will be approximately $5,200 a month. Our payments now to the building fund are more than this amount. The present building we are now using will seat 650 to 700 at each service. By having two morning services a day we can seat 1,300 people a day thereby taking care of our membership. Since only 501 attend church services, we could have a membership enrollment of 2,500 and by using two services a day take care of our membership. All that would be necessary would be to secure a youth director or an associate pastor for our evening services.

I have given much thought and prayer to this building program and I see no solution to building a sanctuary at this time.

After reading his statement, Mr. Tenent made the following motion:

RESOLVED, That we move as expeditiously as possible towards the construction of Unit B.

The motion was seconded by Mr. Harry Johnson. The chairman called for discussion and a number of questions and statements were made. At the conclusion of the discussion, the question was called for. The secretary recorded 79 votes for Mr. Tenent's motion and none against.

Dr. Grant stated the matter would be referred immediately to the Finance Committee and the Architects Committee for action.

The purpose of the call meeting having been accomplished, same was adjourned with a statement by the chairman that the roll call made for the

Official Board's regular meeting would suffice for both it and the call meeting of the Quarterly Conference.

Respectfully submitted,
Earle Billings, Secretary
Special Call Meeting

APPROVED: Quarterly Conference
Dr. Charles W. Grant, Chairman

✣ ✣ ✣

SANCTUARY CONTRACT

Signed May 6, 1963

Another exciting contract was signed on May 6, 1963, with F. T. Thayer Jr., general contractor, for the construction of the Christ Church sanctuary for the sum of $834,805, to be built in 370 working days. This contract was signed by E. R. Richmond Sr., chairman of the Architect and Building Committee, Edgar Tenent, chairman of the Official Board, and James H. Seabrook Sr., chairman of the trustees. The plans were prepared by two architectural firms laboring and collaborating together: James B. Adams, architect, and Thorn, Howe, Stratton and Strong, associated architects.

On the next Sunday, May 12, 1963, following the morning worship, the sanctuary groundbreaking service was held. The congregation assembled on the southeast corner of the property at 4488 Poplar Avenue for the ceremony and they were joined by friends from all over the city; Mayor Henry Loeb was present, and Mr. F. T. Thayer Jr., general contractor, was also there. The event was televised by WMCT television station. The participants in the groundbreaking used gold spades to turn the soil. On this memorable occasion, it was noted that among the crowd, representatives were present from Protestant, Catholic, and Jewish faiths.

✣ ✣ ✣

SANCTUARY

Building Construction Costs

F. T. Thayer, General Contract as modified by change orders Nos. 1–19	$831,509.62
Stained Glass Windows contract with Jacoby Studios	50,000.00
Organ contract with M. P. Moler	70,445.00
Pew contract with Southern Desk Co.	33,885.20

Carpet contract with Southern Rug & Carpet Co. 17,909.10
Tester contract with George L. Payne, Inc. 925.00
Hanging Cross contract with George L. Payne, Inc.
(incl shipping but no installation) 2,333.00
Architect's Fee 58,174.89
Total $1,065,181.81

Miscellaneous Costs

Shutter Windows for Nursery $868.00
Door mats and freight 876.50
Labor to unload organ 99.51
Dixie Sheet Metal—connect blowers to organ .356.35
Seabrook's—drapes, divider and freight 109.68
Communion covers, glasses, etc 152.50
Offering Plates, etc. 146.23
Reserve supply of material to cover pews (2 seats & 2 backs) 55.00
Reserve supply of carpeting (72 yards) 658.80
Supervision fee—Mrs. Bernice Penland 1,000.00
Hanging Cross and Tester (estimate) 1,500.00
Express for Cross 75.50
Seelbinders—Tables & Chairs for the Narthex in Sanctuary 1,738.00
Carrico—8 kneeling pads and kneeling benches 1,030.00
Rogers Church Goods Co.—Candles, burners, lighting tapers 43.40
Cokesbury—2 candle lighters and transportation charges 20.56
Tom Wells, Inc.—Furniture and Accessories for Brides' Room 1,360.87
Hamling Interiors—Brides' Room 37.50
Hamling Interiors—Labor & Installation 4 Roman Shades 80.00
Memorial Bronze—Memorial block for Chapel 42.00
Theater Supply—cords to rope off pews (Est.) .289.00
S. C. Toof & Company—Furniture 5,123,58
Landscaping (spent to date $1,730.96) 7,500.00
Insurance 6,818.44
Total $29,981.42

Approximate Total—subject to minor adjustment $1,095,163.23

October 19, 1967

Mr. Jesse M. Vineyard
c/o Sherman, Vineyard, Walt & Threlkeld
Fourth Floor, Leader Federal Building
158 Madison Avenue
Memphis, Tennessee 38103

Dear Jesse:

In Re Parking for Christ Methodist Church

The business firms which are our tenants in Laurelwood Shopping Center are becoming more and more concerned as weekday activities increase at Christ Methodist Church. On April 12, 13, and 14 the parking situation in the shopping center from the standpoint of our tenants and the people in the area not members of Christ Methodist Church was intolerable.

Many of the people attending this three-day meeting refused to park elsewhere when requested to do so, and many stated that they would never buy anything in the Laurelwood stores, etc.

I am sure you realize, Jesse, it is rent from these merchants that has enabled us to provide the parking area in question without any cost to the church and the rights of these merchants must be protected. I am sure you will remember that this was the intention of the parties at the time our agreement was made. In fact the easement which we gave the church reads as follows:

> It is further understood and agreed by and between said parties that each will cooperate in all unessential particulars to effectuate the respective parking needs of both parties and also agree that the businesses to be located on said land over which said easement is granted shall have priority over said parking at such time as both of said businesses are open for business and the said church is holding services.

We would appreciate it very much if you would take this matter up with the governing body of Christ Methodist Church with the request that all members of the church be notified that they are not to use the parking areas of Laurelwood Shopping Center on week days when the majority of the stores are open for business.

If you will acknowledge receipt of this letter and advise me of the action taken, it will help us in dealing with our tenants.

Cordially yours,
L. Hall Jones
President-Manager

✣ ✣ ✣

Land and Buildings

Brief History
Christ United Methodist Church
By D. A. Noel

In this volume and its companion volumes a chronological history is given of the acquisitions of land and the construction of buildings by Christ United Methodist Church from the date the church was established in June 1955 through March 1998. In an effort to be brief, all details are not given but reference is made to records that can be found in the church archives where a vast volume of additional facts may be found. The accompanying reports are divided into the periods of service by each of the four outstanding senior ministers who have served the church through its history to date.

We have attempted to indicate for each property the approximate dates of acquisition or construction, the approximate costs (for buildings, the costs are usually to include architect's fees, general contractor costs, furnishings, and equipment). There has been no attempt to allocate the total cost of land parcels to the cost of the various buildings that have been constructed thereon.

Also named in association with each building are the Building Committee, the architects, and the general contractor.

The Dr. Charles W. Grant Years, June 1955–June 1969.

1955	Land	4488 Poplar, 6.4 acres
1955	Land and cottage	4370 Poplar
1956	Parsonage	4227 Belle Meade Cove
1958	Fellowship Hall (Later named Rash Building)	
1960	Grant Building	
1962	Land and Two Residences	4448 & 4468 Poplar
1964	The Sanctuary	
1967	Land and Residence	382 East Cherry Circle

First Property Purchase—6.4 Acres, 1955. The first property purchase was 6.4 acres of vacant land at 4488 Poplar. It was on this land that the first permanent building was constructed (the Fellowship Hall, later named the Rash Building). This plot also provided building sites for the Grant Building, the sanctuary, the Beaty Activities Building and the Rogers Youth Center.

The land purchase was made in April 1955 for $95,000 by the original Steering Committee.

Land and Cottage, 4370 Poplar. Also in 1955 Christ Church acquired a lot and cottage located at 4370 Poplar from First Methodist Church by payment of

Upper Left: *4448 Poplar Avenue;* ***Upper Right:*** *382 East Cherry Circle;* ***Bottom Left:*** *Little cottage.*

$7,500 and assumed the mortgage debt of $25,300, total cost $32,800.

In October 1955 a "Little Chapel" was constructed on this property for a cost of about $8,375. The church used the existing cottage and little chapel until May 1960 when the property was sold for $85,000. By this time the newly constructed Fellowship Hall and Grant Building provided adequate space for the activities, which had been housed at 4370 Poplar. (This location is now the site of the Marsonne Apartments.)

Parsonage, 4227 Belle Meade Cove 1956. In February 1956, the church purchased its first parsonage. A special committee composed of Edward R. Richmond, chairman, L. A. Conolly, and Edgar Tenent acquired the property for $33,000 plus an estimated $2,000 for needed repairs. Dr. Grant occupied the parsonage and then Dr. Beaty.

On April 6, 1978, the parsonage was sold to Dr. Beaty for $75,000. About this time it was becoming a frequent choice of churches and pastors to provide pastors a parsonage allowance to purchase a home instead of churches furnishing a parsonage. In this way, ministers could build up home equity.

Later, a lot (#74) on Grove Park Road was purchased. This lot was not used and was sold June 16, 1977, to Morris Mills for $26,000.

First Permanent Building, Fellowship Hall. In August 1955, a contract was signed with Walk C. Jones Jr., architect, to design the first two permanent buildings. Unit "A" was to be the Fellowship Hall (later named the Rash

Building), and Unit "B" was to be named the Grant Building. The estimated cost of the two buildings was $819,483. It was decided that it would not be financially feasible to construct both buildings at once and Unit "A," Fellowship Hall, was to be built first. The Fellowship Hall contained a combination Sanctuary-Social Hall, office areas, classrooms for the Junior Department and a kitchen.

The Building Committee was composed of Everett C. Handorf, chairman, Jesse Anderson, Harry A. Johnson Jr., Lee McCormick, and Jesse Vineyard.

Construction was begun in May 1957, and the building was completed in April 1958. The general contractor was Canfield, Badgett and Scarbrough. The total amount paid to the contractor was $386,880.56. After adding separate contracts for kitchen equipment, $24,771.00, and furniture and fixtures, the total cost was $526,161.34 according to a Finance Committee report dated May 31, 1958. There was no specific allocation to the building cost for land.

Dr. Grant continued as senior pastor through this construction period and two future building projects.

The Grant Building. Unit "B" of the construction plans was to be used for additional classrooms for kindergarten, primary and adult departments, the parlors, and a library.

Walk C. Jones Jr., architect, and the contractor drew the plans for Unit "B" at the same time as Unit "A." The contractor for both units was Canfield, Badgett and Scarbrough. Construction was started March 8, 1959, and completed February 14, 1960. The Building Committee for Unit "B" was composed of Al Lenz, chairman, Ed Richmond Sr., Gil Avery, James Canfield,

Groundbreaking ceremony, first building, Fellowship Hall, April 1, 1956. Left to right: James H. Seabrook Sr., J. E. Underwood (district superintendent), John A. Parsons, Howard Davenport, and Dr. Charles Grant.

Earl Montgomery, and Dennis Earles Sr. The total cost was estimated at $600,000 to include furnishings, etc.

Land and Two Residences, 4448 and 4468 Poplar. In July 1961 the land and residences located at 4448 Poplar and 4468 Poplar were acquired for $142,500.00. These properties located immediately to the west of existing property at 4488 Poplar were acquired for future expansion; however, the two residences were promptly put to use. The house at 4448 Poplar was used as a parsonage for the associate minister and the house at 4468 Poplar was used as a youth center and counseling center.

Later, this land was cleared of the two houses to make room for the construction of the Dunnam Building, Wilson Chapel, and Seabrook Hall (in 1988).

The Sanctuary, 1963–1964. The church sanctuary was designed in classic contemporary style and erected on the prominent northwest corner of Poplar and Grove Park Road in 1963–1964. The first worship service held in the sanctuary, which was designed to seat about 1,500 persons, was on November 1, 1964.

The Building Committee was composed of Edward R. Richmond Sr., chairman, Armistead F. Clay, Everett C. Handorf, Early F. Mitchell, Kenneth Markwell Jr., Jesse D. Wooten, Earl Montgomery, John A. Parsons, and Kemmons Wilson. Architects were James B. Adams, and Ed Thorne of Thorne, Howe, Stratton and Strong.

Construction bids were invited from seven general contractors. The successful bidder was F. T. Thayer Jr., general contractor, who bid $834,805 with completion in 370 days. Groundbreaking ceremonies were May 12, 1963, with completion and occupation November 1, 1964. The total cost of the project including furnishing, equipment, and the organ was approximately $1,115,000.

This is only a summary page of the complicated sanctuary construction. The church archives contain a bound volume (Vol. XI) including plans and details of every phase of the project.

Roundtree Property. In November 1967 the church acquired a lot and residence at 382 East Cherry Circle for $70,000. This property was immediately adjacent to existing land. The music director lived in the house for a time. Presently, the house is known as the Timothy House and it has served for various purposes including as a residence for the youth director.

UNITED METHODIST WOMEN

A History of United Methodist Women

Christ United Methodist Church

Shortly after the organization of Christ Methodist Church, June 26, 1955, the women met to organize the local units of the Woman's Society of Christian Service and the Wesleyan Service Guild.

The Committee for Organization of Christ Methodist Church, Woman's Society of Christian Service was as follows:

Mrs. Charles M. Henderson (Madison Heights)
Mrs. Hugh Carey (Madison Heights)
Mrs. Percy Whitenton (First Church)
Mrs. J. C. Ingram (First Church)
Mrs. Thomas West (St. John's)
Mrs. Richard Taylor (St. John's)
Mrs. Oscar Crofford (Trinity)
Mrs. F. M. Ridolphi (Trinity)
Mrs. J. V. Thomas (St. Luke's)
Mrs. H. C. Shelton (St. Luke's)

This committee met on June 28, 1955, and selected the following officers to be elected to serve for the first year of the organization:

President	Mrs. Percy Whitenton
Vice President	Mrs. Charles W. Henderson
Secretary	Mrs. Jack Caskey
Treasurer	Mrs. Horace Harwell
Assistant Treasurer	Mrs. W. K. Martak
Secretaries:	
Promotion	Mrs. Ned French
Missionary Education	Mrs. Clarence Colby
Christian Social Relations	Mrs. Charles Johnston
& Local Church Activities	Mrs. Fred Ridolphi
Spiritual Life	Mrs. W. J. Templeton
Student Work	Mrs. Sam Mays

Youth Work	Mrs. Charles Tate
Children's Work	Mrs. J. C. Ingram Jr.
Literature & Publications	Mrs. Ray Drenner
Supplies	Mrs. Edgar Tenent
Status of Women	Mrs. Jack Byrne

The Circle Leaders

1. Mrs. Howard L. Davenport
2. Mrs. Richard Taylor
3. Mrs. Russell Reeves
4. Mrs. Robert Holt
5. Mrs. J. T. Canfield
6. Mrs. Hugh Carey
7. Mrs. Ernest Felts
8. Mrs. Ed Richmond
9. Mrs. Merle King
10. Mrs. John Parsons
11. Mrs. D. K. Kelley

✣ ✣ ✣

Mrs. Percy Whitenton (Ethel) had been a very active and capable worker in First Methodist Church. It was her goal to set up the organization of the Woman's Society of Christian Service and the Wesleyan Service Guild according to the guidelines set forth in the *Handbook* so that each member would be able to share in the opportunities for fellowship, and growth in wisdom, understanding, and in her relationship to God. At the meeting, 147 women became charter members, later the report reached 200.

Ethel was a very creative person. One of the examples of her creativity was the Chrismon Tree. She was not only the originator of the idea but the driving force behind the project, making many of the ornaments. Another example of her creative genius and the sharing of her talent was the designing and making of the beautiful casket pall to be used in funerals.

The second president was Mrs. Fred Ridolphi (Rinne) and along with her serving as chairman of the Wesleyan Service Guild was Mrs. Haskell Gass (Ruby). The work along with the membership continued to grow. The women were not only busy with making and paying their pledge to missions, both foreign and home, but there were many places in the life of the new church that needed the services of teaching, telephoning, visiting, and preparing countless meals for church dinners and sandwiches and snacks for the children and youth programs.

Mrs. Ridolphi was a member of the Committee on History, and under the leadership of Mrs. W. J. Templeton (Elizabeth) as chairman, she along with Mrs. Ethel Whitenton kept important records for the history of the church.

The third president was Mrs. Clarence Colby (Margaret), who has the distinction of serving as president of the Woman's Society on two different occasions. The first term was 1957–58 and a later term in 1969–70. The chairman of the Wesleyan Service Guild for this first term was Mrs. V. A. Alexander (Bernice). Margaret Colby had grown up in a parsonage home, being the daughter of Dr. and Mrs. John L. Horton, so it goes without saying that she was well-schooled in Methodism and the work of Methodist Women. During the beginning when the services were held at the Plaza Theater, she and Mrs. Grant served as greeters and welcomed the people as they came to the worship services.

The Wesleyan Service Guild was named for Margaret Colby and was known always as "The Margaret Colby Wesleyan Service Guild."

In 1958, Mrs. Ernest Felts (Helen) became president and was the first person to serve for two years, concluding her term in 1960. During this time there were two persons who served as chairman of the Wesleyan Service Guild. They were Mrs. Sanford L. Jones and Miss Zetta Walker. The beautiful membership teas in which the Woman's Society honored their new members were a highlight of those years.

These were the days before there was a kitchen staff; thus the women served many of the meals. One of the big events each month was the serving of the dinner for the Methodist Men. Before the Fellowship Hall was built, and in the summertime, some of these meals were served on the lawn at the cottage.

Just as the church began with a missionary emphasis, so the Woman's Society gave much support to the work of Wesley House, a Home Missions project begun in north Memphis in 1906, and the Bethlehem Center, a similar project serving the black community in south Memphis and located on Walker Avenue, begun in 1935. Mrs. Charles M. Henderson (Mary) was a member of the Board of Missions and the Woman's Division. She was a member of both boards of these two ministries until her death in 1968. The women of Christ Church had key women and other members of the Woman's Society and the Wesleyan Service Guild who attended the board meetings regularly and kept the groups in active participation with many services and supplies to meet the needs of these institutions as they served these areas of the city. Later on in 1968 the boards of these institutions were consolidated and their ministries under the direction of the United Methodist Neighborhood Center.

Another mission project that was launched in 1966 was the Reelfoot Rural Ministry. This is located in Lake County, Tennessee, an area that has been blighted by people being unable to find work. These persons have been displaced by machines that cultivate and harvest the cotton and other crops. This has received the support of the total church as well as the women. Regularly they need food, clothes, money, and items for conducting classes and recreation programs and other ministries.

On the Executive Committee each year there is a "Key Woman" for the Methodist Hospital Auxiliary. This representative, along with members from the circles, carries suggested items to meet the needs in the hospitals. The membership to the Methodist Hospital Auxiliary is one dollar per year per woman. Great emphasis is placed on each group of Woman's Society, now United Methodist Women, having 100 percent participation.

We cooperate with Church Women United, a citywide organization of the women from all churches in the city, including all denominations. They meet once each month and on an ecumenical basis minister to many needs locally. One of their ministries is to the prisoners in the jails. In 1976 the women of Christ Church began saving books, magazines, and other items to assist and cooperate in this service to others.

Another community service is participation in the R.I.F. Program (*Reading Is Fundamental*). This program is a government program to provide books for children in the city schools that are unable to buy books for reading. It is a matching project and the women of Christ Church are assigned to work with LaRose School.

Each year, beginning in 1953, the women of the Memphis Conference give to the Scholarship Fund at Lambuth College. The income from this increasing fund is used to assist the education of deserving students, preference being given young women planning to enter full-time Christian service under the auspices of the Woman's Division of the Board of Global Ministries. An offering is taken each year as well as an item in the budget to support this scholarship.

It was an exciting event when in 1967 the Woman's Society of the Church entertained the annual meeting of the Memphis Conference Woman's Society and Wesleyan Service Guild. Mrs. James B. Green was the conference president. This was one of the ways we celebrated the opening of the sanctuary and the sharing of Christ Church with others.

The visitors from all over the Memphis Conference were welcomed to Christ Church by the pastor, Dr. Charles W. Grant, the president of the Woman's Society, Mrs. C. B. (Bea) Crofford, and Mrs. Howard (Lorece) Estes, chairman of the Wesleyan Service Guild. The theme of this annual meeting was *In Thy Light We Walk*. We were honored to have on the program Dr. James S. Wilder Jr., president of Lambuth College, Mrs. H. M. (Frankie) Russell, president of the Southeastern Jurisdiction Woman's Society of Christian Service, and Dr. James T. Laney, professor in the Divinity School of Vanderbilt University, later to become president of Emory University.

The women also participated in many services when the Memphis Annual Conference, which includes all the ministers and the laypersons who represent the various churches, met at Christ Church in June of 1965. Bishop H. Ellis Finger Jr. was in his first year as a new bishop and presided over the sessions.

A hundred years ago the women's organization was "The Woman's Mission Society." Later on and for a short period they became two groups. "The Woman's Foreign Missionary Society" and "The Woman's Home Missionary Society." There was even a third group known as "The Ladies' Aid Society;" however, their work consisted mostly of looking after the parsonages. Then in 1940, after the union of the three branches of Methodism, when we became the Methodist Church, the name of the women's organization was changed to the "Woman's Society of Christian Service" and a "Wesleyan Service Guild" for professional and employed women. These organizations for women continued until 1972, when the Women's Division changed the name to "United Methodist Women" and we moved into one inclusive organization.

Statistics tell us that almost half of the women in our nation have entered the working world and are either employed or pursuing careers. This has created some serious obstacles in the number of Methodist Women able to participate in the meetings and program of United Methodist Women. Yet the organization of United Methodist Women in Christ Church has an enrollment of 473 with seventeen circles, or groups. Two of these groups meet at night and are designed for the employed and career woman. In 1980 the president and Executive Committee initiated the use of "service circles," which have gone well and the plan has even been followed by other churches in the conference. The four service groups are as follows:

Group 12	Church Service Group
Group 13	Neighborhood Center
Group 14	Wesley Highland Manor
Group 15	Membership and Visitation

The purpose of these service groups is exactly what the name implies. They minister to the church providing services, articles, and supplies as needed; to the Neighborhood Center in its mission to the needy; the Wesley Highland Manor, a nursing home for the infirm and elderly, where loving concern is a priceless service; and the visitation and cultivation of new and prospective members and a ministry to the shut-ins.

In all of the seventeen groups there is a leader and a study leader. They meet the first Tuesday of each month except July and August. When the business of each group is transacted then the study leader conducts the Bible study on whatever the topic is for the year.

A project that involved more than sixty women, most of them from the United Methodist Women's organization of the church, was begun in 1975: the project of the needlepoint kneeling cushions for the sanctuary. This involved an estimated thirty-nine thousand hours of needlework and 6,379,408 stitches. It was completed and dedicated on May 28, 1978, "To the Glory of God and of His Kingdom."

One of the exciting events that has been initiated in recent years is the Annual Fellowship Day. It began as a part of the Mission Study Series in 1981 and was used to carry out the theme of the study with music, program, and food. It has also been observed as a time of fun and relaxation with a luncheon in a lovely spacious home.

The list of women who have rendered unselfish service to Christ United Methodist Women is innumerable. In conclusion, we will list the members of Christ Church who have served as officers in the Memphis Conference Woman's Society, United Methodist Women, and Southeastern Jurisdiction, in addition to those who have served as local presidents of the Woman's Society of Christian Service, United Methodist Women, and the chairmen of the Wesleyan Service Guild. They are as follows (first for the conference and jurisdiction):

Mrs. C. H. Henderson
Conference Secretary of Missionary Education (WSCS), Secretary of Southeastern Jurisdiction (WSCS), Member of Board of Missions, Woman's Division (8 years)

Mrs. Oscar Crofford
Secretary of Spiritual Life (WSCS), Secretary of Missionary Education and Service (WSCS)

Mrs. Wayne A. Lamb
Secretary of Christian Social Relations (WSCS), Secretary of Missionary Education and Service (WSCS), Secretary of Membership Cultivation (S.E.J.), First President of United Methodist Women

Mrs. C. L. Woodard
Coordinator of Christian Global Concerns (U.M.W.)

Mrs. L. E. Smith
Secretary, Program Resources (U.M.W.)

Chairmen of the Margaret Colby Wesleyan Service Guild

Mrs. J. Porter McClean	1955–1956
Mrs. Haskell Gass	1956–1957
Mrs. V. A. Alexander	1957–1958
Mrs. Sanford L. Jones	1958–1959
Miss Zetta Walker	1959–1961
Mrs. Earl Billings	1961–1963
Mrs. Avis D. Allen	1963–1965
Mrs. Howard Estes	1965–1967
Miss Frances Young	1967–1968
Mrs. W. Floyd Smith	1968–1970
Mrs. Thomas F. Jones	1970–1972

CHARTER MEETING

Woman's Society of Christian Service
Christ Methodist Church
June 28, 1955

Purpose. The purpose of the Woman's Society of Christian Service shall be to unite all the women of the church in Christian living and service; to help develop and support Christian work among women and children around the world; to develop the spiritual life; to study the needs of the world; to take part in such service activities as will strengthen the local church, improve civic, community, and world conditions. To this end this organization shall seek to enlist women, young people, and children in this Christian fellowship, and to secure funds for the activities in the local church and support of the work undertaken at home and abroad for the establishment of a world Christian community.

Membership Ritual

Candles of Love

(Arrange a table with a candelabra in the center bearing three unlighted candles, one blue, one white, and one golden yellow; on the left, a globe of the world and a New Testament; on the right, the Membership Record.)

Chairman of Committee on Membership. Members of the Woman's Society of Christian Service are asked to pledge prayers, service and an annual gift of money to help in sending the light of Christ's love around the world. As we light these "candles of love" for our new members, let us all pledge ourselves anew to the purpose of the Woman's Society. *(Reads Purpose.)*

First Speaker. *(lights candle)* The purity of the white candle represents prayer. Just the central theme of our great work. Praying women really catch the vision of a worldwide family circle.

Second Speaker. *(lights candle)* Blue stands for loyalty. Service requires loyalty. May we be willing at all times to perform to the best of our ability any task that we are called upon to do in His Name in the society, in the church, in the community.

Third Speaker. *(lights candle)* This golden candle signifies our gifts of money. Truly "the Lord loveth a cheerful giver," and women who devotedly pray and willingly serve for the Master's cause are eager to "give till it makes their hearts sing with gladness."

Chairman. May we repeat together the pledge.

Group. I pledge my prayers to bind me closer to Him in whose strength I live; my service in the extension of God's kingdom; my gifts to the support of the Woman's Society of Christian Service.

Chairman Invites New Members to Sign the Membership Record. *An appropriate hymn may be played softly as each one writes her name in the book.*

✣ ✣ ✣

Ethel Mays Whitenton was born in Portsmouth, Virginia, and moved to Memphis when her parents, Harvey J. and Helga Nelsen Mays, were transferred to Memphis with the Virginia-Carolina Chemical Company.

After graduation from Central High School she became a dental technician and continued in this field serving as president of the American Association of

Dental Assistants. Her activities with the American Red Cross brought special commendation.

A person of many talents, she and her husband, Percy Bradford Whitenton, worked tirelessly as a team on all of the fund-raising activities of the church, and as parish visitor, her warm, loving personality brought many new families into the congregation and much happiness to shut-ins.

Mrs. Percy B. Whitenton (Ethel)
First President of Woman's Society of Christian Service Christ Methodist Church, 1955–1956

One example of her creativity was the Chrismon Tree. She was the originator of the idea, the driving force behind this project, and made many of the ornaments. Another was the beautiful pall that she designed to be used in funerals.

Her goal as first president of the Woman's Society of Christian Service was to set up the organization according to Methodist guidelines so that each woman would want to share in the opportunities for fellowship and growth in wisdom, understanding, and in her relationship with God.

EXECUTIVE COMMITTEE
1955–1956

President	Mrs. P. B. Whitenton
Vice President	Mrs. Charles Henderson
Recording Secretary	Mrs. Jack Caskey
Treasurer	Mrs. Albert M. Jones
Assistant Treasurer	Mrs. W. K. Martak
Secretaries:	
Children's Work	Mrs. J. C. Ingram Jr.
Christian Social Relations	Mrs. Charles Johnston
& Local Church Activities	Mrs. Fred Ridolphi
Literature & Publications	Mrs. Ray Drenner
Missionary Education & Service	Mrs. Clarence Colby
Promotion	Mrs. Ned French
Spiritual Life	Mrs. W. J. Templeton
Status of Women	Mrs. Jack P. Byrne
Student Work	Mrs. Sam Mays
Supply	Mrs. Edgar Tenent
Youth Work	Mrs. Charles Tate
Hospital Auxiliary Key Woman	Mrs. Horace Harwell Sr.

Mrs. Fred M. Ridolphi (Rinne)
Second President of Woman's Society of Christian Service Christ Methodist Church, 1956–1957

City Mission Board	Mrs. Richard Kite Mrs. Frank Liddel

✣ ✣ ✣

Rinne Rogers Ridolphi was born in New Albany, Mississippi, daughter of Mr. and Mrs. Lee Rogers. She graduated from Mississippi State College for Women and is married to Fred M. Ridolphi. They have two children; a son, attorney Fred Ridolphi Jr., and a daughter, Corinne, married to Dr. Frank Adams. Rinne and Fred have ten grandchildren.

Rinne is the second president of the Woman's Society of Christian Service of Christ Methodist Church; along with her, serving as chairman of the Wesleyan Service Guild, was Mrs. Haskell Gass (Ruby).

The membership and scope of the work continued to grow. Within the second year of the Woman's Society, the membership grew to a total of 230. The women were busy making their pledges to missions, both at home and foreign. There were many places in Christ Methodist Church that needed the services of teaching, telephoning, visiting, preparing countless meals for church dinners, and preparing sandwiches and snacks for children and the youth groups.

✣ ✣ ✣

Executive Committee
1956–1957

President	Mrs. Fred M. Ridolphi
Christian Social Relations	Mrs. J. W. Pattinson
Vice President	Mrs. Charles Henderson
Student Work	Mrs. Samuel Mays
Recording Secretary	Mrs. Clarence Colby
Youth Work	Mrs. R. J. Drake
Treasurer	Mrs. Frank Walker
Children's Work	Mrs. Charles H. Johnson
Assistant Treasurer	Mrs. J. F. Bigger Jr.
Spiritual Life	Mrs. W. J. Templeton
Secretaries:	
Literature & Publications	Mrs. C. A. Birmingham
Missionary Education & Service	Mrs. Nat Dunn

Promotion	Mrs. Ned French
Status of Women	Mrs. Jack Byrne
Supply	Mrs. Gerald Owens

✣ ✣ ✣

Mrs. Clarence Colby (Margaret)
Third President of the Woman's Society of Christian Service Christ Methodist Church 1957–1958

Margaret Horton Colby was born in a Methodist parsonage in LaGrange, Tennessee, the first of four daughters of Dr. John L. and Ailean Horton.

Her earlier education was received in the Memphis schools, graduating from high school in St. Petersburg, Florida, and receiving her degree from Florida Southern College in Lakeland, Florida. Margaret married Clarence Colby at First Methodist Church in Memphis, Tennessee. They have two children: a son, Clarence (Budd) and a daughter, Irene. Both children are married and have three children each.

Margaret was the third president of the Woman's Society and had the distinction of serving as president on two different occasions. The first term was 1957–1958 and a later term was 1969–1970.

Margaret was well-schooled in Methodism and the work of the Methodist Women having grown up in a Methodist parsonage. During the years when Christ Methodist Church was beginning and services were held in the Plaza Theater, she and Mrs. Grant served as greeters and welcomed the people as they came to the worship services.

The Wesleyan Service Guild was named for Margaret and was known always as the Margaret Colby Wesleyan Service Guild. Mrs. V. A. Alexander (Bernice) was chairman of the Wesleyan Service Guild for the first term.

Margaret has served as Pink Lady for seventeen years at the Methodist Hospital, at the same time serving in several different offices in the Woman's Society, promoting fellowship and growth in wisdom, understanding, and relationship with God.

✣ ✣ ✣

EXECUTIVE COMMITTEE

1957–1958

President	Mrs. Clarence Colby
Christian Social Relations	Mrs. Ray Drenner
Vice President	Mrs. J. V. Cowan

Student Work	Mrs. Frank Prichard
Recording Secretary	Mrs. Ernest Felts
Youth Work	Mrs. R. J. Drake
Treasurer	Mrs. Frank Walker
Spiritual Life	Mrs. Robert Holt
Assistant Treasurer	Mrs. J. F. Bigger Jr.
Literature & Publications	Mrs. Russell Reeves
Secretaries:	
Missionary Education & Service	Mrs. Richard Taylor
Promotion	Mrs. Howard Boone
Status of Women	Mrs. W. H. Grumbles
Supply	Mrs. B. C. Adams

Helen Booth Felts was born in Tupelo, Mississippi, to Mr. and Mrs. George Booth. Her early years of education were in Tupelo. She received a degree from Mississippi State College for Women. Helen married Ernest Felts and they have two children: a son, Ernest, and a daughter Judy.

Helen Felts was elected as the fourth president of the Woman's Society of Christian Service in the year 1958 and was the first president to serve for two consecutive years concluding her term in 1960. During this time there were two persons who served as chairman of the Wesleyan Service Guild: they were Mrs. Sanford L. Jones and Miss Zetta Walker.

One of the highlights of these two years were the beautiful membership teas in which the Woman's Society honored their new members. Before there was a kitchen staff, the women served many of the meals. One of the big events each month was the serving of the dinner for the Methodist Men. Before the Fellowship Hall was built and in the summertime, some of the meals were served on the lawn of the cottage.

Executive Committee
1958–1959

President	Mrs. Ernest Felts
Vice President	Mrs. Sam Mays
Recording Secretary	Mrs. R. K. Weisinger
Treasurer	Mrs. J. M. Meadows
Assistant Treasurer	Mrs. W. H. Grumbles

Secretaries:	
Children's Work	Mrs. Frank Fisher
Christian Social Relations	Mrs. Ray Drenner
Literature & Publications	Mrs. Russell Reeves
Missionary Education & Service	Mrs. James Seabrook
Promotion	Mrs. Howard Boone
Spiritual Life	Mrs. Oscar Crofford
Status of Women	Mrs. Gerald Lewis
Student Work	Mrs. Frank Prichard
Supply	Mrs. B. C. Adams
Youth Work	Mrs. Charles Brown

EXECUTIVE COMMITTEE

1959–1960

President	Mrs. Ernest Felts
First Vice President	Mrs. Sam Mays
Second Vice President	Mrs. Horton DuBard
Recording Secretary	Mrs. Keith Weisinger
Treasurer	Mrs. J. M. Meadows
Assistant Treasurer	Mrs. Lorene McCallum
Secretaries:	
Children's Work	Mrs. Henry Harry
Christian Social Relations	Mrs. William Huff
Literature & Publications	Mrs. Jeans Pattinson
Missionary Education & Service	Mrs. Oscar Crofford
Promotion	Mrs. W. G. Farquhar
Spiritual Life	Mrs. Howard L. Davenport
Status of Women	Mrs. Walter Scott
Student Work	Mrs. Elmo Thompson
Supply	Mrs. Dennis Earles
Youth Work	Mrs. W. C. Armstrong

EXECUTIVE COMMITTEE

1960–1961

President	Mrs. George Atkinson
First Vice President	Mrs. Robert Lee Thomas

Mrs. Ernest Felts (Helen)
Fourth President of the Woman's Society of Christion Service Christ Methodist Church First President to Serve Two Consecutive Years 1958–1959, 1959–1960

Mrs. George Atkinson (Julia)
Fifth President of the Woman's Society of Christian Service Christ Methodist Church 1960–1961

Mrs. Samuel Mays (Eloise)
Sixth President of the Woman's Society of Christian Service Christ Methodist Church 1961–1962

Second Vice President	Mrs. Percy B. Whitenton
Recording Secretary	Mrs. Charles R. Tate
Treasurer	Mrs. J. Marion Meadows
Assistant Treasurer	Mrs. Lorene McCallum
Secretaries:	
Children's Work	Mrs. Henry Harry
Christian Social Relations	Mrs. J. F. Bigger Jr.
Literature & Publications	Mrs. Jeans Pattinson
Missionary Education & Service	Mrs. Oscar Crofford
Promotion	Mrs. W. G. Farquhar
Spiritual Life	Mrs. Frank Walker
Student Work	Mrs. Elmo Thompson
Supply	Mrs. Dennis Earles
Youth Work	Mrs. W. C. Armstrong

✣ ✣ ✣

Eloise Ragsdale Mays, a native Memphian and a charter member of Christ Methodist Church, married Samuel Hardwick Mays in Berlin, Germany, while serving with the 241st General Hospital. They have two children: a son, Samuel Hardy Mays Jr., and a daughter, Melissa Mays Robinson, and three grandchildren.

Eloise helped to set up the original kitchen, served as study leader in the circles, taught in the Sunday school, and worked with the youth.

When Eloise was asked about memorable experiences, she shared Nattie Louise Ruffin's advice on how to get to the church on time, "Dress the night before and stand in the corner." Her second comment told of the loving concern and marvelous cooperation of members that made assuming responsibility a joy.

✣ ✣ ✣

EXECUTIVE COMMITTEE

1961–1962

President	Mrs. Sam Mays
First Vice President	Mrs. Robert Lee Thomas
Second Vice President	Mrs. Oscar Crofford
Recording Secretary	Mrs. George Nowlin
Treasurer	Mrs. Y. O. Mitchell
Assistant Treasurer	Mrs. Harvey Pierce
Secretaries:	
Children's Work	Mrs. William H. Meadows Jr.
Christian Social Relations	Mrs. Roy Edmonds
Literature & Publications	Mrs. Fred Ridolphi
Missionary Education & Service	Mrs. James P. Briggs
Promotion	Mrs. Ralph McCool
Spiritual Life	Mrs. C. H. Cobb
Student Work	Mrs. James Robinson III
Supply	Mrs. Sam Stephenson
Youth Work	Mrs. C. W. Shaw
Chair, Local Church Activities	Mrs. Ernest Felts

✣ ✣ ✣

EXECUTIVE COMMITTEE

1962–1963

President	Mrs. John Tole
First Vice President	Mrs. Oscar Crofford
Second Vice President	Mrs. Ed Richmond Sr.
Recording Secretary	Mrs. George Nowlin
Treasurer	Mrs. Y. O. Mitchell
Assistant Treasurer	Mrs. Harvey Pierce
Secretaries:	
Children's Work	Mrs. William H. Meadows Jr.

Christian Social Relations	Mrs. Richard Taylor
Literature & Publications	Mrs. Fred Ridolphi
Missionary Education & Service	Mrs. James P. Briggs
Promotion	Mrs. Ralph McCool
Spiritual Life	Mrs. C. H. Cobb
Student Work	Mrs. W. C. Armstrong
Supply	Mrs. Sam Stephenson
Youth Work	Mrs C. W. Shaw
Chair, Local Church Activities	Mrs. John Whitsitt

✣ ✣ ✣

Mrs. Richmond, wife of Edward R. Richmond, was a charter member of Christ United Methodist Church, past president of the United Methodist Women, and secretary to the Board of Directors of the Mary Galloway Home.

She was the daughter of the late Dr. and Mrs. William Aycock of Millington, Tennessee, and was a graduate of the University of Tennessee in Knoxville, where she was a member of the Phi Mu Sorority.

For many years, Mrs. Richmond was a home economics teacher at Messick High School. At the time of her death, she was secretary-treasurer of B. R. Richmond and Company, Realtors. She died of a heart attack on April 12, 1975.

✣ ✣ ✣

Executive Committee

1963–1964

President	Mrs. Edward Richmond
Vice President	Mrs. James P. Briggs
Recording Secretary	Mrs. James Canfield
Treasurer	Mrs. B. C. Adams
Assistant Treasurer	Mrs. Hunter Barcroft
Secretaries:	
Children's Work	Mrs. Harry Johnson
Christian Social Relations	Mrs. Richard Taylor
Literature & Publications	Mrs. Sam Stephenson
Missionary Education & Service	Mrs. Ben Carpenter
Promotion	Mrs. Dwight Koenig
Spiritual Life	Mrs. Caruthers Ewing
Student Work	Mrs. W. C. Armstrong

Mrs. John Tole (Helen)
Seventh President of the Woman's Society of Christian Service Christ Methodist Church 1962–1963

Mrs. Edward R. Richmond (Mary)
Eighth President of the Woman's Society of Christian Service Christ Methodist Church Served Two Consecutive Years 1963–1964, 1964–1965

Mrs. Oscar Crofford (Bea)
Ninth President of the Woman's Society of Christian Service Christ Methodist Church Served Two Consecutive Years 1965–1966, 1966–1967

Supply	Mrs. C. P. Harris
Youth Work	Mrs. Orin Johnson
Chair, Local Church Activities	Mrs. John Whitsitt

✣ ✣ ✣

EXECUTIVE COMMITTEE

1964–1965

President	Mrs. Edward Richmond
Vice President	Mrs. Orin Johnson
Recording Secretary	Mrs. James Canfield
Treasurer	Mrs. St. Elmo Newton
Assistant Treasurer	Mrs. Jesse Anderson
Secretaries:	
Campus Ministry	Mrs. Howard Boone
Children's Work	Mrs. Harry Johnson
Christian Social Relations	Mrs. William Osceola Gordon
Missionary Education & Service	Mrs. Mack Hansbrough
Program Material	Mrs. Sam Stephenson
Promotion	Mrs. Dwight Koenig
Spiritual Life	Mrs. Jesse Joyner
Supply	Mrs. C. P. Harris
Youth Work	Mrs. S. W. Parry

✣ ✣ ✣

Executive Committee
1965–1966

President	Mrs. Oscar Crofford
Vice President	Mrs. Ernest Felts
Recording Secretary	Mrs. William Grumbles
Treasurer	Mrs. Jesse Anderson
Assistant Treasurer	Mrs. W. L. Gully
Secretaries:	
Campus Ministry	Mrs. C. K. Robinson
Christian Social Relations	Mrs. Early Mitchell
Membership Cultivation	Mrs. Clarence Colby
Missionary Education & Service	Mrs. Robert Utterback
Program Material	Mrs. Rufus Hayes
Spiritual Life Cultivation	Mrs. William Campbell
Supply Work	Mrs. Charles Newman
Local Church Activities	Mrs. Robert Lee Thomas

✣ ✣ ✣

Executive Committee
1966–1967

President	Mrs. Oscar Crofford
Vice President	Mrs. Orin Johnson
Recording Secretary	Mrs. William Grumbles
Treasurer	Mrs. St. Elmo Newton
Assistant Treasurer	Mrs. Jesse Anderson
Secretaries:	
Campus Ministry	Mrs. Bert Ferguson
Christian Social Relations	Mrs. Early Mitchell
Membership Cultivation	Mrs. Clarence Colby
Missionary Education & Service	Mrs. James Adams
Program Material	Mrs. Rufus Hayes
Spiritual Life Cultivation	Mrs. William Campbell
Supply Work	Mrs. Charles Newman
Local Church Activities	Mrs. Robert Lee Thomas

Mrs. Orin Johnson (Peggy)
Tenth President of the
Woman's Society of
Christian Service
Christ Methodist Church
1967–1968

Mrs. R. K. Weisinger (Joy)
Eleventh President of the
Women's Society of
Christian Service
Christ Methodist Church
1968–1969

EXECUTIVE COMMITTEE
1967–1968

President	Mrs. Orin Johnson
Vice President	Mrs. Emmett Marston
Recording Secretary	Mrs. Jeans Pattinson
Treasurer	Mrs. Jesse Anderson
Assistant Treasurer	Mrs. W. L. Gully
Secretaries:	
Campus Ministry	Mrs. C. K. Robinson
Christian Social Relations	Mrs. David Barcroft
Membership Cultivation	Mrs. Robert Carlock
Missionary Education	Mrs. L. E. Smith
Program Material	Mrs. St. Elmo Newton
Spiritual Life Cultivation	Mrs. Dan Farrar
Supply Work	Mrs. John Jennings
Local Church Activities	Mrs. Ralph Scherr

EXECUTIVE COMMITTEE
1968–1969

President	Mrs. R. Keith Weisinger
First Vice President	Mrs. Clarence Colby

Second Vice President	Mrs. Emmett Marston
Secretary	Mrs. Jeans Pattinson
Treasurer	Mrs. W. L. Gully
Assistant Treasurer	Mrs. Andrew Lasslo
Chairs:	
Christian Social Relations	Mrs. Jim Ellis
Local Church Responsibility	Mrs. Fred Ridolphi
Membership Cultivation	Mrs. Robert Brommer
Missionary Education	Mrs. L. E. Smith
Spiritual Growth	Mrs. LeRoy H. Pope
Supply Work	Mrs. John H. Jennings Jr.

HISTORY OF WORSHIP AT CHRIST METHODIST CHURCH

June 1955–May 1969

by Barbara Melton

The important task of planning worship services was being organized by the church's Steering Committee. A letter of invitation from the Steering Committee was sent on June 14, 1955, to "fellow Methodists," announcing the time and location of the first worship service, the name of the first pastor, and other pertinent information about the new church. On June 24, 1955, a follow-up letter was sent inviting persons to a church conference, for the purpose of formally organizing Christ Methodist Church and to become charter members. A telling commentary about the spirit of the founders of Christ Methodist Church is noticed on the stationery used for these first letters. Across the bottom of the page was written *Divine Worship Service at the Poplar Plaza Theater each Sunday Morning at 11:00* A.M.

On July 14, 1955, Dr. Charles W. Grant sent a letter to new members acknowledging his feelings about being the first pastor of "such a marvelous church with such an ambitious program and promising future." He also addressed the value of divine worship and how important it is for the family to regularly worship together. The letter continued and addressed the importance of Christian service, giving, prayer, and the wonderful enthusiasm prevalent in the congregation.

In October 1955, the first temporary building was constructed on the property at 4370 Poplar and called "The Little Chapel." Here Sunday evening services were held as well as various other meetings of the church.

A Christmas letter to the congregation in 1956 invited families and friends to the following programs and services:

Friday, December 21	Christmas in Song and Story
Sunday, December 23, 10:45 A.M.	Thrilling Christmas Music
	Dr. Grant's Christmas Sermon: God's Gift—Unspeakable, Indescribable, Inexpressible
5:00 P.M.	Christmas Vesper music by Sanctuary Choir, Chapel
Monday, December 24, 5:00–7:00 P.M.	Christmas Eve Holy Communion A come-and-go-as-you-wish communion

In June 1957, a special committee was appointed by Dr. Grant to promote and encourage attendance at Sunday night services. Russell Reeves was named chairman, and the committee included Earl Montgomery, Richard Stratton, Clark Hunt, John Tole, J. V. Cowan Jr., Jack Byrne, and Tom Logan. At a later board meeting it was suggested that the members of the board and the Men's Club should set the example for the entire church by attending the Sunday night services.

An assortment of letters were written by Dr. Grant to the congregation announcing and inviting them to special services: Holy Week, Easter, Loyalty Sunday, and Christmas. On March 1, 1958, the first unit of our church known as the Fellowship Hall was completed. It contained a temporary sanctuary-social hall combination, office area, classrooms, and kitchen. This is presently known as the Rash Building. In a board report in February 1958, Dr. Grant made mention of the numerous items that had been given as memorials, among them the lectern, baptismal font, the brass cross, and the pulpit Bible.

A March 3, 1958, board report first mentions the need for two identical services on Sunday mornings. A unanimous resolution was reached declaring that the church continue with one service until it could be determined that there was a need for two.

In April 1958 a motion was made by Clay Shelton to hold two services for a trial period but after some discussion was tabled.

✣ ✣ ✣

March 1958

On Saturday evening March 1, a prayer vigil was held as a preliminary to the first public worship service in the temporary sanctuary at 4488 Poplar. The sanctuary was open from 7:30 to 9:30 P.M. No offering, no music, no Communion, no preaching, just prayers of thanksgiving to God for all that had been accomplished through prayer and dedication of substance and self. There would be absolute silence throughout the prayer vigil. On March 2, the first service in the Fellowship Hall was held.

Bulletin Excerpt, March 1958

> ***Why is the pulpit in the temporary sanctuary moved to one side?*** For the churches who believe that at each Holy Communion Christ is resacrificed, the altar traditionally has been the center. Following the Reformation the pulpit became the center, symbolizing the centrality and availability of the Word. We believe Christ has been sacrificed *once for all* and that only Christ should be adored in worship, thus the cross becomes the symbol of His reconciling love. The pulpit is the symbol of God's Word to man in Christ. Really, it doesn't matter which is centered; both symbols

mean the same. On the Communion table we have a brass cross and two identical electrified candles, one on either side of the cross. These candles signify the divine and the human nature of Christ and, when lighted, they signify that He is the *Light of the World.* The origin of this usage may be connected with the necessity of using candles at the secret celebrations of Holy Communion in the catacombs. Probably, at first the candles had no other significance. Nevertheless, the symbolism is exalted and worthy of observances in all Christian churches, no matter how simple the form of worship.

MARCH 1958

A special meeting of the Official Board was held to decide if two identical services should be held on Palm Sunday and Easter Sunday. The motion carried unanimously.

OCTOBER 1958

Mr. Bert Ferguson presented a recommendation that the pastor select some laymen from the congregation to assist in the Sunday services. The motion was duly seconded and unanimously adopted.

The Pulpit Supply Committee announced that Rev. Marshall Morris would become the new associate minister.

Mr. John Parsons presented a motion, seconded by Clark Hunt, that two morning services (one at 8:30 A.M. and the other at 10:45 A.M.) begin the next Sunday. The motion carried unanimously. Dr. Grant would conduct the two morning services, and the new associate pastor would have charge of the Sunday evening services.

In a quarterly report to the Charge Conference in 1960, Dr. Grant expressed that he was most deeply concerned about what may be called the spiritual aspects of the church. He reported that, "it is easy to neglect these since there are so many other mundane demands." But he wanted to hold ever before the church the high spiritual ideals that Christ taught and exemplified: the importance of prayer, the strength that comes from thoughtful study of God's Word, the glory of divine worship in which the worshipper gets a glimpse of the beauty of His holiness, the rewards of a disciplined life, the essential elements of Christian stewardship.

A year later, on May 1, 1961, Dr. Grant reported the following concerning the church and worship: The strong heartbeat of the church is that "in Christ Church we must forever do away with mediocrity, must live on tiptoe and possess a clear vision." This means, of course, that "first things must be first," that we must put on a program of education second to none, present a full program of music with such heart appeal that people will cross the city to hear it, and have hours of divine worship that shall meet the spiritual needs of all our people. Dr. Grant then mentioned that the next gigantic undertaking is the construction of the sanctuary.

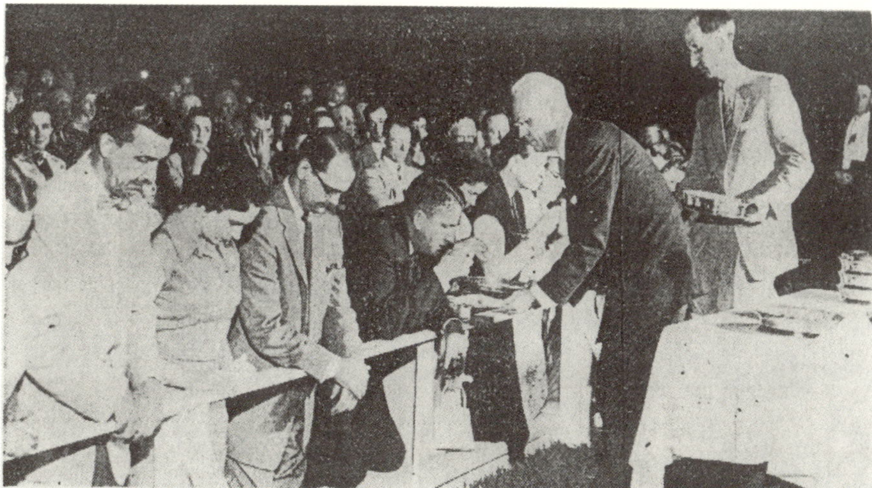

STARLIGHT COMMUNION—More than 250 members of the recently organized Christ Methodist Church gathered last night in front of their temporary office at 4370 Poplar to take part in the church's first communion services. Dr. Charles W. Grant (standing, left), pastor, officiated. He was assisted by communion steward Erie S. Henrich of 270 Goodwyn. The congregation plans a building in East Memphis. —Staff Phot

Communion on the grounds at the little cottage.

Dr. Grant often used the church bulletin to teach and express himself to the congregation. It was mailed to the homes of each member and doubled as a newsletter.

✣ ✣ ✣

Excerpts of Interest

Worship

> ***Quietness in God's House.*** The sanctuary of the church is a holy place. God's Spirit is there to commune with our spirit; to enfold us in His love and to give us strength for the living of these days. Therefore, as we come into the sanctuary of the church, let it be with a prayer in our hearts that we are worthy to meet Him there. Let us come quietly and in reverence, in spirit befitting those who would commune with God. Let us come without whispers and noise. If we must whisper, let our whispers be unto God.
>
> ***Worship.*** The world can be saved from political chaos and collapse by one thing only, and that is worship. To worship is to quicken the conscience by the holiness of God; to feed the mind with truth of God; to purge the imagination by the beauty of God; to open the heart to the Love of God; to devote the will to the purpose of God.
>
> —*Dr. Temple, Archbishop of Canterbury*

Worship is a technique for man's search after God. The elements of praise, prayer, confession, meditation and self-dedication allow the personal attitudes of worship to find expression. Music is the most articulate expression of praise and adoration. The Bible as an inspiring book of life links the contemporary worshippers with the generation of the past. Symbols on the altar and in the church windows are outward signs representative of qualities found in Christian experience. The cross upon the altar is a reminder of the element of sacrifice, which is central to Christian discipleship. Vestments of clergy and choir contribute to the beauty, dignity and reverence in public worship. All these elements of Christian worship are designed to successfully bridge the chasm between man and God. The church is a house of worship. Why not accept the invitation and come to church next Sunday?

✣ ✣ ✣

On April 3, 1961, at the Official Board Meeting of Christ Methodist Church the following motion was made by William Fones and seconded by Richard Oglesby: No person shall be turned away from the services of Christ Methodist Church because of color. The method of seating persons of color desiring to attend services shall be left to the discretion of the Ushers Committee. Motion passed. Resolution adopted. Recorded by H. Clay Shelton, acting secretary.

On November 1, 1964, the sanctuary, with seating capacity of 1,510, was opened for the first worship service. Dr. Grant reported in his quarterly report that, "Now that we are in our new sanctuary we are in a position to have more effective, penetrating and fruitful worship services, the goal of which is total dedication of our total membership." Additionally, in a report from Mrs. William Cazy Smith, chairman of the History and Records Committee, "November 1, 1964 was a momentous day in the life of Christ Church. The long-awaited sanctuary was opened for the first worship service. The soft strains of the organ, starting at 10:35 were a prelude to the service, with Byron Hudson, organist, at the console. Violin notes were also heard as Mrs. John Hendricks played. Seventh-grade boy volunteers, having been trained for the service, served as acolytes. The pew Bibles, a gift from a member, greatly enriched the participation in the worship."

Included in the church's Memorial Plaque Book is a listing of the memorials of stained-glass windows, Communion table, pews, etc. It was a thrilling service to every person present. The seating capacity is 1,510; however, the ushers estimated the congregation on this date to be 1,750. Eighteen new members were added on this date, bringing the membership to 2,001. Mr. Bob Sanford, as choir director, and members of the choir, along with others on the staff of the church made this a memorable service. Bishop Ellis Finger conducted the service for the formal opening of the sanctuary on December 27, 1964, with the declaration that "The Church be open for the worship of God and the service of men."

An interesting letter to the members of the Official Board contained the following information that this writer felt reflected the true spirit of Dr. Grant and his ministry:

> For many years now Mary Anna and I have dedicated Saturday evenings to intercessory prayer, because we feel intercessory prayer is so vital to vibrant and deeply spiritual services on Sunday. We are facing our pre-Easter revival, the challenge is so tremendous and the responsibility so great we feel we need your help in intercessory prayer, therefore, Mary Anna and I want to give you and your wife a personal invitation to join us in the Chapel. You and I know that if we have a spiritual awakening, such must come from God. Usually it is by way of prayer that spiritual awakenings come.

✣ ✣ ✣

Bulletin Cover Sunday April 19, 1964

Ten Commandments for Worshippers

1. Thou shalt not come to service late nor for the Amen refuse to wait.
2. When speaks the organ's sweet refrain thy noisy tongue thou shalt restrain.
3. But when the hymns are sounded out thou shalt lift up thy voice and shout.
4. And when the anthem thou shalt hear thy sticky throat thou shalt not clear.
5. The endemicity seat thou shalt leave free for more must share the pew with thee.
6. The offering plate thou shalt not fear but give thine uttermost with cheer.
7. Thou shalt the minister give heed nor blame him when thou art disagreed.
8. Unto thy neighbor thou shalt bend and, if a stranger, make a friend.
9. Thou shalt in every way be kind, compassionate, and of tender mind.
10. And so, by all thy spirit's grace thou shalt show God within this place.

—*Anonymous*

✣ ✣ ✣

Bulletin Cover, October 1964

> Next Sunday, November 1, 1964, at 10:45 A.M., we will hold our first divine worship service in our new Sanctuary. We are a happy and a grateful people. For many of us it will be one of life's highest hours. To better prepare our hearts for the occupancy of the sanctuary on Saturday, October 1, from 6:00–8:00 P.M. the sanctuary will be open—use front doors, please—and the membership is invited to drop in for prayer and meditation. There will be background music, no speaking. You may remain as long as you wish or make it as brief as you prefer. If we pray with dedication on Saturday evening, then on the Lord's day, we will be better able to give praise with great joy. Let us greet one another in our beautiful sanctuary and together worship our Lord.

✣ ✣ ✣

According to minutes of the board, October 3, 1966, the attendance average for the early service was two hundred. A motion was made and passed to continue these in the Fellowship Hall. Also, a motion was made and passed to hold the Sunday evening services in the Fellowship Hall.

November 7, 1966, minutes of the board report that the 8:30 A.M. Sunday morning service would be moved to the main sanctuary.

On May 2, 1966, the following report was submitted to the members of the Quarterly Conference by Dr. Grant:

> The first 18 months in our new sanctuary remind me of the adolescent boy. You know, he is characterized by long arms, big hands, big feet, and the changing voice. Growth usually comes before coordination is achieved; hence, he is at times clumsy and awkward, with the embarrassment for the up-and-down voice, the break in its pitch within one sentence while speaking. It's a situation that excites both sympathy and disgust, one for which he is not responsible but must pass through, one in which you can see both the man and the child. Out of this situation—because of his physical largeness—you expect strength and maturity but, due to the brevity of the years, you can see lingering lovable childhood.
>
> We have a large sanctuary for our membership. We have an enormous organ and the physical set-up for a tremendous program of music, a truly impressive service of the Sacrament of the Lord's Supper and almost any other type of service one could mention. For the most part the transition, or learning to effectively worship in our new sanctuary, has been made with

smoothness and great appreciation and cooperation on the part of most of our members and friends. There have been moments of awkwardness when, like the adolescent through lack of coordination, things have not been as effective as desired. Most of our people have been like understanding and sympathetic parents of an adolescent. Perhaps on a few occasions some have given way to emotional binges like exasperated parents, but these have been few and far between experiences. After reappraisals and reevaluations, most of these have brought to the church and its program a greater gain, not a loss. Changes for the better have been made and as the needs present themselves, additional changes can be made, always with the idea of upgrading and further enriching our divine worship services.

I do not see how one could have higher goals than we have had since the inception of the church; namely, divine worship services which shall be vitally spiritual, in which every person present has opportunity to participate in singing, reading the Scripture, praying, giving, enjoying Christian fellowship and has a divine confrontation, the climax of which Jesus Christ is crowned as Lord and Master of each worshipper. In many respects this will go down as our best year, for which we thank the membership and praise our Heavenly Father.

✣ ✣ ✣

The big news of 1969 included the change in senior ministers at Christ Church and the change in name for the church from Christ Methodist Church to Christ United Methodist Church. The name change was a result of a General Conference merger of The Methodist Church with the Evangelical United Brethren Church. On June 8, Dr. Grant preached his last sermon at Christ United Methodist Church after receiving another appointment. He had served as the senior minister for fourteen years. In his message to the congregation on his last Sunday as minister, Dr. Grant said, in part, "It has been my great joy to share in the dreams, decisions, the efforts and the rich fellowship of the past fourteen wonderful years as the pastor of Christ United Methodist Church. This Sunday, June 8, brings to a close the pastor-parishioner relationship but Christian friendship can and will continue."

✣ ✣ ✣

Description of Windows

R. Morland Kraus, Designer

Taking his cue from the name of the church, the designer, R. Morland Kraus, has used a Christ theme for these windows. That is, while the two large chancel windows have the traditional placement of the Old Testament on the left and the New Testament on the right as one views them, the Old Testament window is basically Messianic in character pointing to our Lord, while the window on the right contains various Christ symbols.

More specifically, the windows may be described as follows, reading from the top down:

Left chancel window.

> In the left chancel window, the six pointed Creator's Star is seen with six concentric circles, representing the six days of Creation, while the "off-shoot" motion from each circle symbolizes an act of creation. Below this is a burning bush remindful of the Call of Moses, while below this is the Star of David and Branch, starting our Messianic story, Jeremiah 23:5 ". . . I will raise unto David a righteous Branch and a King shall reign," and Jeremiah 33:15, ". . . I will cause a Branch of righteousness to grow up unto David."
>
> Our Lord is also referred to in the next symbol, the Rising Sun and Wings: Malachi 4:2, ". . . But unto you that fear my name shall the Sun of righteousness arise with healing in his wings."
>
> The circle is a symbol of Eternity, while the Cross and Flag represent a banner of righteousness and justice derived from Isaiah 11:10 " . . . There shall be a root of Jesse, which shall stand for an ensign of the people; to it shall the Gentiles seek: and his rest shall be glorious."
>
> The serpent of brass is also a Messianic symbol of Jesus Christ, who in John 3:14 recognized the incident of Moses lifting up this symbol to his people while in the wilderness as a type of His crucifixion: "And as Moses lifted up the serpent in the wilderness, even so must the Son of Man be lifted up."
>
> The water flowing below the Star of David is derived from Zechariah 13:1, ". . . In that day there shall be a fountain opened to the house of David and to the inhabitants of Jerusalem . . ." meaning a fountain for the cleansing of sin. The sun, moon and twelve stars represent Jacob, his wife and twelve sons—Numbers 24:17 ". . . There shall come a star

Right chancel window.

out of Jacob," while the ladder symbolizes Jacob the patriarch.

The Tablets represent the Old Law and the Ten Commandments, and the seven- branch candlestick is a symbol of ancient Old Testament worship of which Christianity is an extension, for Jesus said in Matthew 5:17, "Think not that I am come to destroy the law, or the prophets; I am not come to destroy, but to fulfill."

The right chancel window is devoted to the New Testament. At the top are the Greek letters ICXC, NIKA, meaning Jesus Christ, Victor (Over Death and Sin). The XP or Chi Rho is also a Greek monogram for Jesus Christ, and within circular form may also be seen the Greek letters Alpha and Omega. "I am Alpha and Omega, the beginning and the ending, saith the Lord . . ." Revelation 1:8. The fish is a rebus, meaning "Jesus Christ, Son of God, Savior," which was used extensively by the early Christians.

The sun appears again, but in different form with the IHC monogram, Greek monogram for Jesus. This coincides with the Old Testament reference from Malachi 4:2. The victorious Lamb holding the banner and standing on the book of seven seals (Revelation) is a universal symbol for Our Lord, while below is the cross representing His crucifixion. The circle on the cross contains thorns and a glorious crown suggesting that Jesus is King of Kings. Immediately below is the Easter lily and colors of Dawn representing the purity of Christ and His Resurrection. The descending dove symbolizes the Holy Spirit and Pentecost.

At the base of the window appears the Chalice and Host representing Communion wherein He left us a memorial and commanded us, "This do in remembrance of me," Luke 22:19. The side windows depict Christianity on the march with the pennants or banners (similar to that of the victorious Lamb) flying. The colors were selected for light control and to suggest the rich noble spirit of our faith.

The four balcony windows contain symbols of the four gospel writers suggested by the winged creatures in Revelation and the vision of Ezekiel. Instead of faces the open books (Gospels) appear with the names of the Evangelists. In the "Mark" window, the designer has tried to depict the theme of the gospel as telling of a victorious leader (Christ) with the banner of victory and the Chi Rho and Greek monogram ICXC, NIKA (Jesus Christ, Victor), relating this to the Chancel. Mark's Gospel is said to have been the first that was written. Matthew tells of Christ's lineage from the House of David (Star of David), and in this account may be found the Lord's Prayer.

Luke's Gospel relates the story of that first Christmas when the angels sang "Glory to God in the Highest." The Nativity Star is also shown as well as the Anchor of Hope. St. John tells of the Divine Nature of our Lord and the Kingdom of Heaven. He presents Jesus as the Messiah of the Old Testament, hence the Crown, and the victorious Lamb again, John 1:29, "Behold the Lamb of God."

The chapel windows contain symbols of five events in Our Lord's life, commencing with His Nativity or Incarnation. The other events are His Baptism, Sermon on the Mount, Death and Resurrection.

Upon leaving services it is hoped that inspiration to be found in these windows, and moreover in the Gospels themselves, will lead us to a better life.

R. Morland Kraus is a St. Louis native who studied at Washington University and then won a Louis Comfort Tiffany Fellowship in 1940 for further study in New York. In 1940–41 he was the Carnegie Resident Artist to Hendrix College, teaching and painting, and during the war, he was chief draftsman for the U.S. Army Map Service in St. Louis. Since the war, he has been an instructor at Washington University and has done extensive work in advertising as well as mosaics, stone carvings, and stained glass for churches and other buildings throughout the country.

The Jacoby Stained Glass Studios were founded in 1896 by Herman H. Jacoby, son of Ludwig Jacoby, the first Methodist bishop west of the Mississippi River. Alfred Oppliger joined Mr. Jacoby in this venture, and it is his grandsons, Oliver, Fred Jr., and William who now direct it. Their father, Fred Oppliger Sr., who started as a boy, still remains active although he officially retired some years ago. He is one of only five men to be elected a fellow of the Stained Glass Association of America, a national organization founded in 1903 to promote the finest development of the art and craft in this country.

During three generations' service to the church (and now starting on the fourth) the Jacoby firm has furnished many churches of all denominations and architectural styles throughout the land. Three installations in Memphis, in addition to the new sanctuary of Christ Methodist, include Baron Hirsch Synagogue, First United Lutheran, and the chapel of Idlewild Presbyterian.

At the present time Jacoby men are completing the installation of over two thousand square feet of faceted glass windows in the new one-million-dollar sanctuary of Trinity Methodist Church in Beaumont, Texas, and are about to begin on the faceted glass windows for the new Trinity Methodist Church, Kansas City, Kansas. Space is too limited to mention other installations, but we would add that all the glass used in the windows for Christ Methodist is mouth-blown antique from France, Germany, and West Virginia, being the finest available and noted for its variations in shadings from piece to piece.

✣ ✣ ✣

The Ministry of Music

Music is a medium for messages that make people weep and laugh and wonder and worship. Music walks with young lovers to the altar of marriage. Music is a ladder upon which prayers climb to heaven. Music calls the wanderer home. Music is a comforting companion before an open grave. Music lifts the soul from the depths of despair. Music captures the heart of a king and the heart of a king's servant. Music tells the story that saves. Music is both mystery and miracle, for music is an instrument of God.

The Choir

The role of a church musician is a multifaceted opportunity and responsibility. The majority of a congregation sees the musicians (director, organist, choir members) only at Sunday morning worship, so it is difficult for them to appreciate that there is more involved than merely showing up for church. Countless hours are spent in rehearsal during the week, time needed at home to review notes, the need to leave Sunday school class early to practice or warm up in preparation for the worship service. Church music is a gift from God, which is nurtured (in rehearsals, planning, and preparation), multiplied (as individuals and ensembles), and returned (in worship and service). Music stirs the hearts and minds of both performer and hearer in ways that no other element of worship can. There is an old Quaker proverb that says, "Where many candles are brought together, there is more light." Singing in a choir is much like this proverb. This is one of the greatest benefits of singing in a church choir.

In the Beginning

The first service at Christ Methodist Church was on June 19, 1955, at the Plaza Theater.

Jesse Anderson was the first choir director. Rehearsals were held in the home of Mrs. Herbert (Mabris) Dunkman where she served as accompanist. There were about eighteen members. On Sundays at the theater, the choir sat in front of the congregation facing the stage. When it was time for the music portion of the service, the choir stood, raised their seats, and turned to face the congregation.

Soon Dr. George Muns was employed as a part-time director and Mrs. Byron (Jesalyn) Hudson was added to the staff as organist. Dr. Muns resigned

August 25, 1957, to accept an offer at Delta State College, Cleveland, Mississippi, to become head of the department of music.

Robert L. Sanders Jr. became director on September 1, 1957. The Fellowship Hall Building was opened March 1, 1958. The choir room was located on the third floor. In order to reach the sanctuary, they would descend the steps for the processional. This became a traffic jam of sorts, as worshippers coming in from outside would then be in the way. After services, the choir would then attempt to return to the third floor and again would be forced to work their way through the departing worshippers. There was a door behind the organ leading to a ramp so many decided to leave through there, run down the ramp, and then walk up three flights of stairs to return to the choir room. Even so this was faster than going through the crowd, but we couldn't help but wonder why the architect would design a building with so little consideration for the needs of the choir.* Also the stained-glass windows played havoc on the faces of the women in the choir. Of course they were glad when the sanctuary was built.

*Comment: The Fellowship Hall (today's Rash Building) was built for the purpose its name implies, only to be used temporarily as a sanctuary. Also, in these early years we had to stay within budgetary limits since we had no history for giving.

On October 18, 1964, the cornerstone of the sanctuary was laid. The sanctuary was opened for worship on November 1. At the first service, Mrs. Hudson was at the console of the new organ and Mrs. John (Gloria) Hendricks, a member of the Memphis Symphony Orchestra, played the violin. Built by M. P. Moler, the organ included fifty-five ranks of pipes with electropneumatic action and a movable console. The antiphonal division is located in the balcony but all other pipes are located above and on both sides of the chancel area. The Schulmerich Carillon was installed in 1969 and was a gift from Kemmons Wilson, founder of Holiday Inns, as a memorial to his mother, Ruby Wilson. It is known as the Americana Carillon. It is actually an electromechanical bell in which tiny bronze rods of bell metal are struck by tiny hammers of clappers to produce the tones of either Flemish-tuned or English-tuned bells. The carillon can be played from the keyboard of the organ console or heard exclusively inside the sanctuary. Mr. and Mrs. Jack Renshaw donated the money to cover the purchase price of the organ in honor of their children, Dorothy, Cecile, and Robert Jarrett.

Prior to the completion of the sanctuary, a meeting was held to discuss placement of the choir. It was suggested that the choir be seated on the organ side facing the opposite direction with the director conducting from that side. The idea was to have an unobstructed view of the altar. Also, it was suggested that a screen be placed in front of the choir to hide them from the congregation when they were seated. This was met with dismay among the choir members and the protests were strong. They argued that they only wanted to be heard from the best possible location and this could not be done if the architect and the committee had their say. Finally, the choir's reasoning prevailed and the location was as it is now.

In the early days of the sanctuary, wasps seemed to have found a home in the attic. Occasionally they would descend to the sanctuary during services with the choir being the main target. So it was not unusual for them to land on the shoulders of the choir members, who were dodging them with movements not usually seen at a worship service. To get swatted on your back by a hymnal only meant a wasp had landed there. Maintenance men crawled around in the attic at various times and eventually destroyed their home base. There was nearly always a solo in the order of worship so it was especially difficult to sing with a wasp buzzing around your face. Hopefully, the congregation assumed the body movements of the soloist were due to the emotion experienced in the song.

When Dr. Grant prayed at the worship service, he always began it with the following:

Lean thine arm on the windowsill of heaven and gaze upon thy God.
Then with the vision in thy heart, turn strong to meet thy day.

—Author Unknown

Roger Watson was in the choir and decided to put these words to music. It was effectively done by the choir, and it pleased Dr. Grant.

✣ ✣ ✣

From the Bulletin of November 8, 1964

> The organ prelude is a veil dropped between everyday life and the sanctuary; in crossing the threshold, the music should separate the world without from the world within. Let us cease conversation with each other and use this organ prelude for quiet meditation and communion with God in preparation for the worship service.

Paul D. Shultz joined the staff February 1965 after serving more than twelve years at First Presbyterian Church in Tulsa, Oklahoma. He organized and trained four choirs in addition to the Chancel Choir. On May 30, the combined choirs of 184 voices presented the first Spring Festival of Choirs. Mrs. Hudson resigned, and Kenton Stellwagen replaced her as organist. Paul was a fine Christian gentleman and would give beautiful and meaningful devotionals at staff meetings. His wife, Gerrie, sang in the choir and their daughter, Jennifer, was a member of the youth choir. Their son, James, was a medical student in Dallas. Despite his background and dedication to the music, Paul was not popular with the masses. Some complained that he should be more of a songleader, although he was not hired for that purpose. Paul was more of an introvert, quiet and unassuming but very likeable. So Paul was eventually dismissed, much to the regret of those who knew him well. He composed a benediction response for the choir to sing. From Isaiah 6:8, it became the all-time favorite of the congregation and was often requested even after Paul left.

Kenton Stellwagen was a brilliant musician but somewhat of a character. He did not always adhere to the rules expected of an organist. Sometimes Ken would leave the organ during the sermon to grab a cup of coffee at a nearby coffee shop and once did not get back in time for the closing hymn which had to start without him. Finally Ken had an opportunity to go to Paris to study with the renowned Marcel Dupre who was quite old. Ken was worried for fear Mr. Dupre would die before he could take advantage of this opportunity. Ken was very likable so before he left, a party was given for him at the home of Mr. and Mrs. Wade Smith. Glenn Ragland and Marion Bolks sang a parody to the tune of "I Love Paris." In part they sang:

We'll miss Kenton in the springtime.
We'll miss Kenton in the fall.
We'll miss Kenton every Sunday when we're singing,
Wishing he would look at Paul.

Ken took this very good-naturedly, knowing we were referring to the many times he was not watching when Paul needed his attention. A letter from him during his stay in Paris described his joy to be able to study under the eminent Monsieur Dupre and also with Jean Langlais, a blind organist. It seemed to be the fulfillment of all Ken's dreams.

In April of 1967, Ray Stidham became organist and stayed until December when Emily (Mrs. J. W.) McAllister joined the staff as organist.

Children's and Youth's Choirs in Fellowship Hall. Mrs. Lady Somervell, director.

Jane Taylor, Pat Carson, and Glenn Ragland formed a trio that sang beautifully on many special occasions as well as in worship services for several early years of the church.

An unfortunate situation occurred while Ray was organist. He announced that Van Cliburn and Leonard Bernstein were coming to Christ Church for a concert. Twin pianos were bought for this occasion and everyone was very excited at the thought of having these two musical giants in our midst. However, it was soon learned that none of this was true. Of course, there was a great deal of embarrassment all around. It was learned that Ray was having problems, which was the only explanation for this story.

Emily was a marvelous musician and worked well with Paul. She graduated from the University of Arkansas with a B.S.E. in music education and Memphis State University with a master's degree in organ. She had played organ in churches in Fayetteville, Arkansas; Biloxi, Mississippi; St. Louis, Missouri; and Memphis. She is a certified director of music in the United Methodist Church. In 1972, Emily was elected to Outstanding Young Women of America. When Paul left, Emily resigned out of loyalty to him (August 19 1968).

On September 1, 1968, Mr. and Mrs. Charles H. Noble Jr. began their work in the music department. They had been choir director and organist at First Methodist Church in Sebring, Florida. Mr. Noble was listed as a local preacher and the following groups were under his direction: Chancel Choir, Men's Chorus, Men's Quartet, Children's Chorus Youth Choir, an Interpretative Choir, and a Girls' Ensemble. Additionally, some of his time was to be spent in home visitation and recruitment.

Despite all this, Mr. Noble was not popular with choir members from the very beginning and membership declined. Mr. Noble realized this and resigned to accept a position in Kentucky effective July 1, 1969.

CHOIR DIRECTORS

Jesse Anderson
1955–1956

Paul Shulz
1965–1968

Not Pictured:

Dr. George Muns
1956–1957

Robert L. Sanders
1957–1965

Charles H. Noble
1968–1969

ORGANISTS

Kenton Stellwagen
1965–1966

Ray Stidham
April 1967–December 1967

Emily McAllister
Fall 1968–August 1968

Not pictured:
Mrs. Herbert (Mabris) Dunkman 1955–1956
Mrs. Byron (Jesalyn) Hudson 1956–1957

HISTORY OF THE FRIDAY MORNING MEN'S INTERCESSORY PRAYER GROUP

by Paul McQuiston

In mid-summer 1961 Dr. Charles Grant, "with a vision in his heart," addressed the Methodist Men's evening meeting. He went to great lengths to explain in detail his concept of prayer and his hope for a viable men's prayer group in the church. In his enthusiastic effort to inspire the men at the meeting to accomplish his mission of a prayer proup, Dr. Grant literally preached a sermon:

> From the eighteenth chapter of St. Luke's Gospel we read that Christ was never far away from communion with God through prayer. It was His consistent source of strength and guidance. It was His personal way of giving thanks for the spiritual and material blessings He received. With His simple commission "Men ought always to pray," He opens the way for each of us to find an unlimited source of strength and humility.
>
> He not only opens the way but also by parables and personal examples He gives us prayer patterns to be followed. Most of His prayers were private and unrecorded. His best-known example is our *Lord's Prayer*, which is the most complete prayer we have. In the parable of the Pharisee and the Publican, He lays stress on the most important condition for prayer, sincere humility. Without this quality no prayer can have meaning.
>
> For the past few weeks we have been seeking to find out if there is a feeling of need among men of Christ United Methodist Church for a men's prayer group. We know that the ladies are far ahead of us in this field, and we want to catch up. Our first task is to find out what a prayer group is, how it operates, and what it can do. Tonight, we would like to share our findings with you.
>
> First we have learned that a prayer group is a small, intimate comradeship, united in a common commitment which through regular group discipline seeks spiritual power and direction. It comes into being because of a spontaneous feeling of need in the lives of those who make it up. What is our most basic need? It is the need for relatedness, the need to love. By love we mean a capacity for the experiences of concern, responsibility, respect, and understanding of other persons. But this horizontal relatedness to others is not enough. We also need the vertical relationship with God that gives us the depth to seek and understand salvation. When we establish this double relatedness of man to man and of man to God, we will find salvation. In seeking this relationship we must assume that there is a power more than human that rests in the heart at the innermost core of every man, and that at the same time this power pervades the whole universe, not only pervading it, but giving it being, life, and meaning. We must further assume that this power can come into the world only through the lives of men and women who

seek it and open themselves to it. This seeking and opening has been found far more effective and easier done when people ban together to give mutual assistance in the seeking.

A group of dedicated people banded together in prayer have a latent power that cannot only transform their lives, but also vitalize or revitalize a whole congregation. The power is there, but the conditions for releasing it must be just right.

The first right condition for transforming a collection of individuals into a group with power is fellowship. There must be a feeling of intimacy, a sense of belonging and concern for one another.

The second right condition is mutual strengthening. Even in small, intimate groups, there is power in united action puffing toward a common goal.

A third right condition is mutual enlightenment. Through sharing experiences in Christian witnessing, we find directions for expressing our spiritual powers.

The fourth right condition is corporate inspiration. This is where we gain the confidence in our abilities to grow spiritually and to be stronger witnesses for Christ and His Church.

Having determined what a prayer group is, we need to find out how it operates or functions. For a prayer group to have the intimacy that is its basic strength, it must remain small in numbers. Let me hasten to add that we have room and need for as many prayers in Christ Methodist Church as there are men and women who will respond. The size of each group can be determined by each group as it determines its programs and goals.

Each group can set its goals to fit the intimate talents and needs of its membership. Some groups follow lecture-type devotions; others have panel-type studies; and some become Bible Study Groups. But all prayer groups must spend a large part of each meeting in prayer. The earnestness, sincerity, and humility in our prayers reveal to us our spiritual depths, strengths, weaknesses, and from these we determine our desires to improve our being.

When we see what a prayer group is and how it operates, we can, by maintaining two minimum disciplines, regular attendance and daily private devotions, go as far and as wide as we wish in our quest for salvation. The basic character trait of worship to God is inherent in each of us. The strength of a small, intimate prayer group can be the means of releasing it.

MEN'S PRAYER BREAKFAST

In 1961 when Dr. Grant preached his "prayer sermon" to the men, Christ United Methodist Church had a membership of 1,579. Dr. Grant appointed a three-man committee, consisting of Dr. W. J. Templeton, chairman, Paul G. McQuiston Jr., and Bert Carnahan, to plan and oversee a men's prayer group. The first meeting would be September 22, 1961—a breakfast and devotional meeting lasting from 6:45 until 7:40 A.M. At this meeting Carnahan led the first devotional and then took prayer requests from Dr. Grant, Bill Gully, Dr. Charles Newman, and other men present. At this first meeting, Carnahan focused on the why, where, and how to have a men's prayer group by using the four points for releasing prayer power that Dr. Grant had explained in his organizational and inspirational sermon. Carnahan concluded with his own spiritual autobiography, which created a personal and closer fellowship within the group. Each week the committee members took turns leading the devotionals using as their sources pamphlets, articles, and books dealing with the subject of prayer. One source they used was Rosalind Rinker's book on conversational prayer as a guide for a more meaningful dialogue with God.

As the men's prayer breakfast began to show signs of success, the leaders used more pamphlets to promote a lay prayer movement. The following letter, dated July 31, 1961, was addressed to Dr. Templeton at 235 West Cherry Circle with a copy to Paul McQuiston at 527 North White Station Road:

> Dear Dr. Templeton:
>
> As I mentioned to you in person, I think two good men to assist you in promoting a lay prayer movement will be Bill Gully, 4690 Normandy, and Bert Carnahan, 5111 Sequoia. I shall cooperate in every way.
>
> Cordially, Charles W. Grant
> cc Mr. Paul McQuiston

The first pamphlet, used to encourage a deeper prayer commitment, was mailed by Dr. Grant to each member of the church who had attended a prayer breakfast:

> This personal prayer inventory is being sent to each member of the church who has attended our prayer breakfast. Paul McQuiston and I thought it might prove valuable to you. We trust you can arrange your program to be with us regularly each Friday at 7:00 A.M. It's a very rich and rewarding hour. Whether you attend or not, be sure to remember our ever-increasing church program in your prayers.
>
> Cordially, Charles W. Grant

Paul McQuiston delivered the second devotional on September 29, 1961, and Dr. W. J. Templeton followed on October 6. Dr. Howard Boone gave the October 27, 1961, devotional. Dr. Boone passed out slips of paper and asked each man present to write his prayer request and return it to him for later in prayer time. As years passed, different men filled in from time to time with the devotionals, thus assisting the three-man committee. For instance, David Ben Como could always deliver a quality devotional on short notice. He often used this poem he composed:

Wayfarer's Prayer

I will follow the upward road today;
I will keep my face to the light;
I will think high thoughts as I go my way;
I will do what I know is right.
I will look for the flowers by the side of the road;
I will laugh and love and be strong;
I will learn to lighten another one's load;
This day as I fare along.

This poem is posted in the Bible Class Sunday school room.

C. R. McDaniel voluntarily took the job of calling the regular members when they were absent on Friday morning. As time passed, people's lives changed, thus reflecting changes in the men's prayer breakfast group. Bert Carnahan transferred back to Chicago to work with Cudahay Packing Company, and Paul McQuiston's teaching duties in Jackson, Tennessee, prevented his regular attendance for quite some time. Sewell Dunkin recorded prayer requests each week until Roger Watson voluntarily assumed this duty. He organized a permanent list of prayer requests to be used week after week.

The kitchen staff prepared weekly a buffet-style breakfast, much to the good fortune of the men. A highlight of the breakfasts was Fanny's pastries. On occasions when the kitchen staff took a holiday, the men would undertake the duties of cooking. Marion "Mose" Meadows quickly acquired a reputation for his crisp, delicious bacon.

The Reverend Howard Rash began his ministry at Christ Church in June 1963 as the associate pastor of the church and immediately became an active participant in the Men's Intercessory Prayer Group. Reverend Howard Rash soon began bringing the list of those in hospitals, notices of deaths in our church family, and other communications including prayer requests from the church staff. He gradually assumed responsibility for the devotional leaders by developing a list for each month of the year and scheduling the men to take leadership of the Friday meetings for a month at a time.

In June 1969 Dr. Grant, our beloved founding pastor, originator and regular participant in our Men's Prayer Breakfast Group, was reassigned to the Grace United Methodist Church, Whitehaven, Tennessee.

APPENDIX

The Official Boards, Commissions, and Committees

Board Chairmen and Lay Leaders 1955–1969

James H. Seabrook
Chairman
1955–1957

Howard L. Davenport
Lay Leader, 1955–1957
Chairman, 1957–1959

Dr. Howard A. Boone
Lay Leader
1957–1959

John A. Parsons
Chairman
1959–1961

Dr. W. J. Templeton
Lay Leader
1959–1961

Edgar H. Tenent
Chairman
1961–1963

Robert Lee Thomas
Lay Leader
1961–1962

Board Chairmen and Lay Leaders 1955–1969

George Roberts
Lay Leader
1962–1964

Keith Weisinger
Chairman
1963–1965

Ernest Felts
Lay Leader
1964–1965

Jesse A. Anderson
Chairman
1965–1967

Bert Ferguson
Lay Leader
1965–1967

Ed Richmond Sr.
Chairman
1967–1969

Dr. Tom Shipmon
Lay Leader
1967–1969

THE OFFICIAL BOARD

1955–1956

James H. Seabrook, Chairman, June 1955–1957
Howard L.Davenport, Lay Leader, June 1955–June 1957
Lee McCormick, First Vice Chairman
Fred Ridolphi, Second Vice Chairman
Charles Tate, Secretary
Jesse Anderson
Charles Baker
Roy Barron
Earle Billings
Howard Boone
Jack Byrne
Tom Campbell
James Canfield
Hugh Carey
Jack Caskey
James Clay Jr.
Clarence Colby
L. A. Conolly
Charles Cunningham
Harry F. DeZonia
James Doyle
Dr. Horton G. DuBard
Herbert Dunkman
Ray Drenner
William Drenner
Dennis Earles
J. B. Emerson
Ned French
Haskell Gass
Fred Graham
William Grumbles
E. C. Handorf
B. F. Hardin
C. P. Harris
Henry Harry
Horace Harwell
Leland Helms
John Huckabee
J. C. Ingram Jr.
Harry Johnson Jr.
Charles Johnston
Jesse Joyner
Keith Kelley
Frank Liddell
W. K. Martak
Sam Mays
Porter McClean
Ralph McCool
C. R. McDaniel
J. M. Meadows
Early Mitchell
York Mitchell
Earl Montgomery
D. A. Noel
Frank Prichard
Sam Reid
E. R. Richmond
Lloyd Sarber
Clay Shelton Jr.
Carey Stanley Sr.
H. C. Stroup
W. J. Templeton
Edgar Tenent
Jesse Vineyard
Russell Weaver
Percy Whitenton
W. A. Wren
Paul Yarbrough

Board of Trustees

Howard L. Davenport, Chairman
James T. Canfield
C. P. Harris
C. R. McDaniel
John Parsons
W. J. Templeton
Edgar Tenent

Finance Commission

Hugh Carey
Jack Caskey
Howard L. Davenport
Jesse Joyner
Lee McCormick
C. R. McDaniel
John Parsons
Edgar Tenent

Membership and Evangelism

W. K. Martak, Chairman
Charles Baker
Joanne Dixon
Jac M. Gates
Mrs. Richard Kite
Earl Montgomery
J. H. O'Donnell
Jeans Pattinson

Mrs. W. J. Templeton
Mrs. Percy Whitenton

Committees

Music
Jesse Anderson, Chairman
Ernest Felts
Ned French
Frank Prichard
Henry C. Roberts

Attendance for the Board
Charles Tate, Chairman
Clarence Colby
Herbert Dunkman
Leland Helms
Keith Kelley
Early Mitchell
R. E. Stratton

Audit
D. A. Noel
Donald T. Hall

Collectors and Ushers
W. J. Templeton, Chairman
Roy Barron
Earle Billings
L. A. Conolly
James Doyle
Haskell Gass
Jac Gates
Ernest Hall
J. C. Ingram
Ralph McCool
Charles McVean
Sam Reid
E. R. Richmond
Nelson Wilson

Communion Stewards
Dr. & Mrs. Jesse Suitor, Chairman
Mr. & Mrs. C. A. Birmingham
Mr. & Mrs. Erie Hendrich

Good Literature
J. D. Huckabee, Chairman
Fred Graham
B. F. Hardin
Charles Johnston

House
J. T. Canfield, Chairman
Nat P. Dunn
Porter McClean
J. M. Meadows
W. A. Wren

Insurance
Frank Liddell, Chairman
Charles Cunningham
Frank Fisher
W. A. Wren

Legal Counsel
Jesse Vineyard

Pastoral Relations
James H. Seabrook, Chairman
C. A. Cunningham
Howard L. Davenport
John Parsons
Edgar Tenent

Publicity
William Grumbles, Chairman
James Curry
Barry DeZonia
H. C. Stroupe
Paul Yarbrough

Resolutions
H. Jennings Goza Jr., Chairman
Dennis Earles
Ralph McCool

Church School
Harry Johnson Jr., Superintendent

Commission on Education
William H. D. Fones, Chairman
Ben Carpenter
J. B. Emerson
Mrs. C. P. Harris
Mrs. Leland Helms
Mrs. C. M. Henderson
Harry Johnson Jr.
Sam Mays
W. J. Templeton

M.Y.F.
Corinne Ridolphi

Nominations
Jesse Anderson
Jack Askew
Dr. Howard Boone
Howard L. Davenport
Ernest Felts
Harry Johnson

Lee McCormick
James H. Seabrook
Dr. W. J. Templeton

Architects and Building
E. Handorf, Chairman
Harry A. Johnson Jr.
Lee McCormick

Commission on Missions
William Drenner,
Chairman
Ray Drenner
Dr. Horton G. DuBard
Haskell Gass
William H. Grumbles
Leland Helms
Mrs. Porter McClain
James Seabrook
Charles Tate
Mrs. Percy Whitenton

Stewardship Committee
Howard Boone,
Chairman
James Arnette
Earle Billings
Jack Byrne
James N. Clay Sr.
Jesse Joyner
Y. O. Mitchell
Gerald Owens
C. P. Stanley Sr.
Russell Weaver

Welcome
C. R. McDaniel,
Chairman
Jack Caskey
Harry F. DeZonia
Forest Dowling Jr.
Ray Drenner
C. P. Harris
Horace Harwell
R. H. Norris
Jeans Pattinson
Fred Ridolphi
Percy Whitenton

Junior Official Board
J. B. Emerson, Chairman
C. P. Harris
Harry Johnson
Sam Mays
Clay Shelton Jr.

THE OFFICIAL BOARD
1956–1957

James H. Seabrook,
Chairman
Howard L. Davenport,
Lay Leader, June
1956–June 1957
Jesse Anderson
George Atkinson
Charles W. Baker
Roy W. Barron
Dr. J. F. Bigger Jr.
Earle N. Billings
Harold R. Benson
Dr. Howard Boone
Leon Burkett
Jack P. Byrne
James T. Canfield
Jack B. Caskey
James N. Clay Jr.
L. A. Conolly
Charles A. Cuningham
Moody B. Cunningham
Robert J. Drake
Ray E. Drenner
William E. Drenner
Dr. Horton G. DuBard
James F. Duncan Jr.
Nat Dunn
Sam Dunn
J. B. Emerson
Ernest T. Felts
Frank Fisher
William H. D. Fones
Ned M. French
Jac Gates
William H. Grumbles
E. E. Handorf
C. P. Harris
Henry H. Harry
Leland Helms
Dr. Robert T. Holt
Archie Hoss
Donald T. Hull
Harry A. Johnson Jr.
Charles H. Johnston
D. Keith Kelley
Richard R. Kite
Alfred W. Lenz
Dr. Neil J. Leonard

Frank Liddell
Thomas J. Loberg
William K. Martak
Samuel H. Mays
Ralph McCool
Lee McCormick
C. R. McDaniel
Charles A. McVean
William H. Meadows
William C. Mieher
Early Mitchell
D. A. Noel
Robert H. Norris
James H. O'Donnell Jr.
Felix Overton
John A. Parsons
Jeans W. Pattinson
Dr. Frank Prichard
Russell Reeves
Jack Renshaw
Edward R. Richmond
Fred Ridolphi
Mrs. Fred Ridolphi
George T. Roberts
H. Clay Shelton Jr.
H. S. Spragins
Richard E. Stratton
Dr. Jesse Suitor
Richard Taylor
Charles R. Tate
Dr. W. J. Templeton
Edgar H. Tenent
John H. Tole
James L. Vance
Jesse Vineyard
Keith Weisinger
Percy B. Whitenton
John C. Whitsitt
Harry J. Woodbury Jr.
Jesse D. Wooten
Paul Yarbrough

Board of Trustees
Howard L. Davenport, Chairman
James T. Canfield
C. R. McDaniel
John A. Parsons
Dr. W. J. Templeton
Edgar H. Tenent

Finance Commission
Edgar H. Tenent, Chairman
Hugh Carey
Jack Caskey
Herbert Dunkman
Jesse Joyner
Alfred W. Lenz
Lee McCormick
C. R. McDaniel
Russell Reeves
George Roberts
James Seabrook
Carey P. Stanley Sr.

Ex Officio Members
Howard L. Davenport
Bill Drenner
Mrs. Rosaline Ford
John Parsons
Pastor

Membership and Evangelism
William K. Martak, Chairman
George Atkinson
Charles W. Baker
J. J. Bledsoe
Russell Bramblet
Natalie Dunn
Nick French
Jac Gates
C. P. Harris
Henry H. Harry
Richard Kite
William C. Mieher
Earl Montgomery
Robert H. Norris
James J. O'Donnell Jr.
Felix Overton
Lloyd J. Sarber
Mrs. Richard Taylor
James L. Vance
John C. Whitsitt

Ex Officio Members
Ernest Felts
Harry Johnson Jr.
Mrs. W. J. Templeton

Committees

Music
Jesse Anderson, Chairman
Mrs. L. A. Conolly
Forrest Dowling Jr.
Dr. Frank Prichard
Dr. Henry O. Roberts

Attendance for Board
Charles R. Tate, Chairman
Roy W. Barron
Ned French

Audit
Donald T. Hull
D. A. Noel

Collectors
Dr. W. J. Templeton, Chairman
James F. Duncan Jr.
Sam Dunn
Robert Ford
Haskell Gass
Ernest Hail
Dr. Robert Holt
Archie Hoss
J. C. Ingram Jr.
Charles A. McVean
Felix Overton
Sam Reid
David Stanley

Communion Stewards
Mr. & Mrs. Erie S. Henrich
Dr. & Mrs. Jesse Suitor

Good Literature
Thomas Loberg, Chairman
Robert J. Drake
Charles H. Johnston

House
J. T. Canfield, Chairman
Nat P. Dunn
J. Porter McClean
J. Marion Meadows
W. A. Wren
Paul Yarbrough

Insurance
Frank Liddell, Chairman
Lloyd A. Conolly
Frank Fisher
Horace Harwell
W. C. Mieher

Legal Counsel
Jesse Vineyard

Pastoral Relations
James Seabrook, Chairman
Howard Boone
Howard L. Davenport
John Parsons
E. H. Tenent

Church School
Harry A. Johnson Jr., Superintendent

Commission on Education
William H. D. Fones, Chairman
Ben Carpenter
J. B. Emerson Jr.
Mrs. C. P. Harris
Mrs. Leland Helms
Mrs. C. M. Henderson
Harry A. Johnson Jr.
Sam Mays
W. J. Templeton

Architects and Building
E. C. Handorf, Chairman
Jesse Anderson
Harry A. Johnson Jr.
Lee B. McCormick
Jesse Vineyard

Commission on Missions
William Drenner, Chairman
Ray Drenner
Dr. Horton G. DuBard
Haskell Gass
William H. Grumbles
Leland Helms
Mrs. Porter McClain
James Seabrook
Charles Tate
Mrs. Percy Whitenton

Committees

Publicity
William H. Grumbles, Chairman
James Curry
Barry DeZonia
Harry Woodbury Jr.

Resolutions
H. Jennings Goza Jr., Chairman
Charles Cunningham
Dr. Robert T. Hoit
Dr. Neil J. Leonard
Ralph McCool

Stewardship
Dr. Howard Boone, Chairman
James Arnette
E. W. Atkinson
Earl Billings
Jack Byrne

James N. Clay
Clarence Colby
Harry F. DeZonia
Jac Gates
Richard Kite
C. R. McDaniel
Earl Montgomery
Gerald Owens
Russell Weaver

Welcome
Ernest Felts, Chairman
P. D. Clarkson
Forest Dowling Jr.
Floyd Harvey
R. H. Norris
Jeans Pattinson
Jack Renshaw
Keith Weisinger
Percy Whitenton

Nominating
Jesse Anderson
Dr. Howard Boone
Jack Caskey
Howard L. Davenport
Ernest Felts
Harry Johnson
Lee McCormick
James H. Seabrook
Dr. W. J. Templeton

Temperance
Earle Billings, Chairman
Ray Drenner Sr.
Winfield Dunn
Dr. Charles W. Grant

Scout
Dr. J. F. Bigger Jr.
Sam Dunn
Keith Kelly
Dr. Jesse Suitor
Richard Taylor

Welfare
Mrs. Charles W. Grant
Dr. Neil J. Leonard

District Church Extension
James Seabrook, Chairman
Howard L. Davenport
C. R. McDaniel

Christian Vocations
Mrs. C. M. Henderson
Harry Johnson
Samuel H. Mays
J. H. O'Donnell Jr.

District Steward
James H. Seabrook

Reserve District Steward
Samuel H. Mays

THE OFFICIAL BOARD
1957–1958

Howard L. Davenport, Chairman
Dr. Howard A. Boone, Lay Leader, June 1957–June 1959
Earle Billings, Secretary
Harold R. Benson, Vice Chairman
Lee McCormick, Treasurer
V. Hugo Akin
Jesse A. Anderson
W. C. Armstrong
George Atkinson
Roy W. Barron
Harold Benson
Dr. Jeff Bigger Jr.
Earle N. Billings
J. Fred Bledsoe
Charles C. Brown
Leon Burkett
Dr. Charles Campbell
James T. Canfield
Hugh F. Carey
Ben H. Carpenter
C. C. Carter
Jack Caskey *
James N. Clay Jr.
Clarence Colby
J. V. (Buck) Cowan Jr.
Olen H. Davis
Harry F. DeZonia
Robert J. Drake
William E. Drenner
Dr. Horton G. DuBard
James F. Duncan Jr.
Nat P. Dunn
Sam Dunn
Ernest T. Felts
Bert Ferguson
Frank Fisher
William H. D. Fones

Ned M. French
J. Haskell Gass
Jac Gates
H. Jennings Goza Jr.
Everett C. Handorf
C. P. Harris
Henry H. Harry
O. B. Hayes
Dr. Robert T. Holt
Frank P. Horton
Archie Hoss
O'Neil Howell
Donald T. Hull
Harry A. Johnson Jr.
Charles H. Johnston
Jesse Joyner
Richard R. Kite
Alfred W. Lenz
Tom J. Loberg
William O. Martin
J. Porter McClean
J. Marion Meadows
W. H. Meadows Jr.
W. C. Mieher
Earl Montgomery
R. H. Norris
J. H. O'Donnel Jr.
Felix Overton
Gerald T. Owens
Jeans W. Pattinson
Steve D. Payne
Dr. Frank Prichard
Russell Reeves
Jack Renshaw
Fred Ridolphi
George Roberts
James E. Ruffin
Lloyd J. Sarber
H. Clay Shelton Jr.
Carey P. Stanley Sr.
Richard E. Stratton
Charles R. Tate
Richard B. Taylor
Dr. W. J. Templeton
Robert Lee Thomas
Ed Thom
John H. Tole
James Vance
Jesse Vineyard
Frank Walker
R. Keith Weisinger
Cleo E. Weston
John C. Whitsitt
Jesse D. Wooten
W. A. Wren
Paul B. Yarbrough
Mrs. Clarence Colby, President WSCS

**Ex officio member by virtue of office as Commission Chairman*

Trustees

Howard L. Davenport, Chairman
Moody B. Cunningham
C. R. McDaniel
John A. Parsons
James H. Seabrook
H .S. Spragins
Dr. W. J. Templeton
Edgar H. Tenent

Commission on Membership and Evangelism

R. H. Norris, Chairman
Roy Barron
Harold Benson
J. V. (Buck) Cowan Jr.
Harry F. DeZonia
Sam Dunn
Haskell Gass
Henry Harry
O. B. Hayes
Clark Hunt
Richard Kite
W. K. Martak
Porter McClean
C. R. McDaniel
W. C. Mieher
J. H. O'Donnell
Felix Overton
Richard Taylor
R. L. Thomas
John Tole
John Whitsitt

Ex Officio Members

Dr. Howard Boone
W. E. Drenner
Mrs. P. T. Holt
Virginia Norris
Jeans Pattinson
James Seabrook

Commission on Education

Harry Johnson, Chairman
W. C. Armstrong
J. F. Bledsoe
Ed Carpenter
J. B. Emerson
William H. D. Fones
Keith Kelley
W. O. Martin
D. A. Noel
Richard Stratton
Cleo Weston

Ex Officio Members
Miss Pat Armstrong
Dr. Howard Boone
Barry DeZonia
William E. Drenner
Leland Helms
Mrs. Leland Helms
George Muns
Clay Shelton Jr.
Russell Weaver

Commission on Missions
James Seabrook, Chairman
George Atkinson
Jack Byrne
James Canfield
Hugh Carey
Olen H. Davis
Dr. Horton G. DuBard
Archie Hoss
W. H. Meadows Jr.
Fred Ridolphi
Dr. W. J. Templeton
Frank Walker
Mrs. Percy Whitenton

Ex Officio Members
Dr. Howard Boone
Howard L. Davenport
W. E. Drenner
Jane Fransioli
Jeans Pattinson

Commission on Stewardship and Finance
Jack Caskey, Chairman
James N. Clay Jr.
Howard L. Davenport
Herbert Dunkman
Bert Ferguson
Frank Fisher
Frank Horton
Jesse Joyner
A. W. Lenz
Lee McCormick
Early Mitchell
Earl Montgomery
Gerald Owens
John Parsons
Jeans Pattinson
Russell Reeves
E. R. Richmond
George Roberts
C. P. Stanley
E. H. Stanley

Ex Officio Members
Dr. Howard Boone
Mrs. Rosaline Ford
James Seabrook

District Steward
James Seabrook

Reserve District Steward
Sam Mays

Church School Superintendent
William E. Drenner

Adult Division Superintendent
Russell Weaver

Youth Division Superintendent
Barry DeZonia

Children's Division Superintendent
Mrs. Leland Helms

Church School Secretaries
Leland Helms
H. Clay Shelton Jr.

Lay Member to Annual Conference
Dr. W. J. Templeton

Reserve Lay Member to Annual Conference
W. K. Martak

Committees

Architects and Building
E. C. Handorf, Chairman
Jesse Anderson
Harry Johnson Jr.
Lee McCormick
Jack Renshaw
Jesse Vineyard
Jesse D. Wooten

Attendance for Board
Ned French, Chairman
Charles Tate
W. A. Tate

Audit
Donald Hull
D. A. Noel

Christian Vocations
Pastor, Chairman
Harry F. DeZonia
B. L. Gaddie
Mrs. C. M. Henderson

Harry Johnson Jr.
J. H. O'Donnell Jr.

City Missions
W. E. Drenner, Chairman
Mrs. C. M. Henderson
Mrs. Richard Kite
Mrs. Frank Liddell
James Seabrook

Collectors and Ushers
J. M. Meadows Jr., Chairman
Leon Burkett
James F. Duncan Jr.
Robert Ford
Haskell Gass
Jac Gates
Ernest Hall
Dr. R. T. Holt
Ralph McCool
Charles McVean
David Stanley
James L. Vance
Keith Weisinger

Communion Stewards
Mr. & Mrs. O. F. Gibson
Mr. & Mrs. Erie Henrich

District Church Extension
Howard L. Davenport
C. R. McDaniel
James H. Seabrook

Good Literature
Robert J. Drake, Chairman
Ben Carpenter
Lloyd Conolly
Ernest Felts

House
J. M. Meadows, Chairman
Dennis Earles
Steve D. Payne
Lloyd Sarber
Paul Yarbrough

Insurance
Charles Johnston, Chairman
C. C. Carter
Horace Harwell
Ralph McCool

Landscape
Jesse D. Wooten, Chairman
James Adams
Mrs. H. Davenport
Nat Dunn
Frank Liddell
Mrs. Fred Ridolphi
Ed Thorn
Mrs. Jesse D. Wooten

Legal Counsel
Jesse Vineyard

Music
Clarence Colby, Chairman
Jesse Anderson
Mrs. Lloyd Conolly
Ernest Felts
Dr. Frank Prichard
Wade Smith

Pastoral Relations
James Seabrook, Chairman
Howard Boone
Howard L. Davenport
John Parsons
Edgar H. Tenent

Publicity
W. H. Grumbles, Chairman
Charles Brown
Barry DeZonia
C. P. Harris
Harry Woodbury Jr.

Resolutions
H. Jennings Goza Jr., Chairman
William H. D. Fones
Steve D. Payne
J. E. Ruffin

Scout
Keith Kelley, Chairman
Hugh Akin
Jeff Bigger Jr.
O'Neil Howell
E. R. Richmond Jr.
Richard Taylor
Paul Yarbrough

Temperance
Earle Billings, Chairman
Dr. Charles Campbell
Ray Drenner
Dr. Winfield Dunn

Welcome and Hospitality
C. R. McDaniel, Chairman

A. W. Beasley Jr.
Dr. Charles Campbell
P. D. Clarkson
Floyd Harvey
Donald Lewis
A. J. Westbrook
Percy Whitenton

Welfare
Mrs. Charles Grant, Chairman
Mrs. Neil Leonard
Mrs. Percy Whitenton

Coordinating
Dr. Charles Grant, Chairman
Howard Boone
Jack Caskey
Mrs. Clarence Colby
Howard L. Davenport
W. E. Drenner
Harry Johnson
R. H. Norris
Jeans Pattinson
James Seabrook

The Official Board
1958–1959

Howard L. Davenport, Chairman
Dr. W. J. Templeton, Lay Leader, June 1959–June 1961
V. Hugo Akin
Jesse Anderson
George Atkinson
Gilbert Avery
Harold Benson
Dr. J. F. Bigger
Earle N. Billings
J. Fred Bledsoe
Dr. Howard A. Boone
Charles Brown
Leon Burkett
Jack P. Byrne
Dr. Charles Campbell
Hugh Carey
Ben M. Carpenter
C. C. Carter
Jack Caskey
Clarence Colby
Lloyd A. Conolly
Olen H. Davis
Harry F. DeZonia
Robert J. Drake
Ray Drenner
James F. Duncan Jr.
Herbert H. Dunkman
Sam E. Dunn
Dennis A. Earles
Ernest Felts
Mrs. Ernest Felts
Bert Ferguson
Frank Fisher
William H. D. Fones
Russell E. Garber
J. Haskell Gass
Jac H. Gates
H. Jennings Goza Jr.
Fred Graham
Dr. Charles W. Grant
D. R. Greer
Everett C. Handorf
O. B. Hayes
Leland Helms
Jones A. Holt
Dr. Robert T. Holt
O'Neil Howell
Donald T. Hull
Clark Hunt
Harry A. Johnson Jr.
Keith Kelley
Richard Kite
J. H. Langston
Alfred W. Lenz
Donald Lewis
Thomas J. Loberg
William K. Martak
William O. Martin
Samuel H. Mays
J. Porter McClean
Ralph J. McCool
Lee B. McCormick
Conrad R. McDaniel
Charles A. McVean
J. Marion Meadows
William H. Meadows Jr.
William C. Mieher
Early Mitchell
Earl Montgomery

D. A. Noel
Robert H. Norris
J. H. O'Donnell Jr.
Felix Overton
Gerald T. Owens
Gary Pagels
John A. Parsons
Jeans Pattinson
Russell Reeves
Jack Renshaw
Ed R. Richmond Sr.
Jack Richmond
George Roberts
James E. Ruffin
Lloyd J. Sarber
James H. Seabrook
Carey P. Stanley Sr.
Sam Stephenson Sr.
L. S. Stout
Richard E. Stratton
Richard Taylor
Edgar H. Tenent
Robert Lee Thomas
Ed Thorn
John H. Tole
Frank Walker
Percy Whitenton
John Whitsitt
Kemmons Wilson
Cecil E. Woods
Jesse D. Wooten
W. A. Wren

Board of Trustees
Howard L. Davenport
Conrad McDaniel
John A. Parsons
James H. Seabrook
Dr. W. J. Templeton
Edgar H. Tenent

Commission on Membership and Evangelism
R. H. Norris, Chairman
Roy Barron
Harold Benson
Harry F. DeZonia
Russell Garber
Haskell Gass
D. R. Greer
H. P. Harris
Henry Harry
D. B. Hayes
Jones Holt
Clark Hunt
Richard Kite
J. H. Langston
W. K. Martak
Porter McClean
C. R. McDaniel
W. C. Mieber
J. H. O'Donnell
Felix Overton
Jack Richmond
Richard Taylor
R. L. Thomas
John Tole
John Whitsitt

Ex Officio Members
Dr. Howard Boone
Fred Bledsoe
Mrs. Bea Crofford
Howard L. Davenport
O'Neil Howell
Pastor
James Seabrook
Sue West

Commission on Education
Harry Johnson, Chairman
C. C. Brown
Ed Carpenter
William H. D. Fones
Keith Kelley
Tom Loberg
Reagin Nesbitt
D. A. Noel
Richard Stratton
Elmo Thompson

Ex Officio Members
Fred Bledsoe
Howard Boone
Dr. Charles Campbell
R. J. Drake
Mrs. Henry Harry
Leland Helms
Mrs. Leland Helms
O'Neil Howell
Gary Pagels
Pastor
George Roberts
Harley Tilley
J. L. Waller
Russell Weaver

Commission on Missions
James Seabrook, Chairman
George Atkinson
Jack Byrne
James Canfield
Hugh Carey
Olen H. Davis
Ray Drenner
Dr. Horton G. DuBard

Archie Hoss
W. H. Meadows Jr.
Fred Ridolphi
L. S. Stout
Dr. W. J. Templeton
Frank Walker
Mrs. Percy Whitenton

Ex Officio Members
Lynwood Akin
Fred Bledsoe
Dr. Howard Boone
James N. Clay Jr.
Howard L. Davenport
Ray Drenner
Mrs. Ernest Felts
O'Neil Howell
Pastor
R. L. Thomas

Commission on Stewardship and Finance
Jack Caskey, Chairman
James N. Clay Jr.
Howard L. Davenport
Herbert Dunkman
Bert Ferguson
Frank Fisher
Fred Graham
Jesse Joyner
A. W. Lenz
Lee McCormick
Early Mitchell
Earl Montgomery
Gerald Owens
John Parsons
Jeans Pattinson
Russell Reeves
E. R. Richmond
George Roberts
C. P. Stanley Sr.
E. H. Tenent
Kemmons Wilson

Ex Officio Members
Mrs. Rosaline Ford
Pastor
James Seabrook

District Steward
James Seabrook

Reserve District Steward
Samuel H. Mays

Church School Superintendent
J. Fred Bledsoe

Superintendent Children's Division
Mrs. Leland Helms

Superintendent Youth Division
Ronald B. Thomas

Superintendent Adult Division
Russell Weaver

Church School Secretaries
Leland Helms
J. L. Waller

Lay Member to Annual Conference
Dr. W. J. Templeton

Reserve Lay Member to Annual Conference
W. K. Martak

Committees

Architects and Building
A. W. Lenz, Chairman
Gilbert Avery
Dennis Earles
Jac Gates
Earl Montgomery
E. R. Richmond
Sam Stephenson Sr.

Attendance for Board
Dr. Charles Campbell, Chairman
W. A. Wren

Audit
A. Bryan Bolin
Donald Hull
D. A. Noel
Cecil E. Woods

Christian Vocations
Pastor, Chairman
Barry DeZonia
Dr. Winfield Dunn
Mrs. Charles Henderson
Harry Johnson Jr.
J. H. O'Donnell Jr.

City Missions
Ray Drenner, Chairman
Mrs. Clarence Colby
Mrs. C. M. Henderson
James Seabrook
Mrs. James Seabrook

Collectors and Ushers
W. H. Meadows Jr., Chairman
Jas. F. Duncan Jr.
Robert Ford
Haskell Gass
Jac Gates
Ernest Hall
Dr. R. T. Holt
O'Neil Howell
W. O. Martin
Ralph McCool
Charles McVean
David Stanley
Sam Stephenson Jr.
Charles R. Tate
James L. Vance
Keith Weisinger

Communion Stewards
Mr. & Mrs. R. E. Garber
Mr. & Mrs. O. F. Gibson

Coordinating
Pastor, Chairman
Dr. Howard Boone
Fred Bledsoe
Jack Caskey
Howard L. Davenport
Mrs. Ernest Felts
O'Neil Howell
Harry Johnson Jr.
R. H. Norris
James Seabrook

District Church Extension
Howard L. Davenport
C. R. McDaniel
James Seabrook
Dr. W. J. Templeton

Good Literature
Robert Drake, Chairman
Ben Carpenter
L. A. Conolly
Ernest Felts

House
J. M. Meadows, Chairman
Dennis Earles
Mrs. John Parsons
Lloyd Sarber
Paul Yarbrough

Insurance
Ralph McCool, Chairman
Charles Johnston
Russell Reeves

Landscape
Jesse D. Wooten, Chairman
James Adams
Mrs. Howard L. Davenport
Nat Dunn
E. C. Handorf
Frank Liddell
Mrs. Fred Ridolphi
Ed Thorn
Mrs. Jesse D. Wooten

Legal Counsel
Jesse Vineyard

Music
Tom Loberg, Chairman
Jesse Anderson
Clarence Colby
Mrs. Lloyd Conolly
Ernest Felts
Dr. Frank Prichard
Wade Smith

Nominating
Pastor, Chairman
Dr. Howard Boone
Howard L. Davenport
Harry Johnson
John Parsons
James Seabrook
Dr. W. J. Templeton
Edgar Tenent

Pastoral Relations
James Seabrook, Chairman
Dr. Howard Boone
Howard L. Davenport
John Parsons
Edgar Tenent

Publicity
Gerald Owens, Chairman
Bert Ferguson
Jeans Pattinson

Resolutions
H. Jennings Goza Jr., Chairman
William H. D. Fones
James E. Ruffin

Scout
Keith Kelley, Chairman
V. Hugo Akin
Dr. Jeff Bigger
Sam Dunn

O'Neil Howell
Ed Richmond Jr.
Richard Taylor
Paul Yarbrough

Temperence
Earle Billings, Chairman
Dr. Charles Campbell
Ray Drenner
Dr. Winfield Dunn

Welcome and Hospitality
C. R. McDaniel,
Chairman
A. W. Beasley Jr.
Leon Burkett
Dr. Charles Campbell
P. D. Clarkson
Ned French
Floyd Harvey
Donald Lewis
A. J. Westbrook
Percy Whitenton

Welfare
Mrs. Charles Grant,
Chairman
Mrs. Neil Leonard
Mrs. Percy Whitenton

The Official Board
1959–1960

John A. Parsons,
Chairman
Dr. W. J. Templeton, Lay
Leader, June
1959–June 1961
V. Hugo Akin
Jesse Anderson
William C. Armstrong
George Atkinson
Gil Avery Jr.
Hunter Barcroft Sr.
Bruce Barnes
Harold Benson
Dr. Howard A. Boone
Albert M. Brinkley
Charles C. Brown
Jack P. Byrne
Dr. Charles Campbell
James T. Canfield
Hugh F. Carey
Ben M. Carpenter
C. C. Carter
Jack Caskey
James N. Clay Jr.
Clarence Colby
Lloyd A. Connolly
George M. Darnis
Howard L. Davenport
Harry F. DeZonia
Dr. Horton G. DuBard
Herbert H. Dunkman
Dennis Earles
Mrs. Ernest Felts
Bert Ferguson
Russell E. Garber
Haskell Gass
Dr. B. H. Ginn
Dr. T. E. Goyer
H. Jennings Goza Jr.
Fred M. Graham
Dr. Charles Grant
Walter A. Hackmeister
Everett C. Handorf
Henry Harry
Leland Helms
Jones A. Holt
O'Neil Howell
William S. Huff
Clark W. Hunt
Harry Johnson Jr.
Charles Johnston
Dr. Albert M. Jones
Keith Kelley
Merle D. King
C. P. Knight
J. H. Langston
Dr. Neil J. Leonard
Donald W. Lewis
Thomas R. Logan
Harry S. Lowe
W. K. Martak
Sam Mays
J. Porter McClean Sr.
Ralph McCool
Lee B. McCormick
C. R. McDaniel
J. Marion Meadows
Early Mitchell
Earl Montgomery
Rev. Marshall Morris
Dallas Nelson
D. A. Noel
George Nowlin
Ed Richmond
Dr. Henry C. Robert
James E. Ruffin
Lloyd J. Sarber
James H. Seabrook

H. Clay Shelton Jr.
T. Wade Smith
Carey Stanley Sr.
Harold W. Stewart
Charles R. Tate
Edgar H. Tenent
Robert Lee Thomas
Ed Thorn
Jesse Vineyard
Frank Walker
Keith Weisinger
Percy Whitenton
John C. Whitsitt
John T. Wilkinson
Cecil E. Woods
W. A. Wren
Paul Yarbrough

Ex Officio Members
Alfred Lentz
Brooks H. Shepherd

Commission on Membership and Evangelism
Harold Benson, Chairman
Hunter Barcroft
Jack Byrne
Earle Billings
Dr. Jeff Bigger
James N. Clay Jr.
Torn Curlin
Barry DeZonia
R. J. Drake
Dave Ebersole Jr.
Ernest Felts
Frank Fisher
Haskell Gass
Harry Henry
Jones Holt
Clark Hunt
Earle King
C. P. Knight
J. H. Langston
Donald Lewis
Marion Meadows
W. C. Micher
Charles Ogan
Felix Overton
Wade Smith
Harold Stewart
Elmo Thompson
John Tole
J. D. Weatherford
Percy Whitenton
John Whitsitt
W. A. Wren
Robert Wood

Ex Officio Members
Pastors
George Atkinson
Clarence Colby
Mrs. Howard L. Davenport
Mrs. Horton G. DuBard
D. A. Noel
Dr. W. J. Templeton
Sally Thorn

Education Commission
H. Clay Shelton Jr., Chairman
W. C. Armstrong
Bruce Barnes
Dr. B. H. Ginn
Keith Kelley
Tom Loberg
Tom R. Logan
Sam Mays
Jeans Pattinson
R. E. Stratton

Ex Officio Members
Jas. B. Adams
Dr. C. W. Camp
Harold Holt
Mrs. Laura Parker
Mrs. O. K. Patty
Tom Ragland
Dr. W. J. Templeton
Ronald Thomas
Ed Thorn
Harley Tilley

Missions Commission
George Atkinson, Chairman
C. C. Brown
Dr. Horton G. DuBard
James F. Duncan Jr.
Mrs. Caruthers Ewing
William H. D. Fones
Dr. T. E. Goyer Jr.
H. Jennings Goza Jr.
Mrs. C. M. Henderson
O'Neil Howell
William S. Huff
Harry Johnson Jr.
Dr. Albert Jones
Dr. Neil Leonard
W. K. Martak
D. A. Noel
James E. Ruffin
Richard Taylor
Frank Walker
Mrs. Percy Whitenton

Ex Officio Members
Clarence Colby
Mrs. Oscar Crofford
Mrs. Ernest Felts
Pastors
Dr. W. J. Templeton

Stewardship and Finance Commission
Albert Brinkley, Chairman
Dr. Howard Boone
Jack Caskey
Howard L. Davenport
Herbert Dunkman
Bert Ferguson
Fred Graham
Lee McCormick
C. R. McDaniel
Early Mitchell
Earl Montgomery
John Parsons
Russell Reeves
George Roberts
James Seabrook
Carey Stanley
Edgar Tenent
Keith Weisinger
Kemmons Wilson

Ex Officio Members
Mrs. Avis Allen
George Atkinson
Pastors
Dr. W. J. Templeton
John Whitsitt

Reserve District Steward
Sam Mays

Church School Superintendent
Clarence Colby

Superintendent Adult Division
Harley Tilley

Superintendent Children's Division
Mrs. Richard Taylor

District Steward
James H. Seabrook

Superintendent Youth
Ronald Thomas

Committees

Architects and Building
A. W. Lenz, Chairman
Gil Avery
C. C. Carter
Dennis Earle
Jac Gates
Earl Montgomery
E. R. Richmond

Attendance for Board
Dr. Charles Campbell, Chairman
W. A. Wren

Audit
Cecil Woods, Chairman
D. A. Noel

Christian Vocations
Pastor, Chairman
Mrs W. C. Armstrong
Rev. Marshall Morris
Ronald Thomas

City Missions
Mr. & Mrs. George Atkinson, Chairman
Hugh Carey
Mr. & Mrs. Ernest Felts
Mrs. C. M. Henderson

Collectors and Ushers
Dr. R. T. Holt, Chairman
Hunter Barcroft Sr.
James F. Duncan Jr.
Haskell Gass
Jac Gates
E. W. Hall
Archie Hoss
W. O. Martin
Charles McVean
Lloyd Sarber
Sam Stephenson
Keith Weisinger
Robert T. Wood

Communion Stewards
Mr. & Mrs. R. E. Garber
Mr. & Mrs. O. F. Gibson

Coordinating
Pastor, Chairman
George Atkinson
Harold Benson
Albert Brinkley
Clarence Colby
Mrs. Ernest Felts
John A. Parsons
Clay Shelton Jr.
Dr. W. J. Templeton

District Church Extension
Howard Boone
Howard L. Davenport
Dr. Horton G. DuBard
C. R. McDaniel
James Seabrook
W. J. Templeton

Good Literature
Harry Johnson Jr., Chairman
H. S. Lowe
Fred Ridolphi

Hospital Visitation
George Darms, Chairman
Dr. Chas. W. Campbell
W. A. Hackmeister
O. B. Hayes
John Tole

House
Porter McClean, Chairman
J. T. Canfield
Ben Carpenter
George Nowlin
Paul Yarbrough

Insurance
Jesse Anderson, Chairman
Ralph McCool
Ed Richmond Jr.

Kitchen
Cecil Woods, Chairman
Mrs. Jack Byrne
Mrs. Mae Jennings
Jesse Joyner
Joe McKinney
Mrs. Early Mitchell

Landscape
Mrs. Jesse D. Wooten, Chairman
James B. Adams
Mrs. Howard Davenport
E. C. Handorf
Mrs. Fred Ridolphi
Ed Thorn
Jack Wallace

Legal Counsel
Jesse Vineyard

Music
Jesse Anderson
Dr. Winfield Dunn
Charles Johnston
Mrs. John Parsons
Dr. Henry C. Roberts
Robert Lee Thomas

Nominating
Pastor, Chairman
Dr. Howard Boone
L. A. Conolly
Howard L. Davenport
D. A. Noel
J. H. Seabrook
John Whitsitt

Pastoral Relations
Howard L. Davenport, Chairman
Al Brinkley
J. H. Seabrook
Carey Stanley
Dr. W. J. Templeton

Publicity
Dallas Nelson, Chairman
Bert Ferguson
James H. Seabrook Jr.

Resolutions
John T. Wilkinson Jr., Chairman
Hugh Carey
William H. D. Fones

Scouts
Jack L. Perry, Chairman
James Adams
V. Hugo Akin
Dr. Jeff Bigger
Dr. Howard Boone
James D. Curry
Howard L. Davenport
Mrs. Howard L. Davenport
Nat Dunn
Sam Dunn
E. C. Handorf
Keith Kelley
Frank Liddell
Joe Neeley
John Parsons
Mrs. Fred Ridolphi
Richard Taylor
Edgar Tenent
Ed Thorn
Mrs. Jesse D. Wooten

The Official Board
1960–1961

John Parsons, Chairman, 1960–1961
Dr. W. J. Templeton, Lay Leader, June 1959–1961
William C. Armstrong
George Atkinson
Mrs. George Atkinson
Gil Avery Jr.
Hunter Barcroft Sr.
Harold Benson
Dr. J. F. Bigger
Dr. Howard Boone
Jo Ann Bratton
Albert Brinkley
W. P. Brooks
Jack Byrne
William B. Campbell
James T. Canfield
Jack B. Caskey
James N. Clay
Clarence Colby
Lloyd A. Conolly
George M. Darms
Howard L. Davenport
Barry DeZonia
R. J. Drake
Dr. Horton G. DuBard
James F. Duncan Jr.
Dr. Winfield Dunn
Dennis Earles
Ernest Felts
Frank Fisher
William H. D. Fones
Ned French
Dr. T. E. Goyer Jr.
William H. Grumbles
William L. Gully
Walter A. Hackmeister
Henry H. Harry
Leland Helms
Jones Holt
Dr. Robert T. Holt
Frank Hoover
William S. Huff
Clark W. Hunt
Dr. Albert M. Jones
Charles Johnston
Keith Kelley
Merle D. King
Richard Kite
J. H. Langston
Al W. Lenz
Donald W. Lewis
Thomas J. Loberg
Thomas R. Logan
Dr. William Lovejoy
W. K. Martak
Samuel H. Mays
Dr. Howard McClain
Lee B. McCormick
C. R. McDaniel
W. H. Meadows Jr.
W. C. Mieher
Early Mitchell
Dallas Nelson
D. A. Noel
George Nowlin
Richard S. Oglesby
Felix Overton
Pastors
Jeans Pattinson
Tom Ragland
Russell Reeves
Jack Renshaw
Ed Richmond Sr.
Fred Ridolphi
George Roberts
Dr. Henry C. Roberts
Yerger Robinson
Ralph Scherr
James H. Seabrook
H. Clay Shelton Jr.
T. Wade Smith
Sam Stephenson Jr.
Harold W. Stewart
Charles R. Tate
Richard G. Taylor
Edgar H. Tenent
Elmo Thompson
John H. Tole
Ed Thorn
Dr. Robert Utterback
James L. Vance
Jesse Vineyard
L. T. Warinner
Keith Weisinger
Percy Whitenton
John Whitsitt
John T. Wilkinson
Dr. James L. Wiygul
Cecil E. Woods

Commissions

Membership and Evangelism
Harold Benson, Chairman
Hunter Barcroft Sr.
Dr. Jeff Bigger
Earle Billings
Jack Byrne
James N. Clay Jr.
Tom Curlin
Barry DeZonia
Harry F. DeZonia
R. J. Drake
Dave Ebersole
Ernest Felts
Frank Fisher
Ned French
Haskell Gass
W. L. Gully
Henry Harry
Jones Holt
Clark Hunt
Frank Hoover
Merle King
Richard Kite
J. H. Langston
Donald Lewis
Marion Meadows
W. C. Mieher
Charles Ogan
R. S. Oglesby
Felix Overton
Yerger Robinson
Wade Smith
Harold Stewart
Elmo Thompson
John Tole
J. D. Weatherford
Percy Whitenton
W. A. Wren

Ex Officio Members
Pastors
George Atkinson
Dr. Howard Boone
Miss Sallie Pensbaer
Dr. W. J. Templeton
Mrs. Frank Walker
Mrs. Percy Whitenton

Education
H. Clay Shelton, Chairman
W. C. Armstrong
Earle Billings
Barry Carter
Dr. B. H. Ginn
Keith Kelley
Tom Loberg
Tom R. Logan
Sam Mays
Jeans Pattinson
Tom Ragland
R. E. Stratton

Ex Officio Members
Pastors
Jo Ann Bratton
Clarence Colby
Mrs. R. J. Drake
E. C. Handorf
Don Hawkins
Billy Houston
Jack Keuner
Max S. Long
Ralph McCool
Mrs. Richard Taylor
Dr. W. J. Templeton
Ronnie Thomas
Harley Tilley
John Tole
J. D. Weatherly
John Whitsitt

Missions
George Atkinson, Chairman
Mrs. George Atkinson
Dr. Horton G. DuBard
James F. Duncan Jr.
Mrs. Caruthers Ewing
William H. D. Fones
H. Jennings Goza Jr.
Mrs. C. M. Henderson
O'Neil Howell
William S. Huff
Harry Johnson Jr.
Dr. Albert Jones
Dr. Neil Leonard
Dr. William Lovejoy
W. K. Martak
J. E. Ruffin
Richard Taylor
Elmo Thompson
Dr. Robert Utterback
Frank Walker
Mrs. Percy Whitenton
Robert C. Whitnel Jr.

Ex Officio Members
Dr. Howard Boone
Howard Boone Jr.
Albert Brinkley
Mrs. Oscar Crofford
Pastors
Tom Ragland
Dr. W. J. Templeton

Stewardship and Finance
Albert Brinkley, Chairman
Jesse Anderson
Dr. Howard Boone
W. P. Brooks
Jack Caskey
Howard L. Davenport
Herbert Dunkman
Bert Ferguson
Fred Graham
Lee McCormick
C. R. McDaniel
Early Mitchell
Earl Montgomery
John Parsons
Russell Reeves
George Roberts
Ralph Scherr
James Seabrook
Carey Stanley
Edgar Tenent
Keith Weisinger
Kemmons Wilson

Ex Officio Members
Mrs. Avis Allen
Dr. W. J. Templeton
John Whitsitt

Lay Member to Annual Conference
none elected

Reserve Lay Member to Annual Conference
none elected

District Steward
James Seabrook

Reserve District Steward
Sam H. Mays

Church School Superintendent
Clarence Colby

Assistant Church School Superintendent
Don Hawkins

Superintendent of Adult Division
Harley Tilley

Superintendent of Youth Division
Ronald B. Thomas

Superintendent of Children's Division
Mrs. Richard Taylor

Church School Secretary
Tom Ragland

Literature Secretary
James B. Adams

Committees

Architects and Building
A. W. Lenz, Chairman
Gil Avery Jr.
C. C. Carter
Dennis Earles
Earl Montgomery
E. R. Richmond
Sam Stephenson Jr.

Audit
Cecil Woods, Chairman
W. E. Bartlett
A. Bryan Bolin
D. A. Noel

Christian Vocations
Mrs. W. C. Armstrong
Rev. Marshall Morris
Pastor
Ronald Thomas

City Missions
Mr. & Mrs. George Atkinson, Chairman
Mr. & Mrs. Ernest Felts
Mrs. C. M. Henderson

Collectors and Ushers
Dr. R. T. Holt, Chairman
Hunter Barcroft Sr.
James Duncan Jr.
Haskell Gass
Jac Gates
R. S. Oglesby
Lloyd Sarber
Sam Stephenson Jr.
James L. Vance
L. T. Warinner
Keith Weisinger

Communion Stewards
Mr. & Mrs. R. E. Garber
Mr. & Mrs. O. F. Gibson

Coordinating
Pastor, Chairman
George Atkinson
Mrs. George Atkinson
Harold Benson
Dr. Howard Boone
Albert Brinkley

Clarence Colby
John Parsons
H. Clay Shelton
Dr. W. J. Templeton

District Church Extension
Howard Boone
Howard L. Davenport
Dr. Horton G. DuBard
C. R. McDaniel
James Seabrook
W. J. Templeton

Good Literature
Dr. James Wiygul, Chairman
H. S. Lowe
Fred Ridolphi

Hospital Visitation
George Darms, Chairman
Dr. C. W. Campbell
Mrs. Ernest Felts
W. A. Hackmeister
Dr. J. H. McClain
Mr. & Mrs. John Tole

House
Porter McClean Sr., Chairman
Gil Avery Jr.
J. T. Canfield
Ben Carpenter
George Nowlin
Paul Yarbrough

Insurance
Jesse Anderson, Chairman
Ralph McCool
Ed Richmond Jr.

Kitchen
Cecil Woods, Chairman
Mrs. Jack Byrne
Mrs. Mae Jennings
Jesse Joyner
Joe McKinney
Mrs. Early Mitchell

Landscape
Jesse D. Wooten, Chairman
James B. Adams
Mrs. Howard L. Davenport
E. C. Handorf
Joe Nuismer
Mrs. Fred Ridolphi
Ed Thorne
Jack Wallace
Mrs. Jesse D. Wooten

Legal Counsel
Jesse Vineyard

Library
Mrs. W. B. Campbell, Chairman
Mrs. Frank McAllister
Mrs. S. K. McKenzie
Mrs. Marshall Morris
Mrs. David Parks

Music
Robert Lee Thomas, Chairman
Jesse Anderson
Dr. Winfield Dunn
Charles Johnston
Mrs. John Parsons
Dr. Henry Roberts
Mrs. Marvin Woolen

Nominating
Pastor, Chairman
Howard L. Davenport
Everett Handorf
Donald Lewis
C. R. McDaniel
James Seabrook
Dr. W. J. Templeton

Pastoral Relations
Howard L. Davenport, Chairman
Al Brinkley
J. H. Seabrook
Carey Stanley
Dr. W. J. Templeton

Publicity-Public Relations
Tom Ragland, Chairman
W. P. Brooks
Bert Ferguson
W. H. Grumbles
Dallas Nelson
James Seabrook Jr.

Records and History
Mrs. W. J. Templeton, Chairman

Resolutions
John T. Wilkinson Jr., Chairman

Hugh Carey
William H. D. Fones

Scouts
Earle Billings, Chairman
V. Hugo Akin
Dr. J. F. Bigger
James D. Curry
Sam Dunn
Keith Kelley
Jack Perry
Richard Taylor

Temperance
Dr. W. Lovejoy, Chairman
Lloyd Conolly

Dr. Winfield Dunn
J. H. O'Donnell Jr.

Welcome and Hospitality
W. H. Meadows Jr., Chairman
Donald Lewis
Dr. C. W. Campbell
W. D. Campbell
P. D. Clarkson
Floyd Harvey
Jack Renshaw
Charles R. Tate
Percy Whitenton

Wills and Legacies
Carey Stanley, Chairman

A. M. Brinkley
Caruthers Ewing
Ernest Felts
Dr. Charles Grant
Donald Hull
John Parsons
James Seabrook Sr.

Weekday School
Dr. Charles W. Grant, Chairman
Howard L. Davenport
Harry Johnson Jr.
H. Clay Shelton Jr.

The Official Board
1961–1962

Edgar H. Tenent, Chairman, June 1961–June 1963
Robert Lee Thomas, Lay Leader, June 1961–June 1962
James B. Adams
Jesse Anderson
James Arnette
E. W. Atkinson
George Atkinson
Dr. Richard L. Austin
Hunter Barcroft Sr.
W. E. Bartlett
Harold Benson
Dr. William A. Berry
Dr. J. F. Bigger
Earle Billings
Dr. Howard A. Boone
Jo Ann Bratton
James P. Briggs
Albert Brinkley
Dr. Charles Campbell
William B. Campbell
James T. Canfield
Jean A. Carson
Barry M. Carter
Armistead F. Clay
James N. Clay Jr.
Clarence Colby
George M. Darms
Howard L. Davenport
James A. Davenport
Harry F. DeZonia
Robert J. Drake
Dr. Horton G. DuBard
James F. Duncan Jr.
Herbert Dunkman
Dr. Winfield Dunn
Frank T. Fans
Ernest Felts Sr.
Bert Ferguson
Frank Fisher
William H. D. Fones
Ned French
Haskell Gass
O. F. Gibson
H. Jennings Goza Jr.
Dr. Charles W. Grant
W. H. Grumbles
W. L. Gully
Everett C. Handorf
Henry Harry
Charles E. Hendricks
Dr. Robert T. Holt
Frank Hooker
Archie Hoss

O'Neil Howell
Charles H. Johnston
Dr. Albert M. Jones
Jesse Joyner
Merle D. King
Richard Lamphere
Alfred W. Lenz
Donald Lewis
Thomas R. Logan
Max S. Long Jr.
Dr. William M. Lovejoy
Kenneth Markwell
Samuel H. Mays
Mrs. Samuel H. Mays
J. Porter McClean
Dr. J. H. McClain
Lee B. McCormick
C. R. McDaniel
Marion Meadows
W. H. Meadows Jr.
W. C. Mieher
Rev. Marshall Morris
Dallas Nelson
St. Elmo Newton
George Nowlin
Richard S. Oglesby
Felix Overton
Jeans Pattinson
John A. Parsons
Jack L. Perry
Alan B. Peterson
Joe Pitner
Tom Ragland
R. G. Ramsay
Fred Ridolphi
Ed Richmond Sr.
George Roberts
Dr. Henry G. Roberts
Yerger Robinson
Ralph Scherr
James H. Seabrook Sr.
James H. Seabrook Jr.
James I. Seago
H. Clay Shelton Jr.
J. E. Stafford
T. Wade Smith
Carey P. Stanley Sr.
Sam Stephenson Jr.
Harold Steward
Eugene Stigall
W. F. Stout
Charles R. Tate
Richard G. Taylor
Dr. W. J. Templeton
Bob Wilson

Commissions

Membership and Evangelism
Donald Lewis, Chairman
James B. Arnette
E. W. Atkinson
George Atkinson
Roy Barron
Harold Benson
Dr. J. F. Bigger
Earle Billings
Jack Byrne
Dr. Charles Campbell
W. B. Campbell
Harry F. DeZonia
R. J. Drake
Jas. E. Duncan Jr.
Dr. Winfield Dunn
Dennis Earles
Dave Ebersole Jr.
Frank Fisher
William H. D. Fones
Robert Ford
Haskell Gass
Jac Gates
Henry Harry
Leland Helms
Chas. Hendricks
Raymond Holman
Jones Holt
Frank Hoover
Clark Hunt
Merle King
Richard Lamphere
O. H. Little
W. K. Martak
J. P. McClean Sr.
C. R. McDaniel
Marion Meadows
W. C. Mieher
Gordon Miles
Earl Montgomery
George Nowlin
Chas. Ogan
Richard Oglesby
Felix Overton
Jeans Pattinson
W. F. Stout
Dr. W. J. Templeton
Elmo Thompson
Percy Whitenton

Ex Officio Members
Earle Billings
Howard Boone
Mrs. C. H. Cobb
Mrs. Oscar Crofford
Bobby Fisher
Pastors
Ralph Scherr
Robert Lee Thomas

Education
James B. Adams, Chairman
Barry Carter
James Davenport
Barry DeZonia
William H. D. Fones
O'Neil Howell
Tom Logan
Dr. J. H. McClain
Alan Peterson
Tom Ragland
Yerger Robinson
R. E. Stratton
Dr. Robert Utterback

Ex Officio Members
Pastors
Earle Billings
Jo Ann Bratton
Ben Carpenter
Bobby Fisher
Mrs. Frank Fisher
Mrs. T. E. Goyer Jr.
Claire Hull
Mrs. S. K. McKenziei
Mrs. Charles McVean
Richard Oglesby
Lady Somervell
Dr. W. J. Templeton
R. L. Thomas
Ronald Thomas

Missions
Ralph Scherr, Chairman
George Atkinson
Armistead Clay
James N. Clay Jr.
Dr. Horton G. DuBard
Jack Jayroe
M. H. Meadows Jr.
Dr. Frank Prichard
Fred Ridolphi
J. E. Stafford
John Tole
Jesse Vineyard
Frank Walker
Robert Whitnel

Ex Officio Members
Sally Bailey
Dr. Jeff Bigger
Mrs. Jas. P. Briggs
Mrs. C. M. Henderson
Don Lewis
Lee McCormick
Richard Oglesby
Pastors
Mrs. Ralph Scherr
James Seabrook
R. L. Thomas

Commissions

Stewardship and Finances
Lee McCormick, Chairman
Jesse Anderson
Albert Brinkley
Herbert Dunkman
Bert Ferguson
E. C. Handorf
Jesse Joyner
Al Lenz
St. Elmo Newton
John Parsons
S. G. Ramsey
George Roberts
J. H. Seabrook Sr.
Carey Stanley Sr.
Dr. W. J. Templeton
L. T. Warinner

Ex Officio Members
Mrs. Avis Allen
Jennifer Drake
Pastors
Ed Tenent
S. L. Thomas

Social Concerns
Samuel H. Mays, Chairman
Dr. J. F. Bigger
Dr. Howard Boone
Clarence Colby
W. L. Gully
Archie Hoss
Dr. Albert Jones
J. H. O'Donnell
Dr. Henry Roberts
Eugene Stigall

Ex Officio Members
Mrs. Roy Edmonds
Judy Felts
Pastors
R. L. Thomas

District Steward
Ernest Felts Sr.

Alternate Steward
Richard Taylor

Recording Steward
Harry F. DeZonia

Church School Superintendent
Richard S. Oglesby

Superintendent of Adult Division
Ben Carpenter

Superintendent of Youth Division
Ronald Thomas

Superintendent of Children's Division
Mrs. Thomas E. Goyer Jr.

Church School Secretary and Treasurer
Tom Ragland

Literature Secretary
R. J. Drake

Assistant Superintendent in Charge of Cultivation
Earle Billings

Lay Member to Annual Conference
Howard L. Davenport
J. H. Seabrook

Reserve Lay Member to Annual Conference
Dr. William M. Lovejoy

Home and Hospital Steward
Dr. J. F. Bigger

Committees

Architects and Buildings
E. R. Richmond Sr., Chairman
Armistead Clay
E. C. Handorf
Earl Montgomery
John Parsons
Kemmons Wilson
Jesse D. Wooten

Adult
W. E. Bartlett, Chairman
Charles Hendricks
Archie Hoss
John Whitsitt

Christian Vocations
Pastor, Chairman
Jo Ann Bratton
Rev. Marshall Morris
Mrs. C. W. Shaw
Ronald Thomas

City Missions
Mr. & Mrs. Jack Byrne
Mrs. C. M. Henderson, Chairman
Mr. & Mrs. W. K. Martak

Collectors and Ushers
Haskell Gass, Chairman
Hunter Barcroft Sr.
James P. Briggs
Harry F. DeZonia
J. F. Duncan Jr.
Ned French
Dr. Robert Holt
W. O. Martin
W. H. Meadows Jr.
Gordon Miles
Felix Overton
Joe Pitner
Charles Tate
Dr. W. J. Templeton
J. L. Vance
W. T. Wardlaw
J. D. Weatherford
John Wilkinson Jr.
Dr. R. L. Wooten

Communion Stewards
Mr. & Mrs. R. E. Garber
Mr. & Mrs. O. F. Gibson

Coordinating
Pastor, Chairman
James B. Adams
Dr. Howard Boone
Jo Ann Bratton
Donald Lewis
Sam Mays
Mrs. Sam Mays
Lee McCormick
Rev. Marshall Morris
Richard S. Oglesby
Ralph Scherr

District Church Extension
John Tole, Chairman
Clarence Colby
Dr. Horton G. DuBard

Good Literature
Charles Johnston, Chairman
Dr. William Barry
Mrs. Oscar Crofford
Harold Stewart

Hospital Visitation
W. F. Stout, Chairman
Jean Carson

R. J. Drake
Dr. Albert Jones
John Philbeck
Dr. J. L. Wiygul
W. A. Wren

House
Porter McClean Sr., Chairman
Kenneth Markwell
Earl Montgomery
James I. Seago
Sam Stephenson Jr.

Insurance
Frank Fisher, Chairman
H. H. Dunkman
John Wilkinson Jr.

Kitchen
Marion Meadows, Chairman
Mrs. Ernest Felts Sr.
Ed Hardin
Mrs. May Jennings
Mr. & Mrs. Jesse Joyner

Joe McKinney
Delmer Woodard

Landscape
Ed Thorn, Chairman
James Canfield
A. W. Lenz

Legal Counsel
Jesse Vineyard

Library
Miss Jo Ann Bratton
Mrs. C. H. Cobb
Mrs. Roy Edmonds
Mrs. S. K. McKenzie
Mrs. Marshall Morris
Mrs. Mattie Thomas

Music
T. Wade Smith, Chairman
Merle King
Dr. W. M. Lovejoy
Dr. Frank Prichard
Mr. & Mrs. Charles Tate

Nominating
Pastor, Chairman
Howard L. Davenport
John Erson
Bert Ferguson
William H. D. Fones
Everett Handorf
Ed Richmond

Pastoral Relations
Al Brinkley, Chairman
Harold Benson
Howard L. Davenport
James Seabrook Sr.
Keith Weisinger

Publicity-Public Relations
Bert Ferguson, Chairman
Jean Carson
W. H. Grumbles
Wiley House
Dallas Nelson

The Official Board

1962–1963

Edgar H. Tenent, Chairman, June 1961–June 1963
George Roberts, Lay Leader, 1962–1963
James B. Adams
Jesse Anderson
James B. Arnett
E. W. Atkinson
George Atkinson
R. Lee Austin
W. E. Bartlett
David Bencomo
Harold Benson
Dr. J. F. Bigger
Earle Billings
Dr. Howard Boone
James P. Briggs
Albert M. Brinkley
Dr. Shed Caffey
Dr. Charles Campbell
William B. Campbell
Jean Carson
Barry M. Carter
Jack Caskey Sr.
William Roger Cobb
Clarence Colby Sr.
Hugh L. Cullen Jr.
James D. Curry
Howard L. Davenport

Harry F. DeZonia
Robert J. Drake
James F. Duncan Jr.
Winfield Dunn
Frank Farris
Ernest Felts Sr.
Bert Ferguson
William H. D. Fones
Ned French
Haskell Gass
O. F. Gibson
H. Jennings Goza Jr.
Dr. Charles W. Grant
W. H. Grumbles
E. C. Handorf
Charles E. Hendricks
Dr. Robert T. Holt
Warner Howe
O'Neil Howell
Jack Jayroe
Jesse Joyner
Alfred W. Lenz
Donald Lewis
Phil Lowe
Kenneth Markwell
George Martin Jr.
Samuel H. Mays
Dr. J. H. McClain
Porter McCleanSr.
Lee McCormick
C. R. McDaniel
Paul McQuiston
Marion Meadows
W. H. Meadows Jr.
W. C. Mieher
Gordon Miles
Early Mitchell
Earl Montgomery
Rev. Marshall Morris
St. Elmo Newton
D. A. Noel
George Nowlin Jr.
Richard Oglesby
Felix Overton
John A. Parsons
Jeans A. Pattinson
Jack L. Perry
Alan B. Peterson
Joe Ritner
Tom Ragland
R. G. Ramsay
Russell Reeves
Jack Renshaw
Ed Richmond Jr.
Fred Ridolphi
Yerger Robinson
Ralph Scherr
James Seabrook Sr.
James I. Seago
Raymond Skinner Jr.
J. E. Stafford
Sam Stephenson Jr.
Carey Stanley Sr.
E. E. Stigall
W. F. Stout
Richard G. Taylor
Dr. W. J. Templeton
Robert Lee Thomas
Ronald B. Thomas
Elmo Thompson
Ed Thorn
John H. Tole
Mrs. John Tole
Dr. Robert Utterback
Jesse Vineyard
Frank Walker
William T. Wardlaw
L. T. Warinner
J. D. Weatherford
R. C. Whitnel
John C. Whitsitt
Gene Williams
Dr. James Wiygul
Jesse D. Wooten
W. A. Wren

Commissions

Membership and Evangelism

Donald Lewis, Chairman
James B. Arnette
E. W. Atkinson
George Atkinson
Roy Barron
Harold Benson
Dr. J. F. Bigger
Jack Byrne
Dr. Charles Campbell
W. B. Campbell
Hugh Cullen Jr.
Harry F. DeZonia
R. J. Drake
James F. Duncan Jr.
Dr. Winfield Dunn
Dennis Earles
Frank Fisher
William H. D. Fones
Robert Ford
Haskell Gass
Jac Gates
Henry Harry
Leland Helms
Charles Hendricks
Ray Holman
Jones Holt
Frank Hoover
Clark Hunt
Merle King

Richard Lamphere
O. H. Little
Phil Lowe
W. K. Martak
J. P. McClean
C. R. McDaniel
Marion Meadows
W. C. Mieher
Gordon Miles
Earl Montgomery
George Nowlin
Chas. Ogan
R. S. Oglesby
Felix Overton
Jeans Pattinson
Ray Skinner Jr.
W. F. Stout
Dr. W. J. Templeton
Elmo Thompson
Percy Whitenton

Ex Officio Members
Earle Billings
Jack Caskey Sr.
Mrs. C. H. Cobb
Pastors
Mrs. Ed Richmond Sr.
George Roberts
Ralph Scherr

Education
James B. Adams, Chairman
James Curry
William H. D. Fones
O'Neil Howell
Dr. J. H. McClain
Alan Peterson
Tom Ragland
Yerger Robinson
R. E. Stratton
Ronald Thomas

Ex Officio Members
Earle Billings
Ben Carpenter
Jack Caskey Sr.
Bobby Fisher
Mrs. Frank Fisher
Mrs. Earnie Leachman
Tom Logan
Mrs. Charles McVean
Geo. Nowlin Jr.
Pastors
George Roberts
Dr. W. J. Templeton
Dr. Robert Utterback

Missions
Ralph B. Scherr, Chairman
George Atkinson
Armistead Clay
James N. Clay Jr.
Dr. Horton G. DuBard
Jack G. Jayroe
George Martin Jr.
W. H. Meadows Jr.
Frank Richard
Fred Ridolphi
Mrs. Ralph Scherr
J. E. Stafford
John Tole
Jesse Vineyard
Frank Walker
R. C. Whitnel

Ex Officio Members
Dr. J. F. Bigger
Mrs. Jas. P. Briggs
Jack Caskey
Mrs. C. M. Henderson
Donald Lewis
Lee McCormick
Pastors
George Roberts
James Seabrook Sr.
Dr. Robert Utterback

Trustees
James H. Seabrook Sr., Chairman
Howard L. Davenport
Bert Ferguson
C. R. McDaniel
John A. Parsons
Edgar H. Tenent
Dr. W. J. Templeton

Commissions

Stewardship and Finance
Lee McCormick, Chairman
Albert Brinkley
Jack Caskey
Howard L. Davenport
Charles Dodson
Herbert Dunkman
Bert Ferguson
E. E. Handorf
Jesse Joyner
A. W. Lenz
St. Elmo Newton
John Parsons
R. G. Ramsay
Russell Reeves
George Roberts
James Seabrook Sr.
Carey Stanley Sr.
L. T. Warinner

Ex Officio Members
Mrs. Avis Allen
Jesse Anderson
Earle Billings
Dr. C. W. Campbell
Jack Caskey Sr.
Frank Fisher
Charles Johnston
Early Mitchell
Pastors
John Pickens
R. G. Ramsay
George Roberts
Dr. W. J. Templeton
Edgar Tenent
John Tole
John Whitsitt

Christian Social Concerns
Samuel H. Mays, Chairman
Dr. Howard Boone
Dr. Shed Caffey
Clarence Colby
W. L. Gully
Archie Hoss
Dr. Albert Jones
Paul McQuiston
James H. O'Donnell
Dr. Henry Roberts
Eugene Stigall

Ex Officio Members
James Adams
Mrs. James Adams
Dr. J. F. Bigger
Don Lewis
Lee McCormick
Pastors
George Roberts
Ralph Scherr

District Steward
Ernest Felts Sr.

Alternate Steward
Richard Taylor

Recording Steward
Harry F. DeZonia

Church School Superintendent
Dr. Robert Utterback

Superintendent of Adult Division
Ben Carpenter

Superintendent of Youth Division
Tom Logan

Superintendent of Children's Division
Mrs. Earnie Leachman

Church School Secretary and Treasurer
Tom Ragland

Literature Secretary
R. J. Drake

Assistant Superintendent in Charge Cultivation
Earle Billings

Home and Hospital Steward
Dr. J. F. Bigger

Committees

Architects and Building
E. R. Richmond Sr., Chairman
Armistead Clay
E. C. Handorf
Early Mitchell
Earl Montgomery
John Parsons
Jesse D. Wooten
Kemmons Wilson

Audit
W. E. Bartlett, Chairman
Ben Merchant
Jack Reynolds

Christian Vocations
Dr. Charles Grant, Chairman
Tom Logan
Rev. Marshall Morris
Mrs. C. W. Shaw

City Missions
Mrs. C. M. Henderson, Chairman
Mr. & Mrs. Jack Byrne
Mr. & Mrs. W. K. Martak

Collectors and Ushers
Hunter Barcroft Sr.
J. P. Briggs
Harry F. DeZonia
J. F. Duncan Jr.
Ned French
Haskell Gass
Dr. Robert Holt
W. O. Martin

W. H. Meadows Jr.
Gordon Miles
Felix Overton
Joe Pitner
Charles Tate
Dr. W. J. Templeton
James L. Vance
W. T. Wardlaw
J. D. Weatherford
John Wilkins Jr.
Dr. R. L. Wooten

Communion Stewards
Mr. & Mrs. R. E. Garber
Mr. & Mrs. O. F. Gibson

Coordinating
Dr. Charles Grant, Chairman
James Adams
Jack Caskey Sr.
Donald Lewis
Lee McCormick
Sam Mays
Rev. Marshall Morris
Ralph Scherr
Mrs. John Tole
Dr. Robert Utterback

District Church Extension
John Tole, Chairman
Clarence Colby
Dr. Horton G. DuBard

Good Literature
David Ben Como, Chairman
Dr. William A. Berry
Gene Williams

Hospital Visitation
W. F. Stout, Chairman
Jean Carson
R. J. Drake
Dr. Albert Jones
John Philbeck
Dr. J. L. Wiygul
W. A. Wren

Homes and Hospitals
Dr J. F. Bigger, Chairman
Dr. R. L. Austin
Alan Peterson
Dr. Robert Utterback

House
J. P. McClean Sr., Chairman
Warner Howe
Kenneth Markwell
Earl Montgomery
George Nowlin
Jack Renshaw
James I. Seago
Sam Stephenson Jr.
Ed Thorn

Insurance
Ed Richmond Jr., Chairman
Jesse Anderson
Al Brinkley

Kitchen
Marion Meadows, Chairman
Mrs. Ernest Felts Sr.
Ed Hardin
Mrs. Mae Jennings
Mr. & Mrs. Jesse Joyner
Joe McKinney
Delmer Woodard

Landscape
Mrs. J. H. Seabrook Sr., Chairman
Mr. & Mrs. Joe Nuismer
Mr. & Mrs. Jesse Wooten

The Official Board

1963–1964

Keith Weisinger, Chairman, June 1963–June 1964
George Roberts, Lay Leader, 1963–1964
James B. Adams
Jesse Anderson
W. C. Armstrong
James B. Arnette

Dr. R. Lee Austin
Hunter Barcroft Sr.
David Bencomo
Earle Billings
Dr. Howard A. Boone
James P. Briggs
Jack P. Byrne
Dr. Shed H. Caffey Jr.
Dr. C. W. Campbell
Jack Caskey Sr.
Jean A. Carson
Barry M. Carter
Dr. Percy Clayton
James D. Curry
Howard L. Davenport
Harry F. DeZonia
Robert J. Drake
Dr. Horton G. DuBard
Herbert Dunkman
Frank T. Farris
Bert Ferguson
Frank Fisher
Albert Fulmer
Russell Garber
Haskell Gass
O. F. Gibson
W. O. Gordon
H. Jennings Goza Jr.
Dr. Charles Grant
W. L. Gully
Everett C. Handorf
Henry Harry
Rufus M. Hayes
Charles E. Hendricks
Louis O. Hill
Warner Howe
O'Neil Howell
Robert O. Hyde
Jack Jayroe
Harry A. Johnson Jr.
Orin Johnson
Charles Johnston
Keith Kelley
Merle D. King
Dwight Koenig
Dr. Neil Leonard
Donald Lewis
Phil Lowe
James Markham
Kenneth Markwell
W. K. Martak
George Martin
W. O. Martin
Gerald Maynard
Samuel H. Mays
Porter McClean Sr.
Ralph McCool
Lee McCormick
C. R. McDaniel
Paul McQuiston
Kenneth McRae
J. Marion Meadows
Gordon Miles
Early Mitchell
Earl Montgomery
C. W. Newman
St. Elmo Newton
D. A. Noel
George Nowlin
John W. Parsons
Morgan A. Patton
Jack L. Perry
Joseph A. Pitner
S. G. Ramsay
Rev. Howard W. Rash
Russell Reeves
Ed Richmond Jr.
Ed Richmond Sr.
Mrs. Ed Richmond
W. D. Roberds
James H. Seabrook Sr.
James H. Seabrook Jr.
James I. Seago
H. Clay Shelton Jr.
Raymond Skinner Jr.
Russell Smith
William Cazy Smith
J. E. Stafford
Carey Stanley Sr.
Harold Stewart
Eugene E. Stigall
W. F. Stout
Charles R. Tate
Richard G. Taylor
Dr. W. J. Templeton
Edgar H. Tenent
Robert Lee Thomas
Ronald B. Thomas
Ed Thorn
Jesse Vineyard
Frank Walker
William H. Walker
William T. Wardlaw
Jerry D. Weatherford
Dr. Richard P. White
Percy Whitenton
R. C. Whitnel
John C. Whitsitt
Gene Williams
Kemmons Wilson
W. A. Wren

Commissions

Membership and Evangelism
Robert J. Drake, Chairman
James B. Arnette
Harold Benson

Dr. J. F. Bigger
Mr. & Mrs. W. B. Campbell
Robert Carlock
Mrs. Robert Carlock
Mrs. Ruth Carmichael
Harry F. DeZonia
Jas. F. Duncan
William H. D. Fones
David Foster
Haskell Gass
Henry Harry
Leland Helms
Chas. Hendricks
Ray Holman
Jones Holt
Merle King
Donald Lewis
Phil Lowe
Marion Meadows
George Nowlin
W. F. Stout
Dr. W. J. Templeton
Elmo Thompson
Mrs. Sue Tilley
William T. Wardlaw
Percy Whitenton

Ex Officio Members
Earle Billings
Mrs. Caruthers Ewing
Bert Ferguson
Mrs. Dwight Koenig
Pastors
Don Perry
George Roberts

Education
Ronald B. Thomas, Chairman
Barry Carter
W. O. Gordon
James Hillis
Robert O. Hyde
Max Long
Dr. Thomas H. Shipmon
R. E. Stratton
Richard Taylor

Ex Officio Members
Priscilla Baker
Earle Billings
Dr. Shed Caffey
Ben Carpenter
Jean Carson
Mrs. James M. Doyle
R. J. Drake
Mrs. Clara B. Dunaway
Herbert Dunkman
W. L. Gully
Mrs. John Hendricks
Lora Ellyn Hindman
Harry Johnson Jr.
Earnie Leachman
Mrs. Earnie Leachman
Tom Logan
Gerald Maynard
Mrs. Charles McVean
Ben Merchant
Bob Moses
Pastors
Joe Pitner
Tom Ragland
George Roberts
H. Clay Shelton
Ann Utterback
Dr. R. A. Utterback
Fletcher Zeitner

Missions
Bert Ferguson, Chairman
W. C. Armstrong
Dr. Shed Caffey Jr.
Howard L. Davenport
Dr. Horton G. DuBard
Frank Fisher
Jack Jayroe
Harry Johnson Jr.
Dwight Koenig
George Martin
Gerald Maynard
Mr. & Mrs. Kenneth McRae
Dr. C. W. Newman
Russell Reeves
Ralph Scherr
William Cazy Smith
J. E. Stafford
Jesse Vineyard
Frank Walker
Robert Whitnel

Ex Officio Members
Jesse Anderson
Dr. J. F. Bigger
Earle Billings
Mrs. Ben Carpenter
R. J. Drake
Mrs. Charles M. Henderson
Jim McRae
Pastors
George Roberts
Dr. R. A. Utterback

Trustees
James H. Seabrook Sr., Chairman

Howard L. Davenport
Bert Ferguson
C. R. McDaniel
John A. Parsons

Stewardship and Finance
Jesse Anderson, Chairman
Albert Brinkley
Jack Caskey Sr.
Howard L. Davenport
Dr. Horton G. DuBard
Herbert Dunkman
Everett C. Handorf
Charles Hendricks
Charles Johnston
Keith Kelley
W. K. Martak
Gerald Maynard
C. R. McDaniel
Ralph McCool
Lee McCormick
Early Mitchell
St. Elmo Newton
D. A. Noel
John Parsons
Morgan Patton
John Pickens
R. G. Ramsay
Russell Reeves
James Seabrook Sr.
Harold Stewart
Ed Tenent
Kemmons Wilson

Ex Officio Members
Mrs. Avis Allen
Earle Billings
Jack Byrne
Dr. C. W. Campbell
Frank Fisher
Pastors
R. G. Ramsay
Ed Richmond Jr.
George Roberts
John Tole
John Whitsitt

Christian Social Concerns
John H. Tole, Chairman
Dr. Howard Boone
Jack Byrne
Dr. P. A. Clayton Jr.
Albert Fulmer
Russell Garber
W. L. Golly
Samuel H. Mays
J. H. O'Donnell Jr.
Dr. H. C. Roberts
E. E. Stigall
Charles R. Tate
Dr. W. J. Templeton

Ex Officio Members
Jesse Anderson
Dr. J. F. Bigger
R. J. Drake
Bert Ferguson
Jan McQuiston
Pastors
George Roberts
Mrs. Richard Taylor
Ronald B. Thomas

Committees

Architect and Buildings
Ed Richmond Sr., Chairman
Armistead Clay
Everett C. Handorf
Kenneth Markwell
Earl Montgomery
John Parsons
Kemmons Wilson
Jesse D. Wooten

Audit
W. E. Bartlett
Charles G. Dodson
Ben Merchant
Jack Reynolds

Christian Vocations
Dr. Charles Grant, Chairman
Mrs. W. C. Armstrong
Tom Logan
Rev. Marshall Morris

City Missions
Mr. & Mrs. W. L. Gully
Mrs. C. M. Henderson, Chairman
Mr. & Mrs. Russell Smith

Collectors and Ushers
Dr. Robert T. Holt, Chairman
Paul Ballinger
Hunter Barcroft Sr.
David Bowlin
Harry F. DeZonia
J. F. Duncan Jr.
Ned French
Haskell Gass
Max Long Jr.
William O. Martin

W. H. Meadows Jr.
Gordon Miles
Felix Overton
Joe Pitner
W. D. Roberds
Dr. W. J. Templeton
Dr. J. D. Upshaw
James L. Vance
William T. Wardlaw
J. D. Weatherford
Dr. Richard L. Wooten

Communion Stewards
Mr. & Mrs. R. E. Garber
Mr. & Mrs. O. F. Gibson

Coordinating
Dr. Charles Grant, Chairman
Jesse Anderson
Earle Billings
R. J. Drake
Bert Ferguson
Ronald B. Thomas
John H. Tole

Mrs. Ed Richmond Sr.
Keith Weisinger

District Church Extension
William Cazy Smith, Chairman
Charles Hendricks
Charles Johnston

Good Literature
Louis O. Hill, Chairman
Mr. & Mrs. Rufus M. Hayes

Hospital Visitation
W. F. Stout, Chairman
Jean Carson
Dr. Albert Jones
Dr. Neil Leonard
Charles Tate
Mrs. Percy Whitenton
W. A. Wren

Homes and Hospitals
Dr. J. F. Bigger, Chairman

Dr. R. Lee Austin
Dr. Robert Utterback

Insurance
Ed Richmond Jr., Chairman
Hunter Barcroft Sr.
Orin Johnston

Kitchen
Earl Montgomery, Chairman
Mrs. Ed Richmond Sr.
Ed Hardin
Mrs. Mae Jennings
Joe McKinney

Landscape
Mrs. Jesse D. Wooten, Chairman
Mr. & Mrs. Joe Nuismer
Mr. Jesse D. Wooten
Mrs. James Seabrook Sr.

Legal Counsel
Jesse Vineyard

The Official Board
1964–1965

Keith Weisinger, Chairman, June 1964–June 1965
Ernest Felts, Lay Leader, June 1964–June 1965
John Whitsitt, Vice Chairman
Sam Mays, Secretary
Jesse Anderson
W. C. Armstrong
Hunter Barcroft Sr.
Andrew A. Bellomo
David Bencomo
Harold Benson
Dr. J. F. Bigger
Robert K. Brommer
Jack P. Byrne
Dr. Shed Caffey
Jack Caskey Sr.
Harley Clark
William H. Crump
James D. Curry
Howard L. Davenport
Robert J. Drake
Dr. Horton G. DuBard
James F. Duncan Jr.
Herbert Dunkman
Ernest Felts Sr.
Bert Ferguson

Frank Fisher
William H. D. Fones
Albert Fulmer
Russell Garber
W. O. Gordon
W. L. Golly
Dr. Charles W. Grant
Mack Hansbrough
Henry Harry
Rufus M. Hayes
Louis O. Hill
James A. Holt
Dr. Robert T. Holt
Warner Howe
Robert O. Hyde
Jack Jagoditsch
Doyle Johnson
Harry Johnson Jr.
Orin Johnson
Charles Johnston
Keith Kelley
Merle D. King
Dwight Koenig
Dr. Andrew Lasslo
Donald Lewis
Thomas R. Logan
James B. Markham
W. K. Martak
George Martin
Samuel H. Mays
Ralph McCool
Lee McCormick
Seth McGaughran
C. R. McDaniel
Paul McQuiston
Guest Middleton
Gordon Miles
Early Mitchell
Dr. Charles W. Newman
D. A. Noel
George Nowlin
Felix Overton
Tom Ragland
Rev. Howard W. Rash
Russell Reeves
Ed Richmond Jr.
Mrs. Ed Richmond Sr.
George Roberts
Dr. Henry C. Roberts
Ralph Scherr
James H. Seabrook Sr.
H. Clay Shelton Jr.
Dr. Thomas H. Shipmon
Raymond Skinner Jr.
William Cazy Smith
Sam Stephenson Jr.
Harold Stewart
Dr. W. J. Templeton
Edgar H. Tenent
Ronald B. Thomas
Elmo Thompson
John H. Tole
Dr. J. D. Upshaw
James L. Vance
Jesse L. Vance
Jesse M. Vineyard
William H. Walker
Stanley Wertz
Keith Weisinger
James Westerfield
Dr. Richard P. White
Dr. Richard L. Wooten

Trustees
James H. Seabrook Sr., Chairman
Howard L. Davenport
Bert Ferguson
C. R. McDaniel
John A. Parsons
Dr. W. J. Templeton
Edgar Tenent

Recording Steward
W. K. Martak

Church School Superintendent
Dr. Robert A. Utterback

Adult Division Superintendent
Ben Carpenter

Youth Division Superintendent
Paul McQuiston

Children's Division Superintendent
Mrs. Earnie Leachman

Secretary Treasurer
Tom Ragland
Membership Secretary
Mrs. J. D. Weatherford

Literature Secretary
Robert J. Drake

Commissions

Membership and Evangelism
Robert J. Drake, Chairman
Dr J. F. Bigger
Mrs. Jack Byrne
Mr. & Mrs. W. B. Campbell

Robert Carlock
Mrs. Robert Carlock
Jean Carson
George Darms
James F. Duncan Jr.
William H. D. Fones
David Foster
Haskell Gass
Henry Harry
Leland Helms
Charles Hendricks
Ray Holman
Jones Holt
Clark Hunt
Merle King
Donald Lewis
Marion Meadows
Guest Middleton
Mrs. Guest Middleton
Mr. & Mrs. W. C. Smith
W. F. Stout
Dr. W. J. Templeton
Mrs. Sue Tilley
W. T. Wardlaw

Ex Officio Members
George Atkinson
Jim Duncan
Mrs. Caruthers Ewing
Ernest Felts
Mrs. Dwight Koenig
George Roberts
William Loyd Smith
Elmo Thompson
Percy Whitenton

Education
Ronald B. Thomas,
Chairman
Barry Carter
W. O. Gordon
James Hillis
Robert O. Hyde
Doyle Johnson
Dr. Thomas H. Shipmon
Ray Skinner Jr.
Richard Taylor
Robert Templeton
James Westerfied

Ex Officio Members
Ben Carpenter
Mrs. Robert Condra
R. J. Drake
Ernest Felts
Paul McQuiston
Pastors
Tom Ragland
George Roberts
Dr. R. A. Utterback
Jan Whitsitt

Missions
Bert Ferguson,
Chairman
W. C. Armstrong
Harold Benson
Dr. Shed Caffey
J. L. Davenport
Dr. Horton G. DuBard
Frank Fisher
Harry Johnson Jr.
Dwight Koenig
Dr. Andrew Lasslo
George Martin
Seth McGaughran
Kenneth McRae
Dr. Charles W. Newman
Russell Reeves
Ralph Scherr
Dr. W. J. Templeton
Dr. J. D. Upshaw
Jesse Vineyard
Frank Walker
Dr. James Wiygul

Ex Officio Members
Jesse Anderson
Dr. J. F. Bigger
R. J. Drake
Ernest Felts
Mrs. C. M. Henderson
Pastors
George Roberts
Dr. R. A. Utterback

Stewardship and Finance
Jesse Anderson,
Chairman
Robert Brommer
Jack Caskey Sr.
Howard L. Davenport
Dr. Horton G. DuBard
C. K. McDaniel
John Parsons
John Whitsitt

Stewardship and Finance
Herbert Dunkman
E. C. Handorf
Charles Hendricks
Charles Johnston
Keith Kelley
Tom Logan
W. K. Martak
Ralph McCool
Lee McCormick
Early Mitchell
Morgan Patton
John Pickens

Russell Reeves
George Roberts
James Seabrook Sr.
Harold Stewart
Ed Tenent Sr.
Kemmons Wilson

Ex Officio Members
Mrs. Avis Allen
Ernest Felts
Pastors
George Roberts

Christian Social Concerns
John H. Tole, Chairman
Dr. Howard Boone
Jack Byrne
Dr. P. A. Clayton Jr.
Albert Fulmer
Russell Gather
W. L. Gully
Samuel H. Mays
J. H. O'Donnell
Dr. H. C. Roberts
Charles R. Tate
Dr. W. J. Templeton

Ex Officio Members
Jesse Anderson
Dr. J. F. Bigger
Robert J. Drake
Ernest Felts
Bert Ferguson
Pastors
Ronald B. Thomas

Committees

Architect and Building
Ed Richmond Sr., Chairman
Armistead F. Clay
Everett Handorf
Kenneth Markwell
Earl Montgomery
John Parsons
Kemmons Wilson
Jesse D. Wooten

Audit
Ben Merchant, Chairman
W. E. Bartlett
Harley Clark
Jack Reynolds

Christian Vocations
Mrs. W. C. Armstrong
Dr. Charles Grant
Paul McQuiston
Rev. Howard W. Rash

City Missions
Mr. & Mrs. W. L. Gully
Mrs. C. M. Henderson
Mr. & Mrs. Russell Smith

Collectors and Ushers
Ernest Ball
Paul Ballinger
Robert Carlock
James F. Duncan Jr.
Steve Fransioli Jr.
Ned French
Haskell Gass
Dr. Robert Holt
Merle King
W. O. Martin
W. H. Meadows Jr.
Gordon Miles
Charles Morris
Felix Overton
Joe Pitner
Kenneth Rash
W. D. Roberds
Andrew Sippel
Frank Smith
Dr. W. J. Templeton
W. T. Wardlaw
Jerry Weatherford
Dr. R. L. Wooten

Communion Stewards
Mr. & Mrs. R. E. Garber
Mr. & Mrs. O. F. Gibson

Coordinating
Dr. Charles Grant, Chairman
Jesse Anderson
R. J. Drake
Bert Ferguson
Ed Richmond Sr
George Roberts
Ronald Thomas
John Tole

District Church Extension
William Cazy Smith, Chairman
Charles Hendricks
Charles Johnston

Good Literature
Louis Hill, Chairman
David Bencomo
Mr. & Mrs. Rufus Hayes
Gene Williams

Hospital Visitation
W. F. Stout, Chairman
Jean Carson

Dr. Albert Jones
Dr. Neil Leonard
Charles Tate
Mrs. Percy Whitenton

Homes and Hospitals
Dr. J. F. Bigger, Chairman
Dr. R. Lee Austin
Dr. Robert Utterback

House
Marion Meadows, Chairman
Warner Howe
Kenneth Markwell
George Nowlin
Sam Stephenson Jr.

Insurance
Ed Richmond Jr., Chairman
Hunter Barcroft Sr.
Frank Fisher
Orin Johnson

Kitchen
Earl Montgomery, Chairman
Ed Hardin
Mrs. Mae Jennings
Joe McKinney
Mrs. Ed Richmond Sr.
Stanley Wertz

Landscape
Mrs. Jesse D. Wooten, Chairman
Mr. & Mrs. Joe Nuismer
Mrs. James Seabrook Sr.

Legal Counsel
Jesse Vineyard

Library
Mrs. W. B. Campbell, Chairman
Mrs. C. H. Cobb
Mrs. Howard Rash
Mrs. Mattie Thomas

Music
Dr. W. M. Lovejoy, Chairman
Merle King
Mrs. Frank Liddell Sr.
Dr. Frank Prichard
T. Wade Smith
Mr. & Mrs. Charles R. Tate
Mrs. R. C. Whitnel

Nominating
Dr. Charles Grant, Chairman
Jesse Anderson
Howard Boone
Dr. Horton G. DuBard
Bert Ferguson
C. R. McDaniel
James Seabrook Sr.
John Tole

Pastoral Relations
Dr. Howard Boone, Chairman
Jack Caskey Sr.
Bert Ferguson
Earl Montgomery
John Parsons

Publicity-Public Relations
Dallas Nelson, Chairman
Jean Carson
D. A. Noel

Records and History
Mrs. W. J. Templeton, Chairman
Mrs. Fred Ridolphi
Mrs. Percy Whitenton

Resolutions
Armistead Clay, Chairman
John Whitsitt

Sanctuary Building Fund
R. G. Ramsey, Chairman
Jack Byrne
Dr. Charles Campbell
Frank Fisher
John Tole
John Whitsitt

Scouts
Clay Shelton, Chairman
V. Hugo Akin
Andrew Bellomo
James D. Curry
William H. D. Fones
Roy Perkins
Richard Taylor

Weekday School
Dr. Charles Grant, Chairman
Robert O. Hyde
Harry Johnson Jr.
H. Clay Shelton

Welcome and Hospitality
Dr. Charles Campbell, Chairman
P. D. Clarkson
Mack Hansbrough
Donald Lewis
W. H. Meadows Jr.
C. R. McDaniel
James L. Vance
Jesse Vineyard
Percy Whitenton

Will and Legacies
John T. Wilkinson Jr., Chairman
Carey P. Stanley Sr.

THE OFFICIAL BOARD
1965–1966

Jesse A. Anderson, Chairman, June 1965–June 1967
Bert Ferguson, Lay Leader, June 1965–June 1967
James Arnette
George Atkinson
Hunter Barcroft Sr.
Andrew A. Bellomo
Harold Benson
Earle Billings
Dr. Howard Boone
Robert K. Bommer
Jack P. Byrne
Dr. Charles Campbell
Ben Carpenter
Clarence Colby Sr.
John Curtis
C. Winston Hoover Jr.
Jack Jayroe
Harry A. Johnson Jr.
Orin Johnson
Charles Johnston
Dr. Albert Jones
D. Keith Kelley
Merle D. King
Dwight Koenig
Mrs. Dwight Koenig
Dr. Andrew Lasslo
Alfred W. Lenz
Donald Lewis
Thomas R. Logan
C. Phil Lowe
J. Porter McClean
Ralph A. McCool
H. Clay Shelton Jr.
Dr. Thomas H. Shipmon
Andrew A. Sippel Jr.
William Cazy Smith
J. E. Stafford
Sam L. Stephenson Jr.
W. F. Stout
Charles R. Tate
Richard Tate
Richard G. Taylor
Robert Templeton
Dr. W. J. Templeton
Mrs. W. J. Templeton
Elmo Thompson
Ed Thorn
John H. Tole
Dr. Merlin L. Trumbull
Dr. K. D. Upshaw
Dr. Robert Utterback
Jesse M. Vineyard
William H. Walker
William T. Wardlaw
L. T. Warinner
Keith Weisinger
Stanley H. Wertz
James Westerfield
Percy Whitenton
John Whitsitt
Max D. Winn
Dr. James L. Wiygul
Mrs. Jesse D. Wooten

Board of Trustees
Keith Weisinger, Chairman
E. R. Richmond Sr., Chairman
Howard L. Davenport
Bert Ferguson
C. R. McDaniel
John A. Parsons
James H. Seabrook Sr.
Dr. W. J. Templeton
Edgar H. Tenent

Commissions

Membership and Evangelism
Dr. Thomas H. Shipmon, Chairman

James Arnette
Andrew Bellomo
David Bencomo
Dr. J. F. Bigger
Richard Bolks
Robert Brommer
Ed M. Brooks
Mrs. Jack Byrne
Mr. & Mrs. Robert E. Carlock
Jean A. Carson
James D. Curry
George Darms
Charles W. Dean
Harry F. DeZonia
James F. Duncan
Sewell Dunkin
Donald Farmer
John L. Fletcher
J. Haskell Gass
Roy L. Greenlee
Henry Harry
Leland Helms
Charles Hendricks
Louis O. Hill
Mrs. Louis Hill
Ray Holman
Jones Holt
Winston Hoover
Clark Hunt
Charles Johnston
Keith Kelley
Merle D. King
Donald Lewis
C. Phil Lowe
Emmett Marston
W. K. Martak
George B. Martin
Dr. J. Howard McClain
J. Porter McClean
Ralph A. McCool
James A. McCrory
C. R. McDaniel
Paul McQuiston
J. Marion Meadows
Guest Middleton
Gordon Miles
Charles Montague Jr.
Dr. Charles W. Newman
George Nowlin
John A. Parsons
Sam Pearson
Ed Richmond Jr.
Ralph Scherr
James Seabrook Jr.
H. Clay Shelton
Andrew Sippel Jr.
William Loyd Smith
W. C. "Bill" Smith
J. E. Stafford
W. F. Stout
Charles R. Tate
Robert Templeton
Dr. W. J. Templeton
Edgar H. Tenent
Elmo Thompson
John H. Tole
Jesse M. Vineyard
William H. Walker
William T. Wardlaw
Keith Weisinger
John Whitenton
Percy Whitenton
John Whitsitt
Max D. Winn

Ex Officio Members
Mrs. William B. Campbell
Charlotte Dabbs
Bert Ferguson
Paul McQuiston
Mrs. R. J. Oglesby Sr.
Pastors
Mrs. Tom Ragland
George Roberts

Education
Dr. Andrew Lasslo, Chairman
Hunter Barcroft Jr.
James P. Briggs
Barry Carter
Albert Fulmer
Charles Gaston
W. O. Gordon
Dr. O. B. Harrington
James R. Hillis
Doyle Johnson
Joe Pitner
R. G. Ramsay
Richard Taylor
James Westerfield

Ex Officio Members
Ginna Boone
Mr. & Mrs. Harry Brahm
Robert Carlock
Hugh Colville Jr.
Robert Compton
Mrs. Robert Condra
William H. Crump
Dr. Lesley Dameron
Sewell Dunkin
Ernest Felts
Bert Ferguson
Mrs. O. F. Gibson
Keith Kelley
Mrs. Andrew Lasslo
Sam Mays

Paul McQuiston
Mrs. Charles A. McVean
Randy Oglesby
Pastors
Mrs. Roy Perkins
Tom Ragland
George Roberts
Paul Schultz
Andrew Sippel Jr.
Ray Steiner
Keith Weisinger
James Westerfield
Mrs. Pat Wilson

Missions
Dr. Howard A. Boone, Chairman
George Atkinson
Clarence Colby
William C. Crump
Howard L. Davenport
Dr. Horton G. DuBard
Ernest T. Felts
John Fletcher
William H. D. Fones
Orin Johnson
Sam Mays
W. C. "Bill" Smith

Ex Officio Members
Mrs. James B. Adams
Billy Atkins
Bert Ferguson
Dr. T. Goyer Jr.
Mrs. Frances Lowrie
Pastors

Stewardship and Finance
D. A. Noel, Chairman
Harold Benson
Earle Billings
Jack Caskey
John Curtis
Herbert Dunkman
W. L. Gully
Warner Howe
Tom Logan
W. K. Martak
Lee McCormick
Early Mitchell
Earl Montgomery
John Parsons
Morgan Patton
Ed Richmond Sr.
James Seabrook Sr.
Dr. Merlin Trumbull
Keith Weisinger

Ex Officio Members
Mrs. Avis D. Allen
Dr. Howard Boone
Ben Carpenter
Bert Ferguson
Frank Fisher
Everett Handorf
Jack Jayroe
Dr. Andrew Lasslo
Ben Merchant
Pastors
Dr. Thomas H. Shipmon

Christian Social Concerns
Ben Carpenter, Chairman
R. E. Garber
Mack Hansbrough
Lawrence Hawkins
Harry A. Johnson Jr.
Dr. Albert A. Jones
Dr. Robert A. Utterback
Stanley Wertz
Dr. Richard White
Dr. James L. Wiygul
Dr. Richard L. Wooten

Ex Officio Members
Dr. Howard Boone
Bert Ferguson
Dr. T. E. Goyer Jr.
Mrs. John R. Hartie
Dr. Andrew Lasslo
Mrs. Early Mitchell
D. A. Noel
Jon Parry
Pastors
George Roberts
Dr. Thomas H. Shipmon

Committees

Architect and Building
Ed Richmond Sr., Chairman
Armistead Clay
Everett Handorf
Kenneth Markwell
Earl Montgomery
John Parsons
Kemmons Wilson
Jesse D. Wooten

Audit
Ben Merchant, Chairman
Bryan Bolin

Christian Vocations
Pastor, Chairman
Mrs. Harry Brahm
W. H. Crump
Mrs. James Hindman

City Missions
Mrs. Charles M. Henderson, Chairman
Mr. & Mrs. Moody Cunningham
Mr. & Mrs. Steve Fransioli Jr.

Collectors and Ushers
W. O. Martin, Chairman
Hunter Barcroft Sr.
Dr. Charles Campbell
Dr. Robert Holt
Felix Overton
William T. Wardlaw
Gene Williams

Communion Stewards
Mr. & Mrs. Jack Byrne, Chairman
Mr. & Mrs. W. F. Stout

Coordinating
Pastor, Chairman
Jesse Anderson
Dr. Howard Boone
Ben Carpenter
Mrs. Bea Crofford
Mrs. Howard Estes
Dr. Andrew Lassie
D. A. Noel
George Roberts
Dr. Thomas H. Shipmon

Dietetics
Mrs. Ed R. Richmond Sr., Chairman
Mrs. Robert Lee Thomas
Mrs. Stanley Wertz

Furnishings
Mrs. Bernice Penland, Chairman
William H. Crump

Good Literature
Mrs. Dwight Koenig, Chairman
Mrs. Charles Tale
Mrs. Percy Whitenton

Hospital Visitation
W. F. Stout, Chairman
Jack Byrne
Russell Garber

Homes and Hospitals
Dr. Thomas E. Goyer Jr., Chairman

House
Everett Handorf, Chairman
Al W. Lenz
Earl Montgomery
Roy Perkins
James Seabrook Sr.
Andrew Sippel Jr.
Ed Thorn

Insurance
Frank Fisher, Chairman
Jack Caskey
Frank Liddell Sr.

Landscape
Mr. & Mrs. Jesse Wooten, Chairman
Mr. & Mrs. Joe Nuismer
Mrs. James Seabrook Sr.

Legal Counsel
Jesse Vineyard

Library
Mrs. Lesley Dameron, Chairman
Mrs. Horace Gray
Mrs. Andrew Lasslo
Mrs. Howard Rash
Mrs. W. F. Stout
Mrs. Mattie Thomas

Music
Jack Jayroe, Chairman
Mrs. Ernest Fells
George Roberts

Nominating
Bert Ferguson
Don Lewis
Lee McCormick
John Parsons
Jas. H. Seabrook Sr.
Keith Weisinger

Pastoral Relations
Howard L. Davenport, Chairman
Lee McCormick
C. R. McDaniel
James H. Seabrook Sr.
Keith Weisinger

Publicity–Public Relations
Tom Ragland, Chairman
Mr. Brescia
Dwight Koenig
George Roberts
Ray Skinner Jr.
L. T. Warner

Records and History
Mrs. W. J. Templeton, Chairman
Mrs. Fred Ridolphi
Mrs. Percy Whitenton

Resolutions
William H. D. Fones, Chairman
Armistead Clay

Scouts
W. O. Gordon, Chairman
Al Best
Harry Brahm
H. Jennings Goza Jr.
W. L. Gully

Weekday School
Pastor, Chairman
Seth McGaughran
Ronald B. Thomas
Dr. J. D. Upshaw

THE OFFICIAL BOARD
1966–1967

Jesse A. Anderson, Chairman, June 1965–June 1967
Bert Ferguson, Lay Leader, June 1965–June 1967
James Arnett
George Atkinson
Hunter Barcroft Sr.
Harold Benson
Earle Billings
Richard Bolks
Dr. Howard Boone
James P. Briggs
Dr. Shed Caffey
Dr. Charles Campbell
Dr. William F. Cantrell
Ben Carpenter
Jack Caskey Sr.
Clarence Colby
William H. Craig
Ray G. Holman
Jones Holt
Dr. Robert Holt
C. Winston Hoover
Warner Howe
Jerry Jacobsen
Jack Jayroe
Dr. Albert Jones
William F. Kennon
John C. Kreamer
Dr. Andrew Lasslo
Al W. Lenz
Donald W. Lewis
Morris Liming
Thomas R. Logan
Roy D. McAnally
George Roberts
Ralph Scherr
James Seabrook Sr.
James Seabrook Jr.
Dr. Thomas H. Shipmon
Andrew Sippel Jr.
William Loyd Smith
J. Ed Stafford
Sam L. Stephenson Jr.
W. F. Stout
Mrs. Charles Tate
Robert Templeton
Dr. W. J. Templeton
Edgar Tenent Sr.
Elmo Thompson
Ed Thorn
John H. Tole
Dr. J. D. Upshaw

Board of Trustees
Keith Weisinger, Chairman
Harold Benson
Howard L. Davenport
Lee B. McCormick
John A. Parsons
E. R. Richmond Sr.
Dr. W. J. Templeton
Edgar Tenent

Commissions

Membership and Evangelism
Dr. Thomas H. Shipmon, Chairman

James Arnette
David Bencomo
Richard Balks
Ed M. Brooks
Mrs. Jack Byrne
Mrs. Robert Carlock
Jean A. Carson
George Darms
Charles W. Dean
Harry F. DeZonia
James F. Duncan
Sewell Dunkin
Fred Edick
Lloyd Estes Jr.
Donald Farmer
Henry Foster
Roy L. Greenlee
Henry Harry
Charles Hendricks
Louis O. Hill
Mrs. Louis Hill
Ray G. Holman
Winston Hoover
Clark W. Hunt
Jerry P. Jacobsen
Keith Kelley
Marie King
John C. Kreamer
Donald W. Lewis
Morris Liming
C. Phil Marston
George Martin
James McCrory
Marion Meadows
William C. Mieher Sr.
Gordon Miles
Charles Montague Jr.
Walter Padgett
Sam Pearson
John R. Ragan
Ralph Scherr
James Seabrook Jr.
H. Clay Shelton
Andy Sippel
William Loyd Smith
W. C. "Bill" Smith
J. Ed Stafford
W. F. Stout
Dr. W. J. Templeton
Elmo Thompson
John H. Tole
Jesse Vineyard
William T. Wardlaw
Keith Weisinger
Percy Whitenton
Max D. Winn

Ex Officio Members
George Atkinson
Mrs. William B. Campbell
Bert Ferguson
Paul McQuiston
Mrs. Richard Oglesby Sr.
Pastors
Mrs. Tom Ragland

Education
Dr. Andrew Lasslo, Chairman
James P. Briggs
Barry Carter
Charles W. Dean
Al Fulmer
Charles Gaston
W. O. Gordon
Dr. O. B. Harrington
James R. Hillis
Doyle Johnson
Dallas Nelson
R. G. Ramsay Jr.
Richard Taylor
James Westerfield
Jimmy Young Jr.

Ex Officio Members
George Atkinson
Dr. Howard Boone
Mr. & Mrs. Harry Brahm
Ben Carpenter
Mrs. Robert Condra
James E. Cox
William H. Crump
Sewell Dunkin
Bert Ferguson
Mrs. O. F. Gibson
Mrs. E. Al Herron
Mrs. Charles Johnston
Paul McQuiston
Mrs. Charles McVean
Pastors
Tom Ragland
Dr. Thomas H. Shipmon
Paul Shultz
Andy Sippel
Mrs. Jerry Weatherford
Keith Weisinger

Missions
Dr. Howard A. Boone, Chairman
George Atkinson
Clarence Colby
William Craig
W. H. Crump
Howard L. Davenport
Dr. Horton G. DuBard
Ernest T. Felts
William H. D. Fones

William R. Freeman
Mrs. Pauline Hord
Orin Johnson
Samuel H. Mays
Gordon O. Miles
Kenneth W. Rash
Raymond Skinner Jr.
W. C. "Bill" Smith

Ex Officio Members
Ben Carpenter
Bert Ferguson
Dr. Thomas E. Goyer
Mrs. Charles M. Henderson
Dr. Andrew Lasslo
Mrs. J. S. Lowrie
D. A. Noel
Pastors
Dr. Thomas H. Shipmon
Andy Sippel
Mrs. R. A. Utterback

Stewardship and Finance
D. A. Noel, Chairman
Harold Benson
Earle Billings
Jack Caskey Sr.
John H. Curtis
Herbert Dunkman
W. L. Gully
Warner Howe
Tom Logan
W. K. Martak
Ralph McCool
Lee McCormick
Early Mitchell
Earl Montgomery
John A. Parsons
Morgan A. Patton
James Seabrook Sr.
Edgar Tenent Sr.
Keith Weisinger

Ex Officio Members
Mrs. Avis Allen
George Atkinson
Dr. Howard Boone
Ben Carpenter
Bert Ferguson
Frank Fisher
Everett Handorf
James R. Hillis
Jack Jayroe
Ben Merchant
Pastors
Dr. Thomas H. Shipmon

Christian Social Concerns
Ben Carpenter, Chairman
Dr. Shed Caffey
Dr. William F. Cantrell
James D. Curry
Russell Garber
Mack T. Hansbrough
Lawrence Hawkins
Dr. Albert M. Jones
Roy D. McAnally
Guest Middleton
Dr. Robert A. Utterback
Stanley Wertz
Dr. Richard P. White
Dr. James L. Wiygul

Ex Officio Members
Dr. Howard A. Boone
Bert Ferguson
Dr. Thomas E. Goyer
John R. Hartie
Dr. Andrew Lasslo
Mrs. Early Mitchell
D. A. Noel
Pastors
Dr. Thomas H. Shipmon

Committees

Architect and Building
Ed Richmond Sr., Chairman
Armistead F. Clay
Everett Handorf
Kenneth Markwell
Earl Montgomery
John Parsons
Kemmons Wilson
Jesse D. Wooten

Audit
Ben Marchant, Chairman
Bryan Bolin

Christian Vocations
Dr. Charles Grant, Chairman
Mrs. Harry Brahm
W. H. Crump
Mrs. James Hindman

Church Use
Lee McCormick, Chairman
Harold Benson
E. C. Handorf

City Missions
Mrs. C. M. Henderson,

Chairman
Mr. & Mrs. Steve Fransioli Jr.
Mr. & Mrs. Russell Garber

Collectors and Ushers
W. O. Martin, Chairman
Hunter Barcroft Sr.
Dr. Charles Campbell
Dr. Robert T. Holt
Dr. Charles Newman
Felix Overton
William Wardlaw
Gene Williams

Communion Stewards
Mr. & Mrs. Jack Byrne, Chairman
Mr. & Mrs. W. F. Stout

Coordinating
Dr. Charles Grant, Chairman
George Akinson
Jesse Anderson
Dr. Howard Boone
Ben Carpenter
Mrs. Bea Crofford
Mrs. Howard Estes
Dr. Andrew Laslo
D. A. Noel
Dr. Thomas H. Shipmon

Dietetics
Mrs. Edward Richmond Sr., Chairman
Mrs. Stanley Wertz
Mrs. John C. Whitsitt

Furnishings
Mrs. Bernice Penland, Chairman
W. H. Crump

Good Literature
Mrs. Charles Tate, Chairman
Mrs. E. Al Herron
Mrs. Percy Whitenton

Hospital Visitation
W. F. Stout, Chairman
Mrs. Jack Byrne
Mrs. Russell Garber

Homes and Hospitals
Dr. Thomas E. Goyer, Chairman

House
Everett Handorf, Chairman
A. W. Lenz
Earl Montgomery
Roy Perkins
James Seabrook Jr.
Andy Sippel Jr.
Ed Thorn

Insurance
Frank Fisher, Chairman
Jack Caskey Sr.
Frank Liddell Sr.

Landscape
Mrs. Jesse D. Wooten, Chairman
Mr. & Mrs. Joe Nuismer
Mrs. James Seabrook Sr.

Legal Counsel
Jesse Vineyard

Library
Mrs. E. Al Herron, Chairman
Mrs. Andrew Lasslo
Mrs. Charles Neiman
Mrs. W. F. Stout
Mrs. Mattie Thomas

Music
Jack Jayroe, Chairman
Mrs. Ernest Felts
George Roberts

Nominating
Dr. Charles Grant, Chairman
Donald Lewis
C. R. McDaniel
John Parsons
Ralph Scherr
James H. Seabrook Sr.
Keith Weisinger

Pastoral Relations
Howard L. Davenport, Chairman
Lee McCormick
C. R. McDaniel
James Seabrook Sr.
Keith Weisinger

Publicity and Public Relations
Tom Ragland, Chairman
Matt Brescia
George Roberts
Ray Skinner Jr.

Elmo Thompson
L. T. Warinner

Records and History
Mrs. Percy Whitenton, Chairman
Mrs. Henry Foster
Mrs. Frank Ridolphi

Resolutions
William H. D. Fones, Chairman
Armistead Clay

Scouts
W. O. Gordon, Chairman
Al Best
Harry Brahm
Ben Carpenter
W. L. Gully
Clark Hunt

Day School
Dr. Charles Grant, Chairman
Seth McGaughran
Ronald Thomas
Dr. J. D. Upshaw

Wills and Legacies
William H. D. Fones, Chairman

Chairman of Official Board
Jesse Anderson

Chairman of Commission on Christian Social Concerns
Ben Carpenter

Chairman of Commission on Education
Dr. Andrew Lasslo

Chairman of Commission on Membership and Evangelism
Dr. Thomas H. Shipmon

Chairman of Commission on Missions
Dr. Howard A. Boone

Chairman of Commission on Stewardship and Finance
D. A. Noel

Secretary of Stewardship
Keith Weisinger

Hospitals and Homes Steward
Dr. T. E. Goyer

Church School Superintendent
Andrew A. Sippel

Superintendent Elementary School Children's Division
Mrs. Robert Condra

Superintendent of Preschool Children's Division
Mrs. O. F. Gibson

Superintendent of Youth Division
Mr. & Mrs. Harry Brahm

Superintendent of Adult Division
E. Sewell Dunkin

President of Young Adult Class
J. W. King

Membership Cultivation Superintendent
Paul McQuiston

Chairman of Committee on Christian Vocations
Dr. Charles Grant

President of WSCS
Mrs. Ben Crofford

President of W.S.G.
Mrs. Howard Estes

President of Methodist Men
Jean Carson

Director of Christian Education
Mr. William H. Crump

Director of Music
Mr. Paul D. Shultz

President of M.Y.F.
Miss Lynda Stigall

M.Y.F. Counselors
Mr. & Mrs. James S. Hillis

The Official Board
1967–1968

Ed Richmond Sr., Chairman, June 1967–June 1969
Dr. Thomas H. Shipmon, Lay Leader, June 1967–June 1969
Mrs. Avis Allen
Jesse Anderson
James Arnette
Wade Beckman
Harold Benson
Earle Billings
Ben Birdwell
Richard B. Bolks
Dr. Howard Boone
Harry Brahm
James Briggs
Robert Brommer
Ed Brooks
J. P. Byme
Dr. Shed Hill Caffey
Mrs. Bea Crofford
William H. Crump
James D. Curry
George Darms
Howard L. Davenport
Charles W. Dean
Harry F. DeZonia
James F. Duncan
Sewell Dunkin
Fred Edick
Lloyd Estes Jr.
Donald R. Farmer
Ernest T. Felts
Bert Ferguson
Frank Fisher
William H. D. Fones
Henry Foster
William R. Freeman
Charles B. Gaston
W. O. Gordon
Dr. Thomas E. Goyer
Dr. Charles W. Grant
Roy L. Greenlee
E. C. Handorf
Mack Hansbrough
Dr. O. B. Harrington
Henry Harry
Lawrence Hawkins
Leland Helms
Mrs. C. M. Henderson
Charles Hendricks
Mrs. E. Al Herron
James R. Hillis
Ray Holman
C. W. Hoover
Henry C. Hottum
Thompson Jamieson
Jack Jayroe
Orin Johnson
Mrs. Orin Johnson
Charles Johnston
Dr. Albert Jones
Jesse Joyner
D. K. Kelley
William F. Kennon
Merle King
Kenneth Markwell
Emmett Marston
George Martin
William O. Martin
Samuel H. Mays
Dr. J. Howard McClain
J. Porter McClean
James E. McCrory
E. R. McDaniel
Seth McGaughran
J. Marion Meadows
Ben H. Merchant
Guest Middleton
William C. Mieher Sr.
Gordon O. Miles
Early Mitchell
Charles Montague Jr.
Earl Montgomery
John Muir
D. A. Noel
Felix Overton
Walter Padgett
John Parsons
Sam Pearson
Mrs. Bernice Penland
John Ragan
Tom Ragland
S. G. Ramsay Jr.
Rev. Howard W. Rash
Kenneth Rash
Jack Renshaw
John P. Rhodes Jr.
Mrs. Edward Richmond Sr.
Mrs. Fred Ridolphi
George Roberts
Dr. Daniel Scott Jr.
James H. Seabrook Jr.
James H. Seabrook Sr.
H. C. Shelton
A. A. Sippel Jr.

W. G. Smith
William Loyd Smith
J. E. Stafford
Dr. Robert Utterback
Jesse M. Vineyard
William T. Wardlaw
L. T. Warinner
Keith Weisinger
James Westerfield
Percy Whitenton
John Whitsitt
Max D. Winn
Dr. James Wiygul
Mrs. Jesse D. Wooten
Jimmy Young Jr.

Board of Trustees
Keith Weisinger, Chairman
Harold Benson
E. C. Handorf
C. S. McDaniel
John Parsons
Ed Richmond Sr.
Dr. W. J. Templeton
Edgar Tenent Sr.
Jesse Vineyard

Commissions

Membership and Evangelism
Sewell Dunkin, Chairman
David Bencomo
Mr. & Mrs. Ben F. Birdwell
Richard Bolks
Ed M. Brooks
Mrs. Robert Carlock
Jean Carson
Mr. & Mrs. Clarence Colby
George Darms
Charles Dean
Mr. & Mrs. Harry F. DeZonia
James F. Duncan
Fred Edick
Lloyd Estes Jr.
Donald Farmer
Henry Foster
William L. Gully
Henry Harry
Leland Helms
Charles Hendricks
Mr. & Mrs. Ray G. Holman
Jones Holt
C. M. Hoover
Jerry P. Jacobsen
Mr. & Mrs. C. S. Jasper
Orin Johnson
Keith Kelley
Mr. & Mrs. William F. Kennon
Merle King
Jack Kraemer
Burns Landess
Donald W. Lewis
Mr. & Mrs. Morris Liming
Emmett Marston
George Martin
Sam Mays
Dr. Howard McClain
James E. McCrory
C. R. McDaniel
Marion Meadows
Charles Montague
Felix Overton
Walter Pagdett
Mr. & Mrs. W. Patton
Sam Pearson
John R. Ragan
Mr. & Mrs. Jack Renshaw
John Rhodes
Mr. & Mrs. E. W. Rice
Mr. & Mrs. Ed G. Scott
William Loyd Smith
Ed Stafford
W. F. Stout
Charles Tate
Dr. W. J. Templeton
Elmo Thompson
John H. Tole
Mr. & Mrs. James Westerfield
Percy Whitenton

Ex Officio Members
Mrs. Dan Farrar
Miss Francis McGinnis
Paul McQuiston
Pastors
Mrs. Tom Ragland
Dr. Thomas H. Shipmon

Education
James R. Hillis, Chairman
Dr. Richard Lee Austin
Wade L. Beckman
Ben Carpenter
Herchel Crowley
Dr. O. Brewster Harrington
Paul McQuiston
Ed Richmond

Dr. Fred Wallace
Gene Williams
Jimmy Young

Ex Officio Members
Mr. & Mrs. Harry Brahm
William H. Crump
Mrs. O. F. Gibson
Mrs. John E. Jennings Jr.
Mrs. Charles McVean
Paul McQuiston
Dr. W. C. Newman Jr.
Pastors
Paul Shultz
Andy Sippel

Missions
R. G. Ramsay Jr., Chairman
James Arnette
George Atkinson
Earle Billings
Jack Byrne
Dr. C. Campbell
Clarence Colby
William H. Craig
William H. Crump
H. H. Dunkman
Howard Estes
Ernest T. Felts
Frank Fisher
William H. D. Fones
William S. Freeman
Russell Garber
Mrs. Pauline Hord
Jesse Joyner
Gordon Miles
J. H. Mercer
Early Mitchell
Kenneth W. Rash
James H. Seabrook Jr.
Frank Walker

Ex Officio Members
Mrs. Robert Fields
Dr. Thomas H. Shipmon
Andy Sippel
Mrs. L. E. Smith
Dr. Jeff Upshaw

Stewardship and Finance
John Parsons, Chairman
Jesse Anderson
Harold Benson
Dr. Howard Boone
Jack Caskey
John H. Curtis
Howard L. Davenport
Dan Farrar
Bert Ferguson
Roy Greenlee
Henry Hottum
Warner Howe
Jack Jayroe
D. K. Kelley
Don Lewis
Tom Logan
Emmett Marston
W. K. Martak
Lee McCormick
John Menges
Early Mitchell
Earl Montgomery
John Muir
D. A. Noel
Morgan A. Patton
Ed Richmond
Ralph Scherr
James Seabrook Sr.
H. C. Shelton
Edgar Tenent Sr.
L. T. Warinner
John Whitsitt

Ex Officio Members
Mrs. Avis Allen
Bryan Bolin
Sewell Dunkin
James R. Hillis
Porter McClean
Ralph McCool
Pastors
R. G. Ramsay
George Roberts
Dr. R. A. Utterback

Christian Social Concerns
Dr. R. A. Utterback, Chairman
Dr. Shed Caffey
Dr. William F. Cantrell
James D. Curry
John Davis
Dr. Winfield Dunn
Lawrence Hawkins
Mack Hansbrough
Dr. O. B. Harrington
Tom Jamieson
Dr. Albert Jones
Mrs. Sam Mays
Roy D. McAnally
Guest Middleton
Dr. Dan Scott
Dr. Richard P. White
Dr. James L. Wiygul

Ex Officio Members
Mrs. David Barcroft
Mrs. Pat Bigger
Pastors

Dr. Thomas H. Shipmon
Dr. Jeff Upshaw

Committees

Audit
Ben Merchant, Chairman

Christian Vocations
Dr. Charles Grant, Chairman
Mrs. Harry Brahm
William H. Crump
Mrs. James Hindman

Church Use
Harold Benson, Chairman
Porter McClean
Lee McCormick

City Missions
Mrs. Howard L. Davenport, Chairman
P. D. Clarkson
Mrs. C. M. Henderson

Collectors and Ushers
Dr. W. J. Templeton, Chairman
Ned French

Communion Stewards
Mr. & Mrs. William Campbell, Chairman
Mr. & Mrs. Howard French
Mr. & Mrs. Felix Overton

Coordinating
Dr. Charles Grant, Chairman
Associate Ministers
Bill Crump
Sewell Dunkin
James R. Hillis
Mrs. Orin Johnson
John Parsons
R. G. Ramsay
Ed Richmond
Paul Shultz
R. A. Utterback
Miss Frances Young

Dietetics
Mrs. Leslie McCullough, Chairman
Mrs. Stanley Wertz
Mrs. John Whitsitt

Furnishings
Mrs. Oscar Crofford, Chairman
R. K. Brommer
Bill Crump
Mrs. St. Elmo Newton

District Church Extension
James Seabrook Jr., Chairman
T. E. Goyer
W. C. Smith

Good Literature
William T. Wardlaw, Chairman
Jean Carson
Mrs. E. Al Herron
Mrs. Charles Tole

Mrs. Percy Whitenton
Hospital Visitation
Mr. & Mrs. Percy Whitenton, Chairman
Mrs. J. O. Mitchell
Mrs. Ralph Scherr

Hospital and Homes
Dr. Jeff Upshaw, Chairman

House
Porter McClean, Chairman
Al Lenz
Kenneth Markwell
Earl Montgomery
Roy Perkins
James Seabrook Jr.
Andy Sippel
Sam Stephenson
Ed Thorn

Insurance
Ralph McCool, Chairman
Armistead Clay
Charles Johnston
Merle King
Bob Templeton

Landscape
Jesse D. Wooten, Chairman
Mr. & Mrs. Joe Nuismer

Mrs. James Seabrook Sr.
Mrs. Jesse D. Wooten

Legal Counsel
Jesse Vineyard

Lay Personnel
Dr. Charles Grant, Chairman
Jesse Anderson
Jack Caskey
Bert Ferguson
Lee McCormick

Library
Mrs. Andrew Lasslo, Chairman
Mrs. E. Al Heron
Mrs. Charles Newman
Mrs. W. F. Stout
Mrs. Mattie Thomas

Committees

Music
George Roberts, Chairman
Mrs. Ernest Felts
Early Mitchell
Sam Pearson
Max D. Winn

Nominating
Dr. Charles Grant, Chairman
E. R. McDaniel
Ralph Scherr
James Seabrook Sr.
Dr. Thomas H. Shipmon
Keith Weisinger

Pastoral Relations
Keith Weisinger, Chairman
Howard L. Davenport
Bert Ferguson
D. A. Noel
Ed Richmond
Ralph Scherr
Dr. Thomas H. Shipmon

Publicity
Earle Billings, Chairman
J. A. Massey
Tom Ragland
George Roberts
John W. Stokes
Elmo Thompson

Records and History
Mrs. Fred Ridolphi, Chairman
Mrs. Henry Foster
Mrs. Percy Whitenton

Resolutions
John Wilkinson, Chairman
Ernest Felts

Scouts
Harry Brahm, Chairman
Al Best
Ben Carpenter
W. O. Gordon
W. L. Gully
Clark Hunt

Weekday School
Dr. Andrew Lasslo, Chairman
Nick French
Charles Gaston
Seth McGaughran
Dallas Nelson
Edgar A. Steepleton
Roland Thomas
Dr. J. D. Upshaw

Wills and Legacies
Howard L. Davenport

Superintendent of Youth Division
Mr. & Mrs. Harry Brahm

Superintendent of Adult Division
E. Sewell Dunkin

President of Young Adult Class
J. W. King

Membership Cultivation Superintendent
Paul McQuiston

Chairman of Committee on Christian Vocations
Dr. Charles W. Grant

President of WSCS
Mrs. Ben Crofford

President of W.S.G.
Mrs. Howard Estes

President of Methodist Men
Jean Carson

Director of Christian Education
William H. Crump

Director of Music
Paul D. Shultz

President of M.Y.F.
Miss Lynda Stigall

M.Y.F. Counselor
Mr. & Mrs. James R. Hillis

THE OFFICIAL BOARD

1968–1969

Ed Richmond Sr., Chairman, June 1967–June 1969
Dr. Thomas H. Shipmon, Lay Leader, June 1967–June 1969
Mrs. Avis Allen
Jesse Anderson
John S. Arend
David H. Barcroft Jr.
David Barcroft
David Bencomo
Harold S. Benson
Earle N. Billings
Ben F. Birdwell
Richard G. Bolks
Harry C. Brahm
James P. Briggs
Robert K. Brommer Sr.
J. Mell Brooks Jr.
Ed M. Brooks
Dr. Shed Hill Caffey
William B. Campbell
Dr. William F. Cantrell
Jean Carson
Jack B. Caskey
P. D. Clarkson
Armistead Clay
W. H. Craig
Mrs. Oscar Crofford
Raymond Cummins
James Curry
John H. Curtis
Dr. William Dabbs
Howard L. Davenport
Dr. Horton G. DuBard
James F. Duncan Jr.
E. Sewell Dunkin
H. H. Dunkman
Dr. Winfield C. Dunn
James D. Ellis
Howard Estes
Lloyd D. Sates Jr.
Dan Farrar
Bert Ferguson
William H. D. Fones
Robert Ford
Henry Foster
William R. Freeman
Ned French
J. Albert Fulmer III
Russell Garber
Charles B. Gaston
W. O. Gordon
Dr. Charles W. Grant
Roy L. Greenlee
Ernest W. Hall
Mack Hansbrough
Dr. O. B. Harrington
Henry H. Harry
Leland Helms
Mrs. Charles M. Henderson
E. Al Heron
James S. Hillis
Jones A. Holt
Charles Winston Hoover
C. Henry Hottum
Warner Howe
O'Neil Howell
Harold F. Higgins
Clark W. Hunt
Thompson Jamieson
Rev. James D. Jenkins
Doyle Johnson
Orin Johnson
Charles Johnston
Jesse Joyner
D. K. Kelley
William F. Kennon
Merle E. King
John C. Kreamer
T. L. Lend
H. B. Landess Jr.
Weston G. Lawson
Don Lewis
Morris Limming
Thomas R. Logan

Rev. Charles H. Lynn
Emmett Marston
W. K. Martak
George B. Martin
William O. Martin
James A. Massey
Sam Mays
Dr. J. H. McClain
J. Porter McClean
Wilbur B. McClintock
Ralph McCool
Lee McCormick
Seth McGaughran
Dr. R. Sam McGinnis
Paul McQuiston
Curt Meierhoefer
Joseph H. Mercer
Ben Merchant
Early Mitchell
Joe P. Neeley
Dr. Charles W. Newman
D. A. Noel
Charles Ogan
Felix Overton
Walter F. Padgett
John Parsons
Sam Pearson
Judge Leroy Pope
Dr. Taylor Prewitt
Mrs. Tom Ragland
Rev. Howard W. Rash
Kenneth W. Rash
Jack Renshaw
John Rhodes
Mrs. Fred Ridolphi
George Roberts
E. R. Richmond Jr.
J. P. Rutledge
Ralph Scherr
Dr. Daniel J. Scott
James H. Seabrook Sr.
H. C. Shelton
Dr. Thomas H. Shipmon
A. A. Sippel Jr.
Victor L. Smith
William Cazy Smith
William Loyd Smith
Fullimore Sperry
Harold W. Stewart
W. F. Stout
Charles Tate
Dr. Richard Taylor
Robert Templeton
Dr. W. J. Templeton
Edgar Tenent
Ronald B. Thomas Jr.
Elmo Thompson
Edward Thorn
Roy H. Thurmond
Dr. Jeff Upshaw
Dr. Robert Utterback
Jesse M. Vineyard
Frank Walker
William T. Wardlaw
S. K. Weisinger
Stanley H. Wertz
Percy B. Whitenton
John Thomas Wilkinson
Gene Williams
Donald E. Wilson
Dr. James L. Wiygul
Jesse D. Wooten
Jimmy Young

Trustees

Early Mitchell, Chairman
Jesse Anderson
Jack Caskey
Dr. Winfield Dunn
Lee McCormick
Earl Montgomery
Jack Renshaw
Ed Richmond Sr.
Roy Thurmond

Commissions

Membership and Evangelism

Sewell Duncan, Chairman
John R. Arend
David Bencomo
Richard G. Bolks
Ed M. Brooks
Mrs. Robert T. Carlock
Jean Carson
George Darms
Mr. & Mrs. Charles Dean
Mr. & Mrs. Harry F. DeZonia
James F. Duncan
Fred Edick
Lloyd Estes
Donald Farmer
Robert Ford
Mr. & Mrs. Henry Foster
William L. Gully
Henry Harry
Leland Helms
Mr. & Mrs. Ray Holman
Jones Holt
Winston Hoover
Harold Huggins
Jerry Jacobsen
Mr. & Mrs. C. S. Jasper
Orin Johnson

Merle King
John C. Kraemer
Donald Lewis
Mr. & Mrs. Morris Liming
Emmett Marston
George B. Martin
Sam Mays
Dr. Howard McClain
James E. McCrory
C. R. McDaniel
J. M. Meadows
Charles A. Montague
Charles Ogan
Felix Overton
Walter Padgett
Mr. & Mrs. Jack Renshaw
John Rhodes
Mr. & Mrs. Ernest Rice
J. P. Rutledge
William Loyd Smith
J. E. Stafford
W. F. Stout
Charles Tate
Dr. W. J. Templeton
Elmo Thompson
Mr. & Mrs. James Westerfield
Mr. & Mrs. L. P. Whitenton
Mr. & Mrs. Max D. Winn

Ex Officio Members
Mrs. Russell Garber
Dr. Charles W. Grant
Rev. Charles H. Lynn
Mrs. Y. O. Mitchell
Mrs. Tom Ragland
Dr. Howard W. Rash
Mrs. Ralph Scherr
Dr. Thomas H. Shipmon
Mr. & Mrs. P. Whitenton

Education
James R. Hillis, Chairman
Ben Carpenter
Dr. William Dabbs
Warner Howe
O'Neil Howell
Doyle Johnson
Seth McGaughran
Paul McQuiston
Joe P. Neeley
Dr. Charles Newman
Judge Leroy Pope
Victor L. Smith
Gene Williams
Jimmy Young

Ex Officio Members
Mr. & Mrs. Harry Brahm
Mrs. Robert Condra
James E. Cox
Mrs. O. F. Gibson
Dr. Charles W. Grant
Mrs. John E. Jennings
Rev. Charles H. Lynn
Dr. W. C. Newman
Rev. Howard W. Rash
Paul Shultz
A. A. Sippel
Mrs. Charles McVean
E. R. Richmond
Mrs. J. D. Weatherford

Missions
Keith Weisinger, Chairman
Winston Hoover
James B. Arnett
Earle Billings
Ben Birdwell
J. P. Byer
Dr. Charles Campbell
Clarence Colby
W. H. Craig
Charles Dean
Dr. Horton G. DuBard
James D. Ellis
Howard Estes
Frank Fisher
William H. D. Fones
William R. Freeman
Russell Garber
Gerry Godwin
Roy Greenlee
W. L. Gully
Mrs. Pauline Hord
Thompson Jamieson
Jesse Joyner
T. L. Land
Thomas R. Logan
James A. Massey
Joseph H. Mercer
Gordon A. Miles
Early Mitchell
Kenneth W. Rash
E. R. Richmond Jr.
James H. Seabrook Jr.
William Cazy Smith
Richard G. Taylor
Dr. Jeff Upshaw
Frank Walker
Dr. Jack Williams

Ex Officio Members
Dr. Charles W. Grant
Rev. Charles H. Lynn
Early Mitchell
Rev. Howard W. Rash
A. A. Sippel
Dr. Jeff Upshaw

Stewardship and Finance
John Parsons, Chairman
Jesse Anderson
Harold Benson
Dr. Howard Boone
J. Mell Brooks
Jack Caskey
Ray Cummins
John Curtis
Howard L. Davenport
Herbert Dunkman
Dan Farrar
Bert Ferguson
Roy Greenlee
Winston Hoover
Henry Hottum
Warner Howe
Jack Jayroe
Dr. K. Kelley
Donald Lewis
W. K. Martak
Lee McCormick
Early Mitchell
Earl Montgomery
John Muir
D. A. Noel
Morgan Patton
E. R. Richmond Sr.
H. C. Shelton
Edgar Tenent
L. T. Warinner
John Whitsitt

Ex Officio Members
Mrs. Avis Allen
Harold Benson
Mell Brooks
Shed Caffey
John Curtis
Howard L. Davenport
Charles Dean
Fred Edick
Edward Estes
Dan Farrar
Dr. Charles W. Grant
Roy Greenlee
Mac Hansbrough
Winston Hoover
Morris Liming
Tom Logan
Rev. Charles H. Lynn
Emmett Marston
Sam Mays
Porter McClean
Ralph McCool
Lee McCormick
Ben Merchant
Earl Montgomery
Rev. Howard W. Rash
Jack Renshaw
E. R. Richmond
George Roberts

Social Concerns
Dr. Robert Utterback,
Chairman
David Barcroft
Dr. Shed Hill Caffey
Dr. William F. Cantrell
James Curry
John Davis Jr.
Dr. Winfield Dunn
Mack Hansbrough
Dr. O. B. Harrington
Lawrence Hawkins
Tom Jamieson
Dr. Albert Jones
William F. Kennon
Mrs. Sam Mays
R. D. McAnally
Wilbur McClintock
Curt Meierhoeffer
Guest Middleton
Dr. Taylor Prewitt
Dr. Dan Scott
Harold W. Stewart
Roy Thurmond
Dr. Richard White
Donald Wilson
Dr. James L. Wiygul
C. Lasseter Woodard

Ex Officio Members
Dr. Charles W. Grant
Rev. Charles H. Lynn
Rev. Howard W. Rash
Dr. Thomas H. Shipmon
Dr. Jeff Upshaw

Committees

Audit
Ben Merchant,
Chairman
Harold Benson
Jim Hillis
Kenneth Markwell
Ralph McCool
Lee McCormick
Lynette Oliver
Jack Renshaw
George Roberts

William Loyd Smith
Andy A. Sippel Jr.

Christian Vocations
Dr. Charles W. Grant, Chairman
Mrs. Harry Brahm
William H. Crump
Mrs. James Hindman

Church Use
Harold Benson, Chairman
Porter McClean
Lee McCormick

United Methodist Neighborhood Center
P. B. Clarkson

Collectors and Ushers
Dr. W. J. Templeton, Chairman
Ned French
J. Albert Fulmer III
Ernest H. Hall
Al Heron
Weston Lawson
W. O. Martin
Dr. Sam McGinnis
Fillmore Sperry
Dr. James Wiygul

Communion Stewards
Mr. & Mrs. William Campbell, Chairman
Mr. & Mrs. Howard French

Coordinating
Dr. Charles W. Grant, Chairman
Sewell Dunkin
James R. Hillis
Rev. Charles H. Lynn
John Parsons
Rev. Howard W. Rash
E. R. Richmond
Paul Shultz
Dr. R. A. Utterback
Keith Weisinger

Dietetics
Mrs. Leslie McCullough, Chairman
Mrs. Stanley Wertz
Mrs. John Whitsitt

Church Furnishings
Mrs. Oscar Crofford, Chairman
Robert Kelly Brommer
Mrs. St. Elmo Newton

Good Literature
W. T. Wardlaw, Chairman
Jean Carson
Mrs. E. Al Heron
Mrs. Percy Whitenton

Hospital Visitations
Mrs. Jesse Joyner, Chairman
Mrs. Russell Garber
Mrs. Y. O. Mitchell
Mrs. Ralph Scherr

Committees

Hospital and Homes
Dr. Jeff Upshaw

House
Porter McClean, Chairman
Al W. Lenz
Kenneth Markwell
Earl Montgomery
Roy Perkins
James Seabrook Jr.
Andrew Sippel Jr.
Sam Stephenson
Ed Thorn

Insurance
Ralph McCool, Chairman
Armistead Clay
Charles Johnson
Merle King
Robert Templeton

Landscape
Mr. & Mrs. Jesse D. Wooten, Chairman
Mr. & Mrs. Joe Nuismer
Mrs. James Seabrook Sr.

Lay Personnel
Dr. Charles W. Grant, Chairman
Jesse Anderson
Jack Caskey
Bert Ferguson
Lee McCormick

Legal
Jesse Vineyard

Library
Mrs. E. Al Heron, Chairman
Mrs. Andrew Lasslo
Mrs. Charles Newman
Mrs. W. F. Stout
Mrs. Mattie Thomas

Music
George Roberts, Chairman
Mrs. Ernest Felts
Early Mitchell
Mrs. Tom Ragland
Max D. Winn

Nominating
Dr. Charles W. Grant, Chairman
Howard L. Davenport
Dr. Winfield Dunn
C. R. McDaniel
Marion Meadows
Ralph Scherr
Dr. Thomas H. Shipmon

Pastoral Relations
Keith Weisinger, Chairman
Howard L. Davenport
Bert Ferguson
D. A. Noel
Ed Richmond
Ralph Scherr
Dr. Thomas H. Shipmon

Publicity
Earl Billings, Chairman
J. A. Massey
Tom Ragland
George Roberts
Elmo Thompson

Records and History
Mrs. Fred Ridolphi, Chairman
Mrs. Henry Foster
Mrs. Percy Whitenton

Resolutions
John Wilkinson, Chairman
Ernest Felts

Scouts
Harry Brahm, Chairman
Ben Carpenter
Dr. Winfield Dunn
W. O. Gordon
Earnie Leachman
Mrs. Tom Mann
Mrs. W. P. Shea
Mrs. William Wilder

Wills and Legacies
Roy Greenlee, Chairman

Lambuth Representative
Dr. W. C. Newman Jr., Chairman

Directors—Day School
Dr. Andrew Lasslo, Chairman
Nick French
Charles Gaston
Roy Greenlee
Seth McGaughran
Dallas Nelson
E. A. Steepleton
Ronald B. Thomas
Dr. J. D. Upshaw

INDEX

ABOUT THE AUTHOR

Harry A. Johnson Jr.

Mr. & Mrs. Harry Johnson, 1945.

Harry A. Johnson Jr. and Penny Johnson have been married for fifty-eight years. She has supported him through thick and thin in all of life. She has given as much, if not more, of herself to Christ Church as he has, but has always listened and given her support to him.

Harry retired as a colonel, United States Marine Corps, after forty years of regular and reserve service. He was awarded fourteen medals and ribbons with four battle stars for his participation in the amphibious attack on Tarawa in the Gilbert Islands and the first landing in the Philippines, on the Island of Leyte, to occupy the Philippine Islands.

He completed a year at a naval academy preparatory school in Silver Springs, Maryland, and courses in English and analytical geometry at Siena College before entering the Marine Corps in 1941.

He was an honor student at the Naval War College and the Industrial College of the Armed Forces. He was a graduate of the Marine Corps and Army's Field Artillery Schools, the Command and Staff School at Quantico, Virginia, the Amphibious Warfare Schools at Little Creek, Virginia, and Coronado, California, and he served as commanding officer of reserve units in Memphis for eighteen years, including a Russian intelligence unit.

He was with Seabrook's for twelve years, president of Harry Johnson, Inc., for eleven years, president of Shelby-Skipwith, Inc., for fifteen years, and vice president of Woodson & Bozeman, Inc., for seven years.

In 1991, he organized Commercial and Military Computers, Inc., to sell computer equipment to the United States government worldwide and served as its president for over ten years.

Harry was chairman of the Commission on Education, chairman of the Building Committee, vice chairman of the Official Board, and helped organize and was the first president and a teacher of the Jack Hayes Class at Madison Heights Methodist Church.

He was chairman of the Church School Committee for the Steering Committee that organized Christ Methodist Church. A charter member, he served as the first church school superintendent, and on the first Building Committee, the Nominating Committee, and the Official Board. With Dr. Charles Grant, he established Christ Methodist Day School.

He served as chairman of the Host Committee when the Memphis Annual Conference was held at Christ Church in 1986, 1991, and 1996.

Penny and Harry have traveled extensively in all fifty states, all seven provinces of Canada, and in twenty-three countries in Europe and Asia. Most of the travel was done without reservations in order to enjoy the people and the countries without time constraints. Their pride and joy has been their son Harry III, his wife Patty, their children McKenzie and Kelly; and their daughter Janet and her husband, Dr. Tom Turpin, and their children Mary Kate, Lauren, and Jay.